ANOTHER
END OF THE WORLD
IS POSSIBLE

ANOTHER END OF THE WORLD IS POSSIBLE

Living the collapse
(and not merely surviving it)

Pablo Servigne, Raphaël Stevens and
Gauthier Chapelle

Translated by Geoffrey Samuel

polity

Originally published in French as *Une autre fin du monde est possible: Vivre l'effondrement (et pas seulement y survivre)*. Préface de Dominique Bourg. Postface de Cyril Dion.
© Editions du Seuil, 2018

This English edition © Polity Press, 2021

Polity Press
65 Bridge Street
Cambridge CB2 1UR, UK

Polity Press
101 Station Landing
Suite 300
Medford, MA 02155, USA

ISBN-13: 978-1-5095-4465-3
ISBN-13: 978-1-5095-4466-0 (pb)

A catalogue record for this book is available from the British Library.

Library of Congress Cataloging-in-Publication Data

Names: Servigne, Pablo, author. | Stevens, Raphaël, author. | Chapelle, Gauthier, author. | Samuel, Geoffrey, translator.
Title: Another end of the world is possible : living the collapse (and not merely surviving it) / Pablo Servigne, Raphaël Stevens, Gauthier Chapelle ; translated by Geoffrey Samuel.
Other titles: Une autre fin du monde est possible. English
Description: Medford : Polity Press, 2020. | Includes bibliographical references. | Summary: "How to face the environmental crisis with open eyes and a deeper awareness of what we can do about it"-- Provided by publisher.
Identifiers: LCCN 2020023225 (print) | LCCN 2020023226 (ebook) | ISBN 9781509544653 (hardback) | ISBN 9781509544660 (paperback) | ISBN 9781509544677 (epub)
Subjects: LCSH: Social change--Philosophy. | Crises (Philosophy) | Global environmental change. | Catastrophical, The.
Classification: LCC HM831 .S4813 2020 (print) | LCC HM831 (ebook) | DDC 303.4--dc23
LC record available at https://lccn.loc.gov/2020023225
LC ebook record available at https://lccn.loc.gov/2020023226

Typeset in 10.75pt on 14pt Janson by
Servis Filmsetting Limited, Stockport, Cheshire
Printed and bound in Great Britain by TJ Books Limited

For further information on Polity, visit our website: politybooks.com

Contents

To the survivalists, collapsonauts, and earth activists,
to keep up courage

To Joanna Macy, Ursula Le Guin and Constance de Polignac

To Antoinette R., Laurie L.-M. and Géraldine R.

To Hugo, Antoine and David S. Buckel

To the growing mycelium . . .

There are things that one can only see properly with eyes that have wept.

Henri Lacordaire

Humanity today is like a waking dreamer, caught between the fantasies of sleep and the chaos of the real world. The mind seeks but cannot find the precise place and hour. We have created a Star Wars civilization, with Stone Age emotions, medieval institutions, and godlike technology. We thrash about. We are terribly confused by the mere fact of our existence, and a danger to ourselves and to the rest of life.

Edward O. Wilson, *The Social Conquest of Earth*
(New York: Liveright Publishing, 2012)

What was really needed was a fundamental change in our attitude toward life. We had to learn ourselves and, furthermore, we had to teach the despairing men, that it did not really matter what we expected from life, but rather what life expected from us. We needed to stop asking about the meaning of life, and instead to think of ourselves as those who were being questioned by life – daily and hourly.

Victor Frankl, *Man's Search for Meaning*
(Boston, MA: Beacon Press, 1992)

I no longer believe that we can change anything in the world until we have first changed ourselves.

Etty Hillesum, *An Interrupted Life: the Diaries and Letters of Etty Hillesum 1941–1943* (London: Persephone Books, 1999)

This is not so much a return to the earth as a return to ourselves. A spiritual experience. It is to heal, rediscover and reaffirm ourselves.

Tee Corinne, quoted in Françoise Flamant, *Women's Land. Construction d'une utopie: Oregon, États-Unis, 1970–2010*
(Donnemarie-Dontilly: Éditions iXe, 2015)

You say that there are no words to describe these times, you say that they do not exist. But remember. Make an effort to remember. Or if necessary, invent.

Monique Wittig, *Les Guérillères* (Paris: Éditions de Minuit, 1969)

Acknowledgements

There are paradoxes we would like to do without: writing about the absolute need for nature, meaning and connection . . . while spending long days immersed in books and in front of a screen, cutting off the presence of human and non-human beings who matter.

We feel an immense gratitude to our companions, Élise, Stéphanie and Marine, and for our children, for having understood and accepted this for many weeks, and especially during this tough final marathon. All your love, and ours, is also found in this book! (We know that's not much comfort.)

At the end of this adventure, we would like to thank Sophie Lhuillier and Christophe Bonneuil, for your willingness to take risks and your kindness, as well as the entire Seuil team for your understanding and your patience. We are delighted to walk at your side!

A huge thank you to Dominique Bourg and Cyril Dion for the foreword and afterword, for your presence and your authenticity. Thanks also to both of you for proofreading, as well as to Nicolas Haeringer, Élise Monette, Typhaine Domercq and Denys Chalumeau, for critical and encouraging comments during the writing.

We send our warm thanks to the intrepid cowgirl Charlotte de Mévius, as well as to Hugues Dorzée from the magazine *Imagine demain le monde* and Alexandre Penasse from the journal *Kairos*, for your trust and support throughout these years.

Thanks to you, brothers and sisters who made the mycelium grow: Agnes, Aline, Claire, Clément, Corinne, Étienne, Helena, Josué, Laurent L., Laurent R., Lise, Marine S., Michel-Maxime, Muriel, Nathéa, Raphaël, Sébastien, Tylie, Valérie-Azul, Vincent and many other filaments and spores. Also to you, our families and neighbours, Nelly and Michel, Chantal and Pierre, Nicole and Michel, Brigitte and Philippe, Typhaine and Sam, Yannick and Virginie, Monique, Benoît and Caroline, Anne and Jean-Martin, Luc, Marc Pier, Sébastien and Corentin, for help, in-flight refuelling and encouragement.

Maxi-admiration and ultra-gratitude for daring, sensitivity and inspiration: Zoé Alowan, Jean Claude Ameisen, Jean-Pierre Andrevon, Margaret Atwood, Carolyn Baker, Janine Benyus, Dominique Bourg, Paul Chefurka, Yves Cochet, François Couplan, Ashlee Cunsolo, Alain Damasio, Philippe Descola, Vinciane Despret, Cyril Dion, Michel-Maxime Egger, Arturo Escobar, Christophe Fauré, Monica Gagliano, Rachel and Antoine (Geb-nout), Brian Goodwin, John Michael Greer, Émilie Hache, Marc Halévy, Stephan Harding, Geneen Haugen, Jean Hegland, Émilie Hermant, Perrine and Charles Hervé-Gruyer, Xavier Hulhoven, Bill Kauth, Paul Kingsnorth, Maja Kooistra, Bruno Latour, Charles-Maxence Layet, Ursula Le Guin, Jacques Lucas, Joanna Macy, David Manise, Dennis and Donella Meadows, Edgar Morin, Baptiste Morizot, Marisa Ortolan, Kim Pasche, Bill Plotkin, André Ruwet, Suzanne Simard, Agnès Sinai, Rebecca Solnit, Starhawk, Isabelle Stengers, Valérie-Azul Thomé, Bruno Tracq, Patrick Van Eersel, Patrick Viveret, Francis Weller, Edward O. Wilson, not to mention the precious punk blue tits whose language has finally been deciphered by that fine diplomat and interpreter Alessandro Pignocchi (and one of which ended up perched on the cover of the original French edition).

Thanks to the pessimists-plus and optimists-plus of the social networks, as well as countless collapsonauts who have written touching and often overwhelming messages over the past three years; you have given us immense courage! We haven't given up on answering you . . . before the collapse.

Special mention to the modest genius of an *Earth-Dweller* who wrote on the walls the beautiful sentence (spotted in 2010 at the University of Nanterre) which served us as title: *Une autre fin du monde est possible*. . . . We take this opportunity to make an appeal to the person who sent us the photo . . . please get in touch, for the next version of these thanks.

Finally, thank you to the sacred feminine, to magic, to the witches, to the Shambhala warriors, the New Warriors, to the spirits of the places that have given us hospitality while we were writing, and to all the other-than-humans who amaze us, who give us life and who are relying on us.

Foreword

I remember something I once read, though I cannot recall where. We are in Gallo-Roman Provence, towards the end of the fourth century. A patrician, at the head of a vast estate, boasts of the power of Rome. The same archaeological excavations reveal that shortly after its owner wrote about his pride in belonging to the Empire, the villa and its inhabitants were victims of a barbaric incursion. It seems that the assailants feasted on the spot and celebrated their crime by drinking out of the skull of the former master of the estate. Perhaps it is this sinister side of this story that prevents me from remembering where I read it.

Whether that is the case or not, the elites of that time, like those of today, displayed a mixture of arrogance, naivety and crude cynicism. Like today, the end of the Empire saw a dramatic rise in inequality. We can imagine that after centuries of the Pax Romana, it must have been difficult to imagine anything like the end of the Empire. It's equally difficult for us to admit that after centuries of 'progress', thermo-industrial civilization and its high growth rates could fall apart.

If you have opened this book, you have probably had some intuition of such a collapse. So have I, and I am convinced, too, that the moral and political manifestations of our movement towards collapse can already be seen and felt around us. For several years, we have seen the rise of political leaders with much the same psychological profile, who gain power by skilfully stirring up and playing on fear and hatred. Repellent and pretentious, dishonest and depraved, destroying one after the other the barriers, physical as well as moral, that protect his compatriots from global violence, Trump is the epitome of these new ruling elites. Many of these politicians have been elected and have won the admiration of vast numbers of people. As this shows, the catastrophe, and the movement that carries it forward, has a moral nature before it takes physical form. As in Serge Reggiani's song, the wolves, all too human, were able to enter Paris because they were already there. Human fellow-feeling had already deserted the city.[1] Moral violence precedes and feeds physical violence, but above all it blinds us and disarms us in the face of the physical threats which signal our entry into the Anthropocene.

This is precisely why this book by Pablo Servigne, Raphaël Stevens and Gauthier Chapelle is so important. The industrial 'party' will soon be over. A number of vital issues, under whatever names, will again take centre stage. How this present world ends, and even more what new worlds it will give birth to, will depend very much on the connections which we are able to weave and on how we succeed in imagining our immediate future. In this respect, this book is very valuable. It is not a treatise of 'collapsology', like Pablo and Raphaël's first book,[2] but a book of 'collapsosophy'. It does not aim to convince us of a probable collapse – an exercise which has already been accomplished – but to prepare us internally to face it, and in a way to go beyond it, by preparing from now on for the world that is to come, the world that we would choose to rebuild, on new principles, among the other worlds that might take shape.

Our approach to reality has driven its extreme love of the one-dimensional, its obstinate simple-mindedness, to the point of destruction. Our Paradise here on earth was to be built purely through progress (but what kind of progress?), science (that of Bayer-Monsanto and its 'science-based' approaches?), the quantitative, GDP, growth, competitiveness, efficiency, mastery of the material world (on what scale and for how long?), capitalism, freedom (what kind of freedom? for whom? for what end?), humanity (alone in a lifeless world?). The modern world was to be a world of easily-understood slogans, everything simple and straightforward. All we had to do was to keep on growing, without considering the consequences, to tear ourselves away from nature, to focus more and more on the individual, to automate everything, to go always faster and further ... towards a world where finally we dread the coming of summer for fear of suffocating, or of being the victim of some extreme event, where seeing a ladybird fly has become a rare occurrence, where cities have become refuges of biodiversity because the countryside has been devastated, where the sciences, those of climate or biodiversity, that still seek to understand the world rather than to oversimplify it even more, describe nightmare futures. And so on.

It's time to stop. We have spent too long sliding down the slope of this destructive modernity. It's time to oppose to it our inner world, our emotions and passions, our children, our friends, our networks, our intelligence and our creativity. We can learn again to accept the complexities of reality (or rather of realities). We can learn again that our world is more than just what we can dominate, directly or indirectly, and more even than we can understand. We can restore ourselves with the wisdoms that the world has accumulated through centuries past, without sneering at them, but also without being afraid to create something new. We can bring into being the spirituality, and the spiritualities, that will allow us to remain upright in the coming storm and to rebuild a shared, open house in which we can all live.

Dominique Bourg
Philosopher, University of Lausanne

Preface
Facing the collapse of our world

Don't you think our epoch has a scent of collapse? Something has toppled over, something is dying on a grand scale. There are signs of the end of this world appearing in the speeches of Extinction Rebellion, Greta Thunberg and Antonio Gutierrez, the Secretary General of the United Nations, in conversations at Davos and in commentaries on the fires in Australia and Brazil and now on the Covid-19 pandemic.

This is no longer surprising: the idea that our world can collapse in the coming years is widespread. In February 2020, an opinion poll on 'collapsology'[1] conducted by the Institut français d'opinion publique (IFOP) in five countries (France, United States, United Kingdom, Italy and Germany) found that 56 per cent of British people and 65 per cent of French think that Western civilization as we know it will soon collapse (23 per cent of British people expect it within twenty years, and 9 per cent before 2030).[2]

We are now beyond discussing whether the threat is real or not. Dozens, even hundreds of 'top scientists' agree that global catastrophic risks (GCRs[3]) need to be taken seriously. For the most sceptical readers (and it is normal to be sceptical), we have summarized the scientific works dealing with these risks in *How Everything Can Collapse* published by Polity in April 2020 (in French in 2015[4]).

As we expected, everything is speeding up. Not so long ago, some scientists claimed that a global systemic collapse of our society and of the biosphere was possible in the near future, though without being able to specify a date. Today, we have gone a step further: some top scientists say this is the most likely scenario.[5] The Doomsday Clock, which symbolizes the imminence of a planetary cataclysm, was brought forward in January 2020 to midnight minus 100 seconds.[6] This cold and relentless statement is in line with that of well-known authors from the English-speaking world who have inspired us, such as Donella and Dennis Meadows, Joanna Macy, Jared Diamond, John M. Greer, Richard Heinberg and Naomi Oreskes, to name a few.

In 2015, the rational and scientific approach of collapsology was considered 'pessimistic' by the political establishment and most of the mainstream media. However, the general public was already open to discuss the matter. We have seen a growing number of readers coming to our lectures who had reached similar conclusions: neither 'sustainable development', nor 'green growth', nor promises of wealth redistribution will be able stop the disasters from happening, should business-as-usual prevail. There is no doubt that humanity and the planet are heading down a catastrophic path.

Once people realize the situation, bewilderment strikes to the very roots of the soul. Then, two questions arise over and over again: How do we live through our lives with this constant flow of bad news and disasters? How can we rethink politics in the aftermath of catastrophes? In other words, which 'inner' and 'outer' paths must we explore?

The book you are holding in your hands tries to answer the first question. This is the psychological, metaphysical and spiritual question of our relationship to the world, of interdependencies between humans as well as between humans and non-humans, of meaning, of narratives, of the sacred, and so on. We wrote it during the summer of 2018, when a conjunction of events caused the theme of collapse to go viral in France: the first articles in the mass media, a particularly hot summer, the publication of a study dubbed 'Hothouse Earth' in the *Proceedings of the National Academy of Sciences* (PNAS), the spectacular resignation of the charismatic French Minister of the Environment, Nicolas Hulot, and fifteen days later, the publication of the IPCC's special report on the impact of global warming of 1.5°C. The following autumn saw the almost simultaneous emergence of the powerful movements of the Gilets jaunes ('Yellow Vests') in France, of Extinction Rebellion and Deep Adaptation in the UK, and of course of the Fridays for Future initiated by Greta Thunberg.

Another End of the World is Possible was published the same autumn and added a missing piece to deepen the conversation. Since then, the word 'collapsology' has become an uncontrollable media monster that has slipped away us, feeding on catastrophic news but also on criticism and praise, superficial mumbo-jumbo and scholarly analysis. It has even entered the famous French dictionary *Le Petit Robert*.[7]

The unravelling of the biosphere is bad news. So, do we need to wish for a breakdown of the current social order in order to avoid an even greater collapse of earth systems? This question becomes more relevant than ever with each passing year. The latest news on climate change and mass extinction of species is breath-taking. The European Environment Agency does not disagree with that statement. In a collection of maps published on 10 February 2020,[8] this public body tries to figure out our children's and grandchildren's future in Europe at the end of the century: rising sea levels, torrential rain, droughts, mega-fires. A Hollywood movie featuring all these disasters would hardly be credible.

Since 2018, protests and rebellions have erupted across the globe. And, in the midst of the heated political debates on collapses (biodiversity, climate, geopolitics, finance, etc.), a microscopic coronavirus has unleashed a series of cascading effects: fear and entrenchment, a voluntary slowdown of economic activity, domestic political upheavals, diplomatic and geopolitical crises, shortages of medicines, masks and food, the injection of massive amounts of liquidity into the markets by central banks around the world to stabilize the financial system and avoid a major crash, and so on. Covid-19 has proved to be a huge stress-test for the globalized economy. It is also a stark reminder of what matters deeply in our daily lives, as well as a real-time dress rehearsal for future disasters and psychological mayhem, which will be much more intense. And more unexpectedly, the lockdown of half of the world's population has demonstrated the extraordinary capacity of wildlife to adapt and self-regenerate!

The Covid-19 pandemic also showed that while we have the political power to shut down non-essential businesses, it is not enough to moderate the extent of future global warming. The efforts we must make to avoid a dramatic loss of the vital earth systems that sustain life are immense and we are not yet up to the task. Nonetheless, the real-life experiment of quarantine has at least made it possible to distinguish the essential (e.g., health, food, the local economy, love, mutual aid, the living world) from the trivial (e.g., holidays on the other side of the world, extravagant gadgets, stock market speculation, trendy clothes, advertising, Formula One Grands Prix). In Western countries, it is totally feasible to considerably reduce industrial activities and stop over-consumption while meeting people's basic needs.

Unfortunately, the post-Covid era is demonstrating the inability of political and economic elites to see this health emergency as a historic opportunity to phase out fossil fuels, drastically reduce inequalities and address poverty. Instead, we have witnessed the development and implementation of non-eco-friendly recovery plans as illustrated by the billions of dollars made available to the aeronautics and automotive industries. Moreover, we must bear in mind that whatever the outcome of this crisis, extreme weather events are locked in for the next twenty to thirty years due to climate system inertia. There is a whole process of acceptance and mourning before us.

This book is dedicated to people who find themselves running on a perpetual treadmill of emotions (anger, fear, rage, sadness, grief, guilt, etc.). It may help you to keep up with the times and to transform your relationship to the world. It may provide some 'useful' tools for people who want to contribute to the emergence of new livelihoods built on the ruins of capitalism. It is not a call for an individual journey; the need is to bring people together and reclaim the commons, to imagine collective stories, so as to ride the wave of the next centuries without capsizing. In this sense, the task ahead is fundamentally political. More precisely, the political task is a precondition for devising policies of resilience that can cope with the unpredictable roller-coasters of the Anthropocene, that can manage great 'collapses' and imagine what may come 'after'.

Our generation must therefore work on three fronts simultaneously, as Rob Hopkins says, with our heads, hearts and hands: understanding what is happening (collapso-*logy*), imagining and believing in other worlds (collapso-*sophy*) and gathering the forces of life to lead the fight against destructive powers and to build alternatives (collapso-*praxis*).

After *How Everything Can Collapse*, this book lays the foundations of collapsosophy. It is a step. Everything remains to be written, to be felt, to be shared, and above all, to be done. With wisdom and compassion. With love and rage.

Pablo Servigne, Raphaël Stevens and Gauthier Chapelle

Introduction

Learning to live with it

The idea of a possible collapse no longer seems to worry us much. These days, the realization that global disasters are already happening is more and more widely accepted, as is the understanding that along with them comes the possibility of a global systemic collapse.

The monumental shocks caused by Fukushima, by the successive waves of refugees in Europe, by the terrorist attacks in Paris and Brussels, the large-scale disappearance of birds and insects, the Brexit vote and the election of Trump have seriously ruptured the sense of peaceful continuity that had been reassuring so many of us.

One of the barriers that stops us from accepting this idea of collapse is the caricature that has been made out of it. When we think of collapse, scenes from Hollywood disaster films rush up in front of us, feeding the vision of a single, unavoidable event that will suddenly annihilate everything with which we are familiar. We fear such a moment much as we fear the moment of transition from life to death in our own dying.

This is to forget that there are other, worse things about death. There is its anticipation, having to see others die, or seeing oneself suffer in the eyes of others. The collapse of our civilization will not be a single event or catastrophe, but a series of disastrous events (cyclones, industrial accidents, attacks, pandemics, droughts, etc.), taking place against a backdrop of equally destabilizing gradual changes (desertification, the disruption of the seasons, persistent pollution, the extinctions of species and of animal populations, and so on).

We envisage the collapse of what we call 'thermo-industrial civilization' as a process taking place in many different locations. It has already begun, but it has not yet reached its most critical phase, and we cannot say how long it will continue. It is both distant and close, slow-moving and fast, gradual and sudden. It will involve not only natural events, but also (and especially) political, economic and social disturbances, as well as events at a psychological level (such as shifts in collective consciousness).

This is no longer a Nostradamus-like prediction, nor is it yet another reason for a passive or nihilistic attitude. 'Collapse' is not a fashion, or a new label. However, this is likely to be a period that historians or archaeologists of future centuries will comes to label and to look upon as a coherent whole, or which future intelligent species will regard as a quite specific historical event.

If you think that we are exaggerating to get your attention, just remember what two climate scientists were saying in 2011 at a conference in Oxford about climate goals for the twenty-first century (and keep in mind that greenhouse gas emissions are directly proportional to economic activity). They recommended the following: The emerging countries had to start reducing their greenhouse gas emissions by 2030, then maintain this decline at 3 per cent annually. The developed countries had to reach their peak emissions in 2015 and then decline by 3 per cent annually.[1] If these very ambitious goals were reached (and we already know that they are not being reached), then the world will have *one chance in two* to stay below an average temperature rise of 4°C by 2100 ... which would already be monstrously catastrophic on a global scale. In 2017, BP and Shell were planning (internally, without informing their shareholders, let alone the public) for changes of the order of +5°C average by 2050.[2]

In recent history, there is no example of a society which has been able to reduce its emissions by more than 3 per cent over a short period. Such a reduction would cause an immediate economic recession, unless it had itself resulted from a collapse like that of the Soviet Union in the early 1990s or that of Venezuela after 2016.

For the Earth's non-human population (fauna, flora, fungi and micro-organisms), the rise in temperature will mean mass slaughter. Some populations will just keep shrinking. Whole species will disappear forever. Populations of amphibians, of insects and birds in the countryside, of coral reefs, mammals, big fishes, whales and dolphins ... The last male northern white rhinoceros of the North died in 2018, joining the list of imaginary animals which illustrate the stories we read at night to our children.

The change in attitude over the last few years

All these numbers about catastrophes are easily accessible, and the aim of this book is not to add to them. What interests us here is the change of attitude and of conscious awareness within society in recent years.

One landmark was in 1992, at the Rio Summit, when more than 1,700 scientists signed a common text warning humanity about the state of the planet.[3] At the time, this was a new and even embarrassing development. Some 2,500 other scientists responded by warning society against the 'emergence of an irrational ideology that opposes scientific and industrial progress'.[4] Twenty-five years later, 15,364 scientists from 184 countries co-authored a letter explaining that without swift and radical action, humanity would be threatened with extinction.[5] There was no response to this letter. There is no longer any debate. But what is the nature of the silence that followed? Paralysis, exhaustion, lack of interest?

Among the ruling elites, tongues speak more freely, if discreetly. When any of the three of us speak these days in political and economic circles, we are struck by how people no longer question the facts. In public, though, scepticism has given way to feelings of powerlessness, and often to a desire to find ways of escape.

Many of the richest people in the world are barricading themselves inside 'gated communities', luxurious and highly secure residential enclaves.[6] They are also leaving the big cities: in 2015, 3,000 millionaires left Chicago, 7,000 left Paris and 5,000 left Rome. Not all of them are just seeking to evade taxes. Many are genuinely anxious about social tensions, terrorist attacks or the anger of a population increasingly aware of injustices and inequalities.[7] As Robert Johnson, the former director of the Soros Fund, told the Davos Economic Forum, many hedge-fund managers are buying farms in remote countries like New Zealand in search of a 'plan B', and have private jets at hand, ready to take off and fly them there.[8] Others have built, away from prying eyes and on every continent, gigantic and luxurious high-tech underground bunkers to protect their family from whatever disaster might happen.[9]

All this illustrates what the philosopher and sociologist Bruno Latour has described as an act of secession by a very well-off category of the population. Aware of the risks and of what is at stake, they are seeking to save their skins without worrying about the fate of the rest of the world.[10] To take up his metaphor of a plane and the difficulty of coming to land back on earth, we have entered an area of heavy turbulence. The lights have come on, the glasses of champagne are falling over, existential anguish is returning. Some people open the portholes, see lightning flashing across a dark night sky, and close them again immediately. At the front of the aircraft, some first-class people can be seen putting on their golden parachutes. But what are they going to do with them? Will they jump out into the storm? The economy class passengers then turn to the crew and ask for parachutes, knowing full well that their request is not going to be met. All that they are offered in response is a snack, a movie, some duty-free liquor . . .

Surviving . . . is that all?

Faced by these catastrophic announcements, a frequent (and logical) reaction is to start preparing for the situation in practical terms. How do we eat when there is no food in the shops? How can we get safe drinking water if the taps are no longer working? How do we keep ourselves warm without oil, natural gas or electricity? It is not difficult to find information about these topics; there are thousands of books available.[11]

The word 'survivalism' is generally used to refer to this 'reaction to surrounding anxiety'[12] which leads us to prepare for major disasters by seeking self-sufficiency, in other words, independence from industrial supply systems. In recent years, this movement has developed in a dramatic fashion and in many forms. But the term 'survivalist' now brings together approaches and ways of understanding the world which are so varied that it has become difficult to use the word at all.

In fact, until the 1980s, 'survivalists' mainly meant left-wing ecological communities who were preparing for a nuclear winter. Today, 'survivalism' can just as well refer to people who want to learn to live in wild environments. It can also refer to groups who reject and resent the State, and seek self-sufficiency by withdrawal from its institutions, and hostility to anyone who might threaten their autonomy. These latter groups of 'survivalists', often politically on the far right, are not the only voice within the movement, but they contribute to survivalism's bad reputation. This has led to a vicious circle in which the label is now used more to discredit than to describe anything specific, and this further reinforces the mistrust and tendency to withdrawal of some survivalist groups.

We don't intend to provide here a psychological, sociological or historical analysis of survivalism. However, let's build on the image that many people have of this movement, and the caricatures and clichés that have developed about it, and present the three aspects of our book in the form of stories.

We start with Robinson Crusoe, the famous hero of Daniel Defoe's novel of 1719. Thrown off course by a hurricane, Crusoe's ship is wrecked in South America, not far from the mouth of the Orinoco. He is the only survivor on a deserted island which he calls Despair Island. Despite his misfortune, Robinson manages to build himself somewhere to live, he makes a calendar, grows wheat, hunts, raises goats, and learns to make his own pottery. Cannibals regularly visit the island to kill and eat their prisoners there. When one of the prisoners manages to escape, Robinson welcomes him and they become friends. Robinson had desperately missed one thing: human relationships.

Maslow's 'hierarchy of needs', often depicted as a pyramid, is a theory of motivation developed in the 1940s.[13] This theory argued that the needs of the human being are first of all physiological (hunger, thirst, sleep, breathing, etc.); then came the needs for security, then for belonging and love, then for esteem, and finally, at the top of the pyramid, the need for self-actualization. The survivalist posture essentially puts the emphasis on the base, on the first two floors of the pyramid (physiological needs and security), as a sort of logical, caricature extension of modern thought. One could see it as a reflection of a materialistic, individualistic world, separated from nature and in permanent struggle, seeking the best means (material, that is) to live in a world populated by potential competitors and by living beings of which we ultimately do not know very much. In this world, food, firewood and weapons are obviously the way to safety.

Now let's compare two fables. The first refers to the symbol of the French survivalist network, the ant, as in La Fontaine's fable of the ant and the grasshopper. The ant spends her summer preparing food in anticipation of difficult times, while having to put up with the mockery of the grasshoppers who see no reason to worry about anything as long as the oil is flowing freely . . . But the ant grits her teeth. She becomes resentful and begins to delight in the pleasure that she will have when the hordes of hungry grasshoppers (and city dwellers) implore her forgiveness and pity far too late, and she tells them to get lost. A well-deserved revenge!

Our second fable is that of the Three Little Pigs. All three are preparing for the arrival of the Big Bad Wolf with more or less seriousness, and with a different vision of the threat he will pose. When the wolf destroys the two weaker houses, the first two pigs (or grasshoppers) run to their super-survivalist brother . . . who opens the door for them. Of course, he may well say, 'I told you so!', but this does not prevent them from subsequently sharing a brotherly meal together. The difference between the two fables is that in the second case there was a sense of brotherhood *before* the disaster.

A last story will give some extra colour to our picture. It is told by our friend Kim Pasche, who has been organizing wild nature immersion courses for many years. Despite his remarkable skills, he refuses to be called a 'survivalist', and mischievously says: 'If you put ten survivalists in a forest for a few months, they will kill each other and destroy the forest. If you put ten Native Americans in the same forest, not only will the forest be more beautiful and productive, but they will have formed a tribe, a true community of humans in connection with other living beings.'[14]

We take it for granted that physiological and safety needs are important. Anyone who has not thought of preparation of this kind is only half awake. Yet survival is a precarious, transient state. It is 'a list of facts without a vision'.[15] We can survive for a few days, for a few weeks, but after that? Worse, if we find ourselves in a really bad disaster with this materialist attitude, with the objective of surviving a few weeks at the expense of our neighbours, it's a safe bet that we will all be dead after a year.

These four stories highlight the reasons for writing this book. These are the desire to get ready for living through the consequences of disasters that are happening and will happen in the future, above all by looking for connections between human beings, connections with non-human life, and a meaning for what is happening. For people who cannot imagine continuing to live without a feeling of achievement, of other people's esteem, trust and love, without reasons to share, Maslow's pyramid is apparently turned upside down. Perhaps it would be better to speak of 'Maslow's table',[16] of which each leg is essential for the overall balance of the person . . .

Cultivating edible plants in one's garden, learning to do without fossil fuels and preparing one's family for emergencies are certainly necessary, but they are not enough to 'make a society', that is to say to make us into human beings.

As the American psychologist Carolyn Baker puts it: 'In fact, could not a budding society of emotionally myopic survivalists produce a culture as terrifying and devoid of humanity as Huxley's *Brave New World*?'[17]

We have no desire to see the continued existence of a violent society that selects for the most aggressive individuals. Wanting to live beyond the shocks, and not just survive them, is already to start our preparation with a different attitude, one that looks towards joy, sharing and fraternity.

A branch of collapsology directed towards inner experience

After we put together the facts about a possible collapse in a first book (*How Everything Can Collapse: A Manual for Our Times*),[18] we can see several directions that are open for 'collapsologists' who want to move onwards. The most important, it seems to us (though not the most urgent one), is that of collective action, in other words of developing realistic, bold and courageous political proposals. However, before we act, and even before we propose courses of action, there are still things we need to understand and an inner journey we need to make. That journey involves coming to terms with the psychological aspects of climate change or other global disasters.[19]

Here we face a huge challenge. Even to be interested in these subjects in their scientific or sociological forms brings with it some risk for our mental health. As for people who take this question head-on and make it the central direction of their lives, they are confronted (and will be for a long time) with very strong demands, both psychological and in their relations with others, as well as in their social and political commitments.

Those who have thought about how bad the situation might get 'will not have an easy time coping with it, but they are not as apt to be overwhelmed by it as those who refuse to contemplate it'. [20] Between the person who is ready for action and the one who remains in denial, there is a whole range of people with various problems: those who just live through catastrophic events at a physical level, those who feel that something is wrong but cannot find the words for it (weak cognitive dissonance), those who know but cannot act in the way that they would wish (acute cognitive dissonance), and those who know and act but are exhausted or discouraged.

During these years of discussions with the public, we arrived at the same conclusion as that described by Carolyn Baker, who has accompanied many people struggling with the prospect of collapse: once the penny drops, most people don't want to see more and more evidence (even if it was important to begin with); they want above all to learn how to live with the collapse. They become 'collapsonauts'.

So, preparing oneself for this future does not just involve material and political aspects. It also has psychological, spiritual, metaphysical and artistic dimensions. The questions which the disasters pose for us are difficult to come to terms with. If we want to continue thinking about the collapse, if we seek to act, to make sense of our lives, or just to get up in the morning, it is important not to go crazy. Crazy with isolation, crazy with sadness, crazy with rage, crazy from thinking too much about it, or crazy from continuing one's little routines while pretending not to see.

Some people think of this psychological dimension as a matter for women, or as a luxury reserved for fragile city dwellers who have known nothing but comfort. It's not like this at all. The psychological challenge is a primordial one, and it affects all social classes, all peoples, all cultures. What do we say to the Sudanese refugee who suffers from anxiety or post-traumatic stress in a camp in Libya or in Calais? That his suffering is negligible? What do we say to the family of a young hyper-sensitive Belgian student who commits suicide because he has seen too much? How do we help the engineer in charge of oil-well drilling, who is reluctant to return to work every morning after kissing his children? How can you keep your spirits up as an activist trying to block a development project, when you create new ways of living in the territory you are defending, and you get bulldozers and grenades in reply?

The purpose of collapsology is not to state certainties that will crush any possible future, nor to make precise predictions, nor to find 'solutions' that can 'avoid a problem', but to learn to live with the bad news and with the changes that they foretell, sudden or gradual, so that we can find the strength and the courage to do something that will transform us, or, as Edgar Morin would say, will bring about our metamorphosis.

Expanding out to 'collapsosophy'

The Canadian Paul Chefurka is one of the community of 'collapseniks' (popular bloggers who are trying to make sense of the coming collapse).[21] He has a striking talent for explaining complex subjects, and has given us a very simple but illuminating scale for describing the growth of awareness.[22] 'When it comes to our understanding of the current global crisis,' he says, 'each of us seems to fit somewhere in a continuum of awareness that can be roughly divided into five stages.'[23]

At Stage 1, people do not seem to see any fundamental problem. If there is a problem, it is that there is not enough of what we have already: growth, jobs, wages, development, etc.

At Stage 2, people become aware of one or another fundamental problem (with a choice between themes such as climate, overpopulation, peak oil, pollution, biodiversity, capitalism, nuclear power, inequalities, geopolitics, migrations, etc.). This 'problem' grabs all of their attention, and they sincerely believe that if it can be 'solved', everything will be as it was before.

At Stage 3, they have become aware of several major problems. People who have arrived at this stage spend their time prioritizing one campaign or cause over another and convincing others of specific priorities.

At Stage 4, the inevitable conclusion is reached, they become aware of the interdependence of all of the world's 'problems'. Everything becomes appallingly systemic, in other words it can't be solved by a few individuals or by miraculous 'solutions', and it can't be dealt with by politics as currently conceived. 'People who arrive at this stage tend to withdraw into tight circles of like-minded individuals in order to trade insights and deepen their understanding of what's going on. These circles are necessarily small, both because personal dialogue is essential for this depth of exploration, and because there just aren't very many people who have arrived at this level of understanding.'[24]

Finally, at Stage 5, people change their point of view irrevocably. They no longer see a 'problem' that calls for 'solutions' but a *predicament* (a situation like death or an incurable disease, from which we cannot extricate ourselves, and which we cannot resolve). This requires them to find ways in which they can learn to live with it as well as possible. At this stage, they realize that the situation encompasses all aspects of life, and that it will profoundly transform them. They can begin to feel completely overwhelmed: they see that the people around them are not interested in what is happening, that the global system is not responding fast enough, and the earth as a whole is suffering intensely. Practically everything is brought into question. This is not only exhausting, but can cut people off from whatever stable and reassuring emotional environment they have. 'For those who arrive at Stage 5, there is a real risk that depression will set in.'[25]

Chefurka says that there are two principal ways to react to this unpleasant situation, though they are in no way mutually exclusive. We can engage in an 'outer' path: politics, transition towns, the establishment of resilient communities, etc.; or in an 'inner', more spiritual path. Such an inner path does not necessarily involve adherence to a conventional religion. If anything, the contrary may be true. 'Most of the people I've met who have chosen an inner path have as little use for traditional religion as their counterparts on the outer path have for traditional politics.'[26]

Within this transforming landscape, 'collapsology' involves analysing and synthesizing the many studies which have been conducted on this inextricable global situation in a transdisciplinary manner. This is a process of opening up the disciplines and breaking down the walls between them, and is summed up well by Spinoza's advice regarding human behaviour: 'Do not make fun, do not lament, do not hate, but understand.'[27] Collapsology could become a scientific discipline in its own right, but it would become truly official only if universities opened chairs in collapsology, if students and researchers in the field got funding, offered symposia and perhaps set up an *Open Journal of Collapsology* (complete with an editorial board) . . .

This collapsological approach, which is essentially rational, is necessary because it makes it possible to dispel the confusion surrounding the subject and, in particular, to remain credible with people who are aware of the subject but not yet convinced. But it is far from enough, because it does not tell us what to do. It does not tell us how to distinguish the good from the bad, how to cultivate powerful convictions, strong values, abundant imagination and a strong common desire. Scientific tools are relevant but they are not sufficient to encompass an issue as complex and multi-faceted as a collapse (which also includes the collapse of thought systems). In other words, by Stage 5 of the growth of awareness, *collapsology is no longer sufficient*.

In recent years, we have enriched our own scientific project through more awareness of human feeling and subjectivity, and this has led us to become involved with ethical, spiritual and metaphysical issues. We think that these are also part of the 'first aid kit' that we will need to open as we face this storm of unpredictable duration. Dominique Bourg, the French philosopher who wrote the Foreword to this book, says much the same in different words in his own book, *A New Earth*:[28] the only choice we have left to us is to rethink our way of seeing the world, in other words, of being in the world.

We propose using the term 'collapsosophy' (from '-sophy' = wisdom) for the whole body of behaviours and positions that arise out of this unavoidable situation (the collapses that are taking place and of the possible global collapse) and which depart from the strict domain of the sciences. The same process of opening out and of breaking down walls that is involved in collapsology is found here too, in a broader opening to questions of ethics, the emotions, and the imagination, and to spiritual and metaphysical questions. We do not aim to choose any particular camp, more to look for complementarities and connections which can be woven between all these areas, so as to help us in undergoing these external and internal transformations.

We are aware that this is not the usual approach in the scientific and political world (or at least it is not discussed openly), and that it can cause discomfort as well as enthusiasm. But it seems to us that we cannot do without it. To quote the American writer John Michael Greer: 'The recognition that these two transformations, the outer and the inner, work in parallel and have to be carried out together is the missing piece that the sustainability movements of the Seventies never quite caught.'[29] He also notes that 'it's not the technical dimension of the predicament of industrial society that matters most just now. It's the inner dimension, the murky realm of nonrational factors that keep our civilization from doing anything that doesn't make the situation worse, that must be faced if anything constructive is going to happen at all.'[30]

In these uncertain times, the voices of scientists are more important than ever. It is time for them to redouble their efforts and the rigour of their work, but also to find the courage to speak with their hearts, and to engage fully in the challenges that face us, with all the subjective and personal factors which that implies. Some of them are doing it already, for example the astrophysicist Hubert Reeves in the 2018 French-Canadian documentary by Iolande Cadrin-Rossignol, *La Terre vue du cœur* (*Earth: Seen From the Heart*).[31]

The disasters that lie ahead of us may lead to the suffering and even death of thousands or millions of human beings in ways that can easily be foreseen ... not counting the other living species. If we shut ourselves off from all of this and look towards the future without compassion, we risk losing both any reason to live and our own humanity. If, in contrast, we take the decision to plunge body and soul into our coming predicament, with compassion and courage, then we need to learn to equip ourselves materially, emotionally and spiritually, in order to avoid madness, or again losing our empathy for the suffering around us. The idea of this book is to explore the changes that we can make inside our heads and our hearts, in order to be able to work with the world of our time. Or, as Carolyn Baker puts it, 'we must ask: Who do I want to be in the face of collapse? What did I come here to do?'[32]

Breaking down walls

It has already been some years since we formed the desire to make as many people as possible come to understand the scientific work on this subject. We haven't yet lost our spirits, or hope, or our reason. We appreciate now that going beyond the strict scientific framework has been a great help for us on this journey. It has even been a source of joy.

Both the partial collapses that are taking place already and the possible systemic collapses of the future are opportunities for transformation. We remain convinced that it is possible to understand, to speak and to live the catastrophes and the sufferings that they generate without giving up joy or the possibility of a future.

This book tells of our discoveries in the fields of disaster psychology but also of our encounters on the paths of 'collapsosophy'. It is aimed at people who want to navigate this balance of light and dark, without giving up their clarity of vision or their sense of reality, but also without renouncing their sense of a future which may be joyful, and in any case is *of this earth*. Because the question asked by Bruno Latour is the question of our generation:

> Do we continue to nourish dreams of escaping, or do we start seeking a place on the earth that we and our children can inhabit? Either we deny the existence of the problem, or

else *we look for a place to land*, to come to earth. From now on, this is what divides us all, much more than our positions on the right or the left side of the political spectrum.[33]

In this book, we report on streams of thought that may be unfamiliar to many readers. We also make connections between areas that may at first seem to have nothing to do with each other. We are aware that this could upset some people. Reading these pages will ask of you a spirit of openness, curiosity and understanding. But this is the nature of a transdisciplinary enterprise (see chapter 4).

This attitude of openness also involves a mistrust of the taken-for-granted labels, clichés and caricatures that are used mainly to discredit: survivalist, snowflake, fascist, leftist, new age, mystic, etc. These labels should not prevent us from looking at the complexity (or the emptiness) that may be hidden behind them.

Treat this book as a visit to a huge wild vegetable garden. Feel free to walk around and pick up what you like, or to learn about what you do not know. There is colour and life, there are fruits ready to pick and connections which still can't be seen. And like the Kogi Indians, fill two saddlebags. Fill the one on the right with what speaks to you and suits you; fill the one on the left with what you disapprove of or what seems irrelevant today, so that you can come back to it later.

In the first part of the book, we explore the impact that the coming disasters may have on our mental health, as well as the ways in which we can recover. How do we absorb this news and this understanding? How do we get used to living with it, over the coming decades? How should we announce it to those around us? Do hope and optimism still make sense?

In the second part, we explore three ways of changing our outlook on the world, so as to help us find meaning, or at least to step aside a little. Why and how can we change our relationship to science and knowledge? Why and how can we open ourselves up to other ways of seeing the world developed by other cultures which are less 'thermo-industrial'? More generally, isn't it time to change the stories we tell ourselves?

And in the third part, we enter more deeply into 'collapsosophy'. We start by approaching the essential question of the connections which we shall need to weave with ourselves, between ourselves, and with other living beings. Then we open up to questions that give meaning to our time and to our lives: the process of growing up and 'becoming an adult', the male–female relationship, the return to the wild, and the ways in which we can go through all of this together.

The impetus of this book is to explore, beginning from the knowledge, experiences and intuitions which each person already has. It is to share the joy of learning further, to provoke moments of realization, to explore our shadows, to meet with people who take us out of our comfort zone, to begin a dialogue with trees, rivers and salamanders, to accompany each other through suffering and mourning, and to participate together in the emergence of what is going to happen.

Part One

Recovery

What man can feel himself at one and the same time responsible and hopeless?
Antoine de Saint-Exupéry, *Flight to Arras,* trans. L. Galantière
(San Diego, CA: Harcourt Brace & Co, 1986)

1

Experiencing the impact

You can always turn off the TV, but the news keeps on coming. It is difficult to avoid hearing about the catastrophes from around the world, and when one stops ignoring them or tries to imagine the repercussions, the news is overwhelming. It turns everything upside down. The world as we imagine it is breaking up, we no longer know what to believe in, our emotions come to the surface. We have always found it striking that in survivalist manuals, essays on the Anthropocene, presentations about the climate, political meetings, with a few rare exceptions,[1] little is said about our feelings, except to discuss people's fear, and the fear of fear. The range of emotions is much wider than that, however, and they have a fundamental impact on the ways in which we think, talk and see the future, and on how we act.

During or after a disaster, psychological trauma affects only a few people directly. However, feelings affect everyone. Emotions are not just 'options' that many men never really acquired or that girls use to spice up their evenings when watching a chick flick. They have a tremendous influence on our judgements and decisions, and they are one of the main triggers of human behaviour.[2] They change our perception of risk[3] and can affect our political preferences.[4]

To realize that it is too late to limit global warming to 'less than 2°C' and that the consequences are and will be catastrophic, to see the massive decline of animal populations, to discover toxic molecules in the blood of babies, all this causes feelings of fear, anger, sadness, resignation, guilt, helplessness, which disrupt the superficial denial that is our daily life.

There is the news in books and newspapers, but there are also the disasters themselves, that are already physically affecting thousands of people. Floods, droughts, tsunamis, vast bushfires, shortages, dead areas in the oceans, decimated populations of insects, birds, fish or large herbivores, and the rest of it. They have already brought about, and they still cause, real and considerable damage to people, populations or social classes. They all cause both physical and psychological shocks that we will have to continue to deal with in the course of this century.

It will be necessary to forge a heart of steel (though bamboo might be more useful, depending on the circumstances[5]) to endure the storms to come. This chapter explores the psychological aspects of disasters, and more specifically the reactions they cause in us.

Living through the disasters

Whether disasters are natural, caused by industry or result from terrorist acts, they can be sudden, overwhelming and often deadly. They kill, cause injury, depress, cause insanity, lead to sorrow and despair, fear, stress, lack of feeling, etc. They cause huge shocks to both body and spirit.

A global increase in the level of mental trauma

After disasters, the media take stock of human losses and quantify the material damage. The economic damage amounts to millions or billions of euros or dollars, and the victims number in the dozens, hundreds or thousands. Hurricane Katrina in 2005 killed 1,836 people[6] and cost the American taxpayer the trifling amount of $160 billion,[7] or nearly 1 per cent of the country's GDP. In 2011 at Fukushima, after the earthquake and tsunami, there were 15,828 dead, 6,145 injured, 4,823 missing and more than one million homes destroyed.[8] The cost was estimated at $626 billion, about three times the Japanese government's first estimate.[9]

Such disasters affect millions of people every year (about 162 million in 2005, 330 million in 2010[10]). In the United States, for example, 13–19 per cent of adults experience at least one disaster in their lifetime.[11] These numbers are increasing worldwide in the face of climate change and increasing population density.[12]

If the number of deaths is relatively low compared to the number of people affected (in 2010, 0.1 per cent of the 330 million people affected died), what happens to the survivors?

Behind these cold, dry figures is hidden another reality, often forgotten and yet of vital significance: the psychological consequences of a disaster last even longer than the physical traumas.[13] Their intensity and frequency will continue to increase. To know how to understand, manage and treat these types of traumas is fundamental to prepare us for future shocks.

During such an event, the first reactions are paralysis, denial, action (saving loved ones, for example) or flight. The shock can cause intense stress, then more lasting reactions such as anxiety, irritability, despair, apathy, loss of self-esteem, guilt, depression, confusion, insomnia, eating disorders or difficulties in making decisions.

Some people continue to react to the initial shock long after the danger has passed. When the reaction to trauma interferes with daily life, mental health professionals speak of 'post-traumatic stress disorder' (PTSD). In recent decades, hundreds of psychiatric studies have been conducted on this topic.[14] They show that symptoms can take up to six months to appear. Specific social categories, including women and children, are more vulnerable.[15] Note also that PTSD is not the only severe symptom; other major problems can include depression, generalized anxiety and panic attacks.[16]

A catastrophic event can also lead to serious but less visible disorders. In a recent study around Fukushima, researchers at Harvard University were able for the first time to compare the health of a population before and after a major disaster.[17] It emerged that in people over sixty-five years of age, the rate of dementia almost tripled, mainly because of the loss of neighbourhood ties.

Gradual disruptions are also effective in disrupting our mental health. For example, in the USSR, as early as the 1970s, well before the Union was dissolved on 26 December 1991 in a 'strangely peaceful atmosphere, without Kalashnikov fire or missile threats',[18] the country was already in serious decline. All the countries in the Soviet bloc suffered the consequences of these processes of economic, social and political collapse.[19] An entire generation was marked by the experience of drastic fluctuations in available resources and by the increasing uncertainty appearing in all facets of life.[20]

This period of collapse was characterized by an accelerating decline in life expectancy. For example, in Russia, between 1992 and 1994, men lost more than six years (from 63.8 to 57.7 years) and women over three years (from 74.4

to 71.2 years). The causes? Increased stress, a failing health system, infectious diseases, suicides, homicides, as well as road accidents and excessive alcohol consumption, especially in Russia for adolescents and young adults.

The suicide rate for men aged fifty to sixty, which increased sharply after 1992, was strongly correlated with the state of the economy (as measured by GDP). For women, it was found to be closely linked to alcohol consumption. Alcoholism played a major role in this social and health chaos, especially for people who were not solidly supported psychologically by those around them. The number of murders tripled between 1988 and 1994 and remains today among the highest in the world. Ninety per cent of the murderers are men, often under the influence of alcohol, and 30 per cent of their victims are women, often raped.

Climate change can be just as deadly and traumatic, itself taking the form of extreme violence, with its consequences of anger, suffering, loss and pain, and thousands of casualties, often much like war in its effects. For example, in India over the last thirty years, the rises in temperature and the subsequent agricultural losses have caused deep despair and 60,000 suicides.[21] A recent study projects that uncontrolled climate change (of over 4°C) could produce between 9,000 and 40,000 suicides in the United States and Mexico in 2050.[22] This increase would represent a change in suicide rate comparable to that induced by an economic recession.

Moreover, as the editorial of a special issue of the climatology journal *Nature Climate Change* notes, there is another subject which is growing fast, if little studied: that of loss, mourning, grief and despair caused by the progressive change in landscapes and ecosystems.[23]

After experiencing 'ecological losses', people can experience what the Canadian researcher Ashlee Cunsolo and the

Australian Neville R. Ellis have called 'ecological grief'. 'Ecological grief is a natural response to ecological losses, particularly for people who retain close living, working and cultural relationships to the natural environment.'[24] There are two contexts in which this ecological grief emerges: disappearance or physical destruction (of species, familiar places, ecosystems, etc.) and the loss of the kinds of knowledge related to these places.

Physical destruction includes, for example, the loss of a home or loved ones as a result of a hurricane,[25] but also the slow degradation of the environment (called 'slow violence'), often ignored because it is not seen as an emergency.[26] Cunsolo and Ellis give the example of Australian farmers, who, seeing the wind turning the land into desert, felt reactions (depression, anger, anxiety, even physical pain) proportional to their 'sense of belonging and connection to the territory'. Here we encounter the concept of 'solastalgia',[27] the malaise and pain associated with the memory of a place of life (territory and ecosystem) which has been destroyed or degraded.[28] This sense of desolation is, for example, frequently felt by migrants.

Regarding the loss of kinds of knowledge, disasters or global changes destroy the knowledge and practices built in relation to a territory and the living beings within it, especially for cultures and populations that have close relations with the natural world. This results in a loss of identity, and consequently in deep feelings of grief.[29] This is the situation for the Australian farmers studied by Ellis, who can no longer predict the seasonal cycle, or pass on this knowledge, and who are therefore worried about the future of their families. The same is true for the Inuit, who can no longer travel on the ice to gather food at their habitual locations. The older generations 'no longer trust their knowledge'[30] and also suffer from having been unable to protect a territory that was under their responsibility. Shame, guilt and helplessness come to gnaw at them.

The plunge into the Anthropocene will only accentuate this feeling of ecological grief. This experience, which so far has been entirely neglected by the scientific or political discourse on climate change, is still difficult to address publicly.[31] To recognize its existence is at least a beginning, as the Australian philosopher Clive Hamilton points out. This is a first step towards recognizing a fundamental connection between us and the biosphere, a connection that we must identify and accept, and of which we have to take care. Feeling sadness after a disaster is not only a sign of good mental health, but also a sign of a deep attachment to the earth.

We should not imagine that scientists do not feel these emotions. Those who are interested in the causes and consequences of disasters (terrorism, armed conflict, genocide, migration, climate change, natural disasters, etc.) are working on a regular basis with a traumatizing research object, but they are not necessarily prepared for the psychological consequences.

Professor Dale Dominey-Howes, of the Natural Hazards Research Group at the University of Sydney, gives a moving description of the impact on these researchers: both the results of being in contact with the location affected, and with the testimonies of survivors, and also the indirect effect of seeing their colleagues experience these kinds of trauma.[32] He urges us to monitor the emotional state of scientists and alerts his colleagues to these risks, which have scarcely been documented. In fact, this is an issue for everyone, as we are reminded by the psychologist Émilie Hermant:

> Finally, I want to repeat that life in industrial civilization is inherently traumatizing. Of course, there are thousands

of veterans among us who suffer from post-traumatic stress disorder, but I have never met a single person who did not have one or another form of trauma in his or her body. Do I need to warn you that the trauma caused by the collapse will most certainly wake up these past traumas that you already carry in your body, unless that is, you find a way to come to terms with them beforehand?[33]

Storms of emotions present and to come

It isn't just trauma that we will have to deal with. The Anthropocene is also a rich source of so-called 'negative' emotions. These are emotions that our culture generally encourages us to neglect so that they don't get in the way of our rational mind's search for 'solutions'. As the situation gets worse, however, we are likely to have to face a growing flood of such emotions.

Sadness can overwhelm us when we lose something we love. Gardens of our childhood, the swallows of our countryside, orang-utans and old-growth forests, whales, sharks and clean oceans, mountain glaciers and Arctic sea ice – new items are constantly added to the litany. When sadness grows to the point where it can seem there is no limit to the losses, it can shift into despair, even into nihilism.[34]

Anger (and sometimes violence, but we should not confuse them with each other) springs up to help us defend a territory or an identity which has been attacked or violated. But it is also a form of expression of pain and suffering, and can also indicate great sensitivity towards injustice. Anger can also mean a willingness, a rage to live, and even to live together. One of the authors of the report to the Club of Rome, Donella Meadows, aptly noted: 'With half-suppressed anger, I tend to swing out and do something impetuous and ignorant. But a fully felt, grounded, familiar anger can move me through a lifetime commitment to make things better.'[35]

Fear is ambiguous too. It is very common when it comes to imagining your family living in a chaotic world without drinkable water or medicines (something which is already happening in many areas). While fear is more of an animal reaction, immediate and explosive, like that of prey in front of a predator, anxiety and anguish are much more sneaky and hidden. They can arise to paralyse us when we need to start moving. Finally, there are collective fears, passed on from history and from the memories we share: the fear of scarcity, of other people's violence, of ideologies or religions.[36]

Fear, when connected to feeling helpless and vulnerable, can lead to denial, paralysis and suppressing one's emotions. Studies dealing with the effects of fear on engagement against global warming are inconclusive.[37] Some studies suggest that fear does not promote engagement, others suggest the reverse. Altogether, there is really no clear correlation between fear and support for campaigns against global warming.[38]

Many people find it difficult to express their emotions They may be afraid of suffering (of being swept away by their feelings), of despair (and of no longer being able to find a reason to live), of appearing morbid in front of others (people expect you to be 'positive'), of appearing ignorant or unconvincing next to supposedly 'objective' experts, of upsetting other people, or just of seeming weak and not in control of their emotions.[39]

The most frequent reaction to such fears is to repress your feelings, to prevent these so-called 'negative' emotions from emerging instead of 'positive' emotions such as joy or enthusiasm. Often people say that an excessive focus on the negative impacts of climate change (i.e. a severe 'diagnosis') without really focusing on solutions (a plausible 'treatment') would put the public off.[40]

We should not try to escape from our feelings. They are
the logical and healthy response of human beings witnessing
the destruction of what they hold dear. It is tempting to try
to reject these negative emotions, to be wary of them, to take
them for bad counsellors. But what if they were not so bad
for us?

For example, they might stimulate the search for information, a fundamental step in getting moving.[41] They might
also be important in helping us to create a desirable image
of the future. A study of coastal communities in California
already affected by climate change, by the psychologist
Susanne Moser, showed that the factors that mattered most
in creating a vision for the future were people's attachment
to the place where they were living, and their emotional
reactions to climate change. These were far more significant
than technical solutions.

This goes even further. For more than forty years, the
work of Joanna Macy, environmental activist and eco-
philosopher, has shown that to stop hiding the facts from
oneself, to allow oneself to express what one holds to be
true, causes a renewal of energy, and a kind of freeing up of
enthusiasm which can lead to genuine joy.

Scientists, too, are affected by this pressure to avoid so-
called 'negative' feelings. Those who study climate change
or the destruction of biodiversity can be severely affected
by despair but avoid showing it in public because they feel
uncomfortable revealing their feelings, and under pressure
to display objectivity and to maintain an emotionless style of
discourse whatever the personal cost.[42]

The philosopher Clive Hamilton analysed this pose of
scientific neutrality a decade or so ago:

Behind the facade of scientific detachment, the climate scientists themselves now evince a mood of barely suppressed

panic. No one is willing to say publicly what the climate science is telling us: that we can no longer prevent global warming that will this century bring about a radically transformed world that is much more hostile to the survival and flourishing of life.[43]

As an editorial in the journal *Nature Climate Change* points out, it is easier to study climate change than it is to consider the mental health of researchers whose field of study involves global disasters and transformations[44] and immerses them daily in anxiety-provoking data, while they are exposed to the denial, apathy or even hostility of the general public. It's a good recipe for depression.

Worse, these scientists are understandably more sensitive to the environment than most people, and this leaves them more exposed to bad news and negative feelings, even while their professional culture requires them not to express their emotions and to stay as neutral as possible. This is an exhausting situation that has, for example, led Camille Parmesan, a researcher of international status, and a specialist in the effects of climate change on biodiversity who also co-authored the Intergovernmental Panel on Climate Change (IPCC) reports, to declare herself publicly 'in a state of professional depression'.

If this field of study is still at an embryonic stage, the scientific community is finally realizing its importance. As the psychologist Susan Clayton summarizes, 'Research should explore strategies to help [researchers] cope with these emotions. Their motivation and their empowerment are important for all of us.'

The historian of science Naomi Oreskes has shown how this culture of feigned indifference has led climatologists to convey an understated version of climate hazards.[45] She argues that scientists should be more vocal about their concerns.[46]

For the philosopher Sabine Roeser, the situation is clear: emotions are 'the missing link in effective communication about climate science'.[47] We need to express them.

For how can one not feel touched when climatologists can no longer contain their tears in the face of fear and helplessness? For us, this type of message is much more powerful than simply reading a (cold) summary of IPCC reports intended for policy makers. All of this resonates precisely with our own experience of collapsologists, and of their exchanges with the public. As Oreskes sums it up, 'How can you communicate danger without emotional emphasis? How can you tell someone that he or she should be worried when you don't sound worried yourself?'[48]

Giving people the bad news

There are two kinds of bad news, news about a disaster that has already occurred (the death of a loved one, the loss of a house, a plane crash, etc.) and news about an event that has not yet happened. Announcing a collapse of bird populations is of the first kind. Announcing (or becoming aware) of a probable collapse of our civilization is of the second. These words by themselves can cause another collapse, that of our inner world.

If there is one area where dreadful announcements are regularly made to people, it is that of health.[49] We probably have some lessons to learn from the experiences in this area of both doctors and nursing staff, and also those of patients and their relatives.

Telling people that their future has gone

In 2013, the Australian philosopher Clive Hamilton described his own moment of realization. It was not understanding something new – he already knew a lot about the subject – but an emotional realization. The shock went from head to heart, and the body started to take action.

> For some years I could see intellectually that the gap between the actions demanded by the science and what our political institutions could deliver was large and probably unbridgeable, yet emotionally I could not accept what this really meant for the future of the world. It was only in September 2008, after reading a number of new books, reports and scientific papers, that I finally allowed myself to make the shift and to admit that we simply are not going to act with anything like the urgency required. Humanity's determination to transform the planet for its own material benefit is now backfiring on us in the most spectacular way, so that the climate crisis is for the human species now an existential one. On one level, I felt relief: relief at finally admitting what my rational brain had been telling me; relief at no longer having to spend energy on false hopes; and relief at being able to let go of some anger at the politicians, business executives and climate sceptics who are largely responsible for delaying action against global warming until it became too late. Yet capitulating to the truth initiated a period of turmoil that lasted at least as long as it took to write this book.[50]

Cunsolo and Ellis speak of a third type of ecological suffering, that connected to the loss of an anticipated future.[51] Whether sudden or chronic in nature, it comes from a change in how we imagine our future (or our lack of a future), and particularly affects young people. It is similar to what has been called 'pre-traumatic' stress disorder, the psychological consequences of living with fear about the future.[52]

One can suffer the harmful effect of the lack of a future as a result of the news of climatic disasters or of ecosystem collapses. In medicine, the news of an incurable disease, whether fatal or not, has a similar effect.

Huntington's disease is a degenerative genetic disease. It is rare and incurable, and its severe symptoms, which usually appear in mid-life, can quickly lead to death.

Émilie was stunned when she was told she had the condition. She was not yet forty years old and had no symptoms. But the genetic test indicated a number, a certainty. 'I was enveloped in a sphere of pure loneliness, a white and silent nucleus, that abrupt and radical removal from the world . . . the slightest idea, the slightest concept is annihilated by the absolute purity of this loneliness.'[53]

Then there was the refusal to believe for months, the 'crossing the desert', and the idea of suicide as the last act of resistance or freedom. There was also anger at the medical institution for having put in place such a violent test and for not having provided support, not being up to the demands of the situation. 'The doctors I met with were both terrified and fascinated by what they were having me do. And from this strange vantage point, the best they could offer me was depressing and corrosive stereotyping.' She remembers the doctors' phrases: 'your life is a coin toss, a matter of heads or tails, it's going to be so difficult for friends and family, there's no treatment, you are very healthy for now but when you get worse you will come and work on your disability with us, what's that – you plan on adopting a child?! . . . [expression of horror/sympathy]'.[54]

Émilie calls them 'tragic spells', which 'make you rot, reducing the multiplicities of tomorrow into a narrow, monolithic, flat, diagnosed sick future that stops the mind from the business not of grieving but creativity'.[55]

This inhibiting and reductive effect on the future is also something often described as the first stage experienced by those who plunge into the collapse on their own. If the person undergoing this phase in turn becomes the messenger of the collapse, before having been able to metabolize the announcement, she too runs the risk of falling into 'tragic spells': 'But you don't understand, you have to stop making children, everything is going to collapse!'

The Dingdingdong Collective, which Émilie founded, was formed around people involved with Huntington's disease: the sick and the future sick, relatives, caregivers and philosophers, including Isabelle Stengers and Vinciane Despret. The intention behind this collective is to improve the situation of those affected by the disease.[56]

A genetic test says something about a person's future. It is not a diagnosis of a *present* state of health, but information about a future state, and it has the power to make people sick, 'infected by information that is both abstract and hopeless'.[57]

Like the test for Huntington's disease, the news of a possible collapse of our civilization can be encountered in solitude, through a book or in front of a screen. This brings about a stressful situation from which it can be difficult to extricate yourself, particularly when the people around you don't want to hear about it, which is not unusual in a society where expressing feelings is so taboo outside the private sphere. On the other hand, even if these people felt themselves alone when faced with the news and its final nature, they may very well quickly and spontaneously find themselves sharing it with others, and wanting to do so.

By contrast with the doctors' reliable and objective measurement, one can't demonstrate with any certainty that the collapse will take place, let alone accurately predict the onset of symptoms.

However, the two announcements are comparable in their impact. Despite the uncertainty, a person may be very deeply convinced of the imminence and severity of collapse. As with the genetic test, this belief becomes a formidable 'destiny-making machine', to use the Dingdingdong Collective's expression. Even worse, if one thinks of these issues as specific moments, as final destinations, the incurable disease and the collapse can exercise a tremendous power of attraction. For the philosopher of science, Katrin Solhdju, quoted by the collective, 'the problem is not where the story ends (all mortals share in that), but the path along which it drags so powerfully those it touches'.[58]

For the Dingdingdong Collective, the 'revelation does not inform you, quite the contrary: it transforms you. It can either make you sick or make you better: it all depends on what you do with it.' The test can be a revelation in a positive sense, as much as a curse.[59]

'How do you prevent this knowledge from becoming poisonous?'[60] How, after being paralysed, to become again the actor and creator of one's own life?

The approach which the group suggests – and we agree with them in relation to the collapse – is to create a more 'positive' culture of illness, based on concrete experiences and knowledge, rather than fears and abstract ideas. 'The antidote wasn't that hard to make. It consisted of a slow and gradual reinjection of everything that might have been eroded by the test: doubt, uncertainty, hesitation, the maybes, what-ifs, and feel-your-ways.'[61]

There are three lessons to be learned from this parallel with Huntington's disease. The first is to stop 'fighting against the disease', because that doesn't lead anywhere very positive. On the contrary, experience suggests we would be better off learning to dance with the illness, as with death, or with our shadows. And Émilie adds an important point (which we will describe in our own journey when we get to chapter 7): the ability to make the antidote grew from 'humility towards the disease, an *a priori* humility'.[62]

A second lesson is that we cannot just announce that 'it's all ruined' (and even less without specifying exactly what is ruined). The community of people engaging with the disease, let's call them the disease-'users' (patients, relatives, caregivers and other concerned people), have learned to trust in 'pragmatism (following what this experience could teach us) rather than determinism (knowing in advance what would happen)',[63] if only to protect themselves against the following kind of situation: Just after his illness is announced to a man, the doctor tells his wife that 'he's done for'. Fifteen days later, the doctor is surprised to find her weighing seven kilos less. She explains to him that she has been like this ever since the announcement where he told her that her husband was 'done for'. He then replied: 'Don't get yourself into such a state: it could take twenty-five years!'[64]

The third lesson is that, after either type of news, you have to regain your self-confidence by creating, exploring and sharing experiences. 'You don't recover through the energy of loneliness and despair but through working together.'[65]

How to announce the bad news?

Before taking the point of view of the doctors, we should ask if the patients really want to know. It depends on the disease, but overall the answer is 'yes'. According to ten or so studies, between 96 and 98 per cent of American and European patients would rather that their doctors communicate the bad news clearly and honestly, even in the case of cancer.[66]

When it comes to the collapse, it's another matter. Admittedly, the people who come to collapsology lectures do want to know. They will leave in a state somewhere between battered and relieved. But when you want to convey the message *outside people in this group*, disillusionment and misunderstanding are very common. In general, people do not want to know, they refuse to believe and assume you are depressed, irrational or just want to stop them enjoying themselves.

What is the doctors' point of view? Leaving aside the dreaded test for Huntington's disease, how do doctors announce the bad news? Can they help us learn how to talk about global disasters?

In a 1984 article, the oncologist Robert Buckman was one of the first to pose the problem of bad news from the care-giver's perspective. His definition of bad news fits very well with the collapse: 'Any information likely to alter drastically a patient's view of his or her future.'[67]

For doctors, this exercise is difficult and delicate. First, there is the fear of being blamed or judged negatively, of showing one's own emotions, of setting off uncontrollable reactions, fear also of one's own death, or of not being able to suggest solutions to the person one is speaking to.[68] For some, it is a burden in terms of accountability (how to be honest with patients and how to treat their legitimate emotions adequately),[69] which makes for an additional stress factor, especially if the patient is young and the situation life-threatening.[70] We find such fears among those who want to be able to talk about collapse to those close to them as well, and even more so when the people they want to speak to have young children.

For many years, doctors were not trained for this. Most of them went through it badly and made mistakes that left patients suffering. As we have seen, a clumsy approach to the announcement can increase the patients' confusion, distress or anger and have a lasting impact on their ability to heal. But, by contrast, when the announcement is done with sensitivity, it can help understanding, acceptance and action.

There are several things we can learn from these episodes. The first is that patients consider their doctors to be one of their most important sources of psychological support. This makes it crucial that doctors respond empathetically to the patients' emotional reactions: that they maintain a warm and human posture, that they speak in such a way as to relieve their patients' emotional distress and that they allow the patients to express their feelings.[71] Such empathy reduces the patients' isolation, expressing solidarity with them, and validates the patients' feelings or thoughts as normal and understandable.[72]

Secondly, in what they say, doctors should be careful to strike a balance between hope and honesty. This is an important skill for collapsologists as well. The challenge is to inspire hope (or rather encourage them not to give up hope prematurely), while speaking the truth.[73]

Thirdly, a clear, informative and practical style of speaking is essential. Doctors are advised to choose their words wisely, to avoid medical jargon and to provide explicit evidence if their patients want it. The news should be given gently, but directly, clearly, and without detours or euphemisms. For example, it's better to say 'he is dead' or 'she is dead' rather than 'he is gone' or 'she is no longer with us'.[74]

The important thing is to connect with the person who is at the receiving end, without providing ready-made solutions, miracle formulas or vague ideas. Ecologists and journalists (and for that matter elected officials) could learn something useful from the experience of doctors. Talking about collapse is stressful for those who are transmitting the news, and also for those who hear it. It is vital to learn how to give and receive bad news. Because it's a safe bet that there will only be more of it.

Ecologists and climatologists have much the same issues. In 2015, the Tyndall Centre for Climate Change Research in the UK published a report called 'The challenge of communicating unwelcome climate messages'.[75] It concluded that 'emotional and psychological implications [must be] acknowledged and handled sensitively', something which never happens with scientific communications. The authors also advocated something we have seen with the doctors: truth and lucidity. 'Instead of highlighting a range of impacts, the seriousness of which is uncertain, it is more effective to say: "There is an awful possible future and we can't rule it out"'.[76]

When scientists are in possession of highly toxic knowledge, they have a great responsibility. To get through to the greatest number of people, they must learn to find the approach that contains as many antidotes as possible. Presenting bad news takes us beyond the domain of scientific knowledge; it is also an emotional, ethical, philosophical and even artistic question. It is not the preserve of academic researchers. This makes it essential to create bridges both between the specialists of the scientific disciplines concerned, and also with other areas. Beginning from this need for transdisciplinarity, we can also build groups of people who are concerned about the global disasters, collapse-'users' (collapsonauts), so that the transformative impact of the news can also help us move beyond the initial state of paralysis.

2

Regaining our spirits

Chapter 1 focused on the negative impact of the disasters that may be ahead. It is important to know, though, that many survivors of disasters recover quite well from their traumatic experience, or seem barely to experience traumatic effects at all. Such people have remarkable resources when it comes to getting back to life after a disaster or finding a life again after experiences that might be deeply traumatizing for others. They spontaneously rediscover their psychological balance within a few weeks or months after a disaster.

Resilience after disasters

This is not to deny the seriousness of what happens to some victims. However, as George Bonanno, professor of clinical psychology at Columbia University (USA) notes, the proportion of traumatized rarely exceeds 30 per cent of the survivors.[1] In other words, more than 70 per cent of the victims are resilient.[2]

Two questions then come to mind: How is it that these survivors are so resilient? And especially, what can we learn from this resilience about how to take care of those who are traumatized?[3]

Return to life

According to a study published in 2010 by the Bonanno team, there are several parameters that affect people's resilience: *proximity* to the location of the disaster (the closer we are, the less resilient we are); *gender* (in some studies, women have developed less resilience than men because their experience has been more traumatizing); *age* (young people can develop more symptoms but are on average more resilient); *financial resources* (the poorest suffer significantly more, comparing across social classes and also between countries); *preparation*, including whether they have already undergone a disaster of the same type, which acts as a kind of 'vaccination'; *personality*, also including genetic factors; *access to reassuring information* (the media and the government can play a positive or negative role in relation to fear).[4]

In preparing for disasters, religious or spiritual practices[5] and also the practice of mindfulness (which has proven very effective)[6] are important, helping to reduce anxiety while fostering relationships of altruism and sharing and offering meaning for the events people may undergo.

Finally, it is well established that the most important factor for resilience (from the first minutes after the tragedy) is the closeness and helpfulness of family and neighbours (or even strangers) who can aid in overcoming fear, give care and bring touches of joy and optimism.

Disaster sociologists have shown how most natural disasters lead to a striking rise in spontaneous mutual help, both between neighbours and between people who do not already know each other, along with other prosocial acts.[7] However, the frequency, spontaneity and quality of such prosocial behaviour depend on the quality of the social network *before* the disaster, and also on whether the network itself does not collapse during the disaster.

Informal connections, particularly between neighbours, often provide the first assistance. After the earthquake, the tsunami and the nuclear accidents in Japan in March 2011, survivors mentioned that many elderly and infirm people were rescued by neighbours, friends or family. They may also help with advice, emotional and psychological comfort, financial assistance, or assistance with urgent tasks.[8]

So what best predicts the resilience of a population is not the intensity of the damage, the population density or the economic capital, but the *social capital*.[9] There is one other small detail: we should distinguish the support people *receive* from the support that they *perceive*. Surprisingly, the latter is much better correlated with recovery than the former, and is one of the clearest factors behind post-disaster resilience.[10]

After the failures in the management of the L'Aquila earthquake of 6 April 2009 in Italy, some researchers have emphasized the importance of what they call *community resilience*: 'Greater attention should be given to understanding, recognizing and strengthening the capacities of local communities and the resilient social processes they put into action in order to address the negative social and economic impacts they experience during crises.'[11]

To summarize, collective preparation for disasters requires two ingredients: the establishment of a network of professionals to treat the traumatized (*recovery*) and the recognition that others will move spontaneously into healing themselves, mutual aid and self-management (*resilience*). This last point also suggests that we should do all we can to assist these qualities so they can be expressed more easily.

It is also worth mentioning a quite striking phenomenon. In the 1990s, researchers Richard Tedeschi and Lawrence Calhoun of the University of North Carolina (USA) noticed some very positive changes among those who had been traumatized: a greater joy in life, a new meaning to their existence, better rapport with others and even . . . yet more children.[12] We know well that crises can destroy us, but they can also make us grow. What is new in this case is the discovery and measurement by psychiatrists, psychologists, social workers and disaster management specialists of what they call *post-traumatic growth*. The writer and former financial trader Nassim Nicholas Taleb calls this *antifragility*: living organisms, when faced with some kinds of shocks, do not just recover from them, they become stronger.

Of course, this needs to be qualified. In competitive situations, there are always the better equipped who come out on top and the less well equipped who can't cope and who end up suffering. The same is true for a disaster: the more resilient can easily turn it into an opportunity or even a force for change, while the more vulnerable receive the full force of the impact, and may not be able to cope at all.

The need to anticipate

Before disasters, the main work consists in maintaining or recreating active, frequent social connections. Within communities (neighbourhood, family, district, ecovillage, etc.), the challenge is to learn to cultivate relationships of reciprocity and trust, along with habits of mutual assistance. Once these habits have taken form, behaviours of sharing, mutual aid, solidarity and altruism can emerge more easily *during* and *after* a shock.[13]

After the disaster, these connections enable victims to make their needs better known, thereby helping them to avoid leaving the region and speeding up efforts at reconstruction.[14] Through fostering a stable psychological and emotional environment, all this strengthens local resilience at both family and community levels.

In contrast, when people experience uprooting, relocation, displacement, refugee camps and migrations, these all contribute to fragmentation of social ties and to weakening of individuals. Anything that promotes an attachment to a territory (social connections included) is therefore desirable. And if migration is necessary, we suggest following the recommendations of a 2014 American Psychological Association report on the consequences of climate change: when putting together kits to use in case of emergency, in addition to food, water and medicines, they also advised looking after people's psychological health by including 'spiritual or religious items, pictures, or blankets and toys for small children [. . .], recreational items such as books or games, and paper and writing instruments to journal or write down important information'.[15]

We might also think about developing antifragile capabilities directly in contact with real disasters, by participating in rescue and reception missions or reconstruction efforts. When we see other people injured, our brains react as if we were injured ourselves.[16] This spontaneous reaction will be all the stronger when traumas are already inscribed in our 'autobiographical memory' and we have developed the capacities to put ourselves consciously in the place of the other (mentalizing or 'theory of mind'[17]).

Living and dancing with the shadows

Suffering, grief, death and mourning are important parts of our humanity. They are pillars of group life. However, our society displays a kind of phobia towards them. Our general approach is to sweep them under the carpet, not to bother others with such things and to avoid expressing them in public. We remember the embarrassment some felt at the tearful, and very moving, words of the Tuvalu representative at the 2009 climate summit in Copenhagen.

We will probably have to deal more and more with these dark parts, so why not become more competent? This section is an invitation to dive into the dark areas of the soul and discover their power to save.

Suffering as connection

Suffering is everywhere: the death of a parent, of a child, of a partner, a friend's suicide, the end of a relationship, a sister's cancer, a teenager who becomes an alcoholic, a father's violence, the suffering of a soldier who has come back from the war, of a family that has lost one of its members in a terrorist attack; major breaks in life such as a change of job, moving house or forced relocation, a serious accident; and finally the craziness of the world.

Suffering is more than a natural reaction to a loss, it is an *initiation* into loss, into the impermanence of the world. What you wanted to be is no longer possible. What was there before no longer exists. For the ecopsychologist Joanna Macy, 'As a society we are caught between a sense of impending apocalypse and the fear of acknowledging it. In this "caught" place, our responses are blocked and confused.'[18]

The American psychotherapist and author Francis

Weller has accompanied people for years on these painful paths.

> It was through the dark waters of grief that I came to touch my unlived life. ... There is some strange intimacy between grief and aliveness, some sacred exchange between what seems unbearable and what is most exquisitely alive. Through this, I have come to have a lasting faith in grief.[19]

Weller has developed rituals and a striking interpretative framework to help us learn how to tame these shadows. He sees it as vital to go through the pains and suffering – what he calls the 'work of grief' – and, especially, to be accompanied on this journey, in order to be able to let go entirely. Weller's work is about *unpacking* the sorrows, one after the other, until the person feels fully alive again.

Francis Weller and Joanna Macy join in the observation that the two major problems of our civilization are *amnesia* and *anaesthesia*. Amnesia because our society has 'sadly turned the ritual of life into the routine of existence'.[20] We have lost what Weller calls the *commons of the soul*, those 'primary satisfactions that sustained and nourished the community and the individual for tens of thousands of years'. Forgetting these languages has left us lost, confused, frightened ... and also, paradoxically, made us much more vulnerable when faced by loss. The consequences of this amnesia are depression, anxiety and loneliness.

Anaesthesia because the pain is too big and too difficult to manage. We try to fill these gaps with bandages against grief: alcohol, drugs, work, consumption, the screen, etc., all the time knowing perfectly well that we are not made to live superficial, resigned and meaningless lives. Anaesthesia increases our suffering. 'Sorrow, pain, fear, weakness and vulnerability' are forced 'into the underworld, where they fester and mutate into contorted expressions of themselves, often coated in a mantle of shame.'[21]

It is easy simply to refer to all this as 'depression', but for Weller, depression is not a 'static' state, it is 'non-metabolized' suffering that becomes toxic to the soul. The latter refuses to go further until we are truly willing to plunge into the shadows.

The demand that one should 'feel good', the need to appear positive and the requirement to be happy can put an enormous pressure on us. This is why Weller finds grief subversive: 'It is an act of protest that declares our refusal to live numb and small. [. . .] Because of that, grief is necessary to the vitality of the soul. Contrary to our fears, grief is suffused with life-force.'[22] As Joanna Macy says, 'The heart that breaks open can contain the whole universe.'

To go through these sufferings can fully reconnect us to our feelings and our capacity to love. This also has positive consequences for our health, our creativity and our sense of being alive. Even better, this immersion into our depths forces us to give meaning to our suffering, which is, we might add, the goal of all therapy, according to the Belgian ecopsychotherapists Vincent Wattelet and Nathalie Grosjean.

But the biggest benefit of this work with grief lies somewhere else: in welding together communities. Sharing one's grief with others can bring about deep comfort, through knowing one's self surrounded by others, and through creating a common understanding. You may have noticed, for example, the outbursts of solidarity and communion after the attacks in Paris, the desire and the warmth of being together. 'What our indigenous ancestors had to sustain them through the dark times was ritual and community. Our work is to embrace and refine both, instead of intractably clinging to a "positive attitude" in the face of out-of-control, incalculable abuse and devastation.'[23]

In isolation and loneliness, this journey can devastate us. This is why this work on pain is done together, through listening, and with good tools (rituals). 'Facing grief is hard work . . . It takes outrageous courage to face outrageous loss. This is precisely what we are being called to do.'[24] This is the basis of the Cancer Help Program that Weller is involved in. At the end of a sharing session, he says, there is the feeling that everyone's suffering is shared and that we must deal with it together. These rituals are a way to honour and then heal the grief we are facing and will face. In the end, these feelings can become travelling companions.

The originality of Weller's work consists in having identified (and so allowed us to deal with collectively) five types of loss (of which only the first is well known). These 'gates of grief' help us to name and recognize types of suffering, and thus function as a five-way compass to learn how to navigate these abysses.

The *first gate* focuses on what we love. It can be summarized as follows: 'Everything we love, we will lose.' Suffering helps keep your heart open to the love of what you have lost. 'Grief and love are sisters, woven together from the beginning . . . There is no love that does not contain loss and no loss that is not a reminder of the love we carry for what we once held close.'[25]

The *second gate* is more surprising: it is the places in ourselves that we do not care for, that we have not loved and for which we feel shame.[26] These 'pieces of soul [that] live in absolute despair' are fragile places that have never felt compassion, kindness, warmth (neither ours, nor that of others). We hide them, because we feel that *they are not worth grieving over.* For Weller, this gate is important because 'we cannot grieve for something that we feel is outside the circle of worth'.[27]

The *third gate* is that of 'the sorrows of the world' (see also the 'ecological sufferings' of the previous chapter). These are more and more frequent, and are often cited by patients of Weller's Cancer Help Program. 'What I have come to see is that much of the grief we carry is not personal; it doesn't arise from our histories or experiences.'[28] This grief shows that we know deeply that we are not separated from the world and that we live interdependently: when we destroy habitats, kill animals or cause irreparable pollution to the land, it affects us directly. The problem is that the suffering of the world is vast and extends far beyond us. How can we remain sensitive and receptive to all the assaults on the biosphere? To stay present, to keep your eyes open, requires courage, conviction and support. 'What we most need to do,' says the Buddhist monk and activist Thich Nhat Hanh, 'is to hear within us the sounds of the Earth crying.'[29]

The *fourth gate* concerns what we expected and did not receive from the 'tribe'. For thousands of generations as hunter-gatherers (the essence of our species' history), we have been biologically and culturally shaped to feel part of a community of humans and other living beings.[30] Today we are almost completely cut off from this enlarged identity, and this creates a powerful sense of loss, the existence of which we barely suspect.

And, finally, the *fifth gate* is ancestral grief. This grief, passed down through the generations, hides in the structure of our cells and derives from the trauma of our personal ancestors (abandonment, rapes, suicides, etc.) as well as from major collective traumas such as wars, pogroms, witch hunts, and the like. There are many of these sufferings endured by our ancestors that have not been digested and from which we have not been freed.

Twenty years after his first grief rituals, Weller notes that things have changed: there is a real breakdown in our collective denial, something which he puts down to an increasing awareness of the irreversible damage caused by our civilization. 'Our personal experiences of loss and suffering are now bound inextricably with dying coral reefs, melting polar caps, the silencing of languages, the collapse of democracy, and the fading of civilization.'[31]

Mourning as metamorphosis

The idea that the emotions which collapse brings up can be understood through a mourning process is a real liberation. It gives us an immediate realization that both relieves us and allows us to realize: 1. that the emotions we are undergoing are natural; 2. that this is a long, dynamic and complex process; and 3. that it will lead eventually to a more serene place, the famous 'state of acceptance'.

The schematic process proposed by Elisabeth Kubler-Ross, with its five stages (denial, anger, bargaining, depression and acceptance) is useful because we can quickly see that it involves movement, and so helps us accept that people we are close to may be at different stages in the process.

The psychiatrist and specialist in mourning, Christophe Fauré, has revisited the stages of mourning in the light of his own long experience in psychiatry and a very intense spiritual life.[32] He describes a succession of four large temporal phases, somewhat different from the Kubler-Ross stages.

The first is the phase of *denial, shock* and *paralysis*. Even if we have prepared for it, when death actually occurs, reason is derailed and refuses to admit the facts. During this phase, which takes time, the emotional anaesthesia allows us to enter mourning at our own pace, without being overwhelmed, while waiting for the right time for the process to continue. This is also a stage of restlessness and dealing with affairs which helps avoid too direct a confrontation with our interior state and with grief. This is the time of collective rituals, such as burials, which provide social 'validation' for the entry into mourning. Then comes a strong phase of emptiness, where we pass a point of no return in accepting the loss 'physically', through an emotional discharge: endless sadness, extreme anguish.

The second phase, *waiting*, *avoidance* and *searching*, is tinged with confusion and disorientation. Our inner bonds with the dead person are still intact, and this leads to avoidance behaviour (such as hyperactivity) and a constant search for signs and objects related to him or her, in order to 'find the dead person at any cost and to annul his death, the idea of which is still intolerable'.[33]

The third phase is *destructuring*. Our pain reaches a paroxysm in which inner connections break down and points of reference disappear. We badly need meaning and connection, but we may also sometimes feel injustice, and sink into despair, fear or anger (or nihilism or revolt, either against others or against ourselves).

The fourth phase is *restructuring*. This last step is also emotionally challenging. We realize that the scar is the sign of not having forgotten, and we agree to live with it. Then the 'possibility of a return to life'[34] and of an end to mourning opens up. This is the moment of 'redefinition of the relationship with others and the world; redefinition of the relationship to the deceased; redefinition of the relationship with oneself'.[35] How to find our place in a world where everything has just been devastated? Who are we, socially and personally? In any case, 'there is potentially a space to live, where we can begin again with something new. The last stages of mourning perhaps consist in looking for and developing this new space.'[36] This is a process that can be started even before the death, if we are prepared.

These schemas of Kubler-Ross and Fauré may seem rigid and even normative for people who do not live through them as specified (which is not uncommon, and also quite natural). They should not be taken as norms, but as points of reference.

Christophe Fauré also invites us to go beyond the generally accepted idea that mourning is a kind of 'work' that we have to do. It is certainly a 'period of mental, personal and emotional transition for someone learning to live again in a context of loss',[37] but this is a *natural* response to the loss of a loved one, or of a place, a memory, an image to which we are attached, an imagined future or a way of life. Psychiatry uses the metaphor of a wound: mourning is a process of forming a scar over it. Even if it can happen spontaneously, we can still take care of it, bring our attention and intention on the wound, so that the process proceeds as well as possible. The wound will close, but the scar will remain for all our life, as a memory of our grief.

We find the idea of mourning interesting because it allows us to see the process of becoming aware of collapse in terms of finding meaning through a metamorphosis, through new stories. Death and illness allow us to contact a radical loneliness that challenges our certainties and beliefs. If you have been through a serious illness or accident, you will have experienced this kind of initiation: habits are shattered, certainties collapse, and to get back on track, you have to give meaning to what has happened. This is what the collective Dingdingdong calls 'being cunning' (*ruser*): thinking up stories that get you moving again and give you life, continuing to repeat them over and over, until you have become calmer.[38]

A difficult aspect of mourning is that of finding peace. In relation to collapse, this is particularly significant for people who are angry with society. 'The slow work of mourning, does it not consist in making peace with the departed, despite everything that remains to be shared and forgiven? Is not this an essential condition for allowing oneself, to live in freedom and calm again?'[39] But how can one forgive the brutality of our thermo-industrial civilization towards the most vulnerable (humans and other-than-humans)? Perhaps this has to be done through collective processes (rituals?) of redressing injustices and/or recognizing fault and responsibility.[40]

Some people try to go through it in advance, like Clément Montfort, director of a web series about the collapse, NEXT[41]: 'It is vital to go through the stage of realizing what has already been lost. I would rather go through the phase of depression and deep sadness, today, so as to be more adaptable and solid tomorrow. I'm making this series for people who are at this stage.'[42] For people like this, it is even already possible to open up several kinds of mourning: for what we hold onto within this thermo-industrial civilization (and also for what we hate), but also of what we care about *outside* this civilization and which it has worked to destroy, sometimes beyond repair. To know afterwards that you are able to go through these difficult inner trials greatly strengthens your courage.

At bottom, the question of the collapse is a magnifying mirror in which we see our shadows and our relationship to death. If someone is not (yet) able to talk about the collapse, they probably should not be forced to do so. Everyone goes at their own pace in this type of process.

To grow up and become fully competent women and men, we must confront death face-to-face or, as the Sufi poet Rumi put it, 'die before dying'. In the context of the Anthropocene, 'we have to learn how to die not as individuals, but as a civilization'.[43]

3

Moving on

In our times, caught between an increasingly devastated planet and our culture's nonstop messages to keep happy and keep busy, a phrase like 'moving on' can sound false. We would not encourage a return to the growth-orientation, or to a comforting denial of reality. Nor are we suggesting that once we are through the difficult 'inner transition', it will be simple to arrive at a world of peace and mutual assistance. Thinking like this just keeps the difficult emotions away for a little longer.

In this chapter we suggest rather that we keep looking for a better approach, one which aligns our heads and our hearts, in the company of our shadows, but also one which lets in the light of this devastated world. It's not a question any longer of trying to find 'solutions' so that our lives can go on as they are, but of accepting and preparing ourselves for the possibility of losing what we are holding on to, so that we are fully available for what is to come (including conflict and action).

Many young people nowadays are aware of global disasters. Already in 2007, 27 per cent of Australians aged ten to fourteen were worried that the world might end before they became adults.[1] Was their pessimism inappropriate? For that matter, was it really pessimism? And what is hidden behind the instructions to stay happy and the blind optimism of older generations?

We suggest dwelling for a little on those two apparently 'positive' notions, optimism and hope. Both can be useful, but they also bring with them pitfalls and evasions.

Mistrusting optimism

The optimist wants everything to improve, and thinks that the future will be better. We can distinguish between two kinds of optimists. First the clear-sighted ones, who are familiar with the problems and who are fighting daily to improve the situation or help others. We can call these people 'optimists-plus'. This is a good way to be. Being optimistic has many benefits for their personal health, such as living longer or having less risk of a heart attack,[2] while they are also contributing through their activity to the health of their whole community.

Optimists become more of a problem when they refuse to admit the downside of things and get annoyed at others who see more clearly. Let's call these people 'optimists-minus'. They demand that everything should be positive, and only positive. It's as if patients with generalized cancer, not wanting to hear about their illness – let alone that they might be dying – were to ask the doctors just to stick to the good news! Between denial and the fear of suffering, there is a great temptation to sweep unpleasant things under the carpet.

But what the optimists hate above all are the pessimists who tell them that 'everything is done for'. They are quite right about this. We can call this type the 'pessimists-minus'. If they learn that they have cancer, they are convinced that they are about to die. Even worse, they will tell other people affected by cancer that they are definitely going to die quickly. This is really not helpful.

There is another category, however, which is more difficult to discern. These are the 'pessimists-plus'. They stay very aware of the bad news, they see a lot of it on the horizon (maybe too much), and they prepare themselves for future disasters because they take them seriously, making it possible to avoid or mitigate them. This is what the philosopher Jean-Pierre Dupuy calls 'enlightened doomsaying'.[3] The icing on the cake: such people avoid a trap into which optimists-plus can fall, that of sinking into depression when their positive vision of the future fails to take shape.[4]

Was the German sociologist Ulrich Beck (1944–2015) an optimist? Beck became famous for creating a general theory of global risk in the 1990s, and argued that major disasters could produce an 'anthropological shock' capable of reorienting worldviews and provoking radical political change. He argued that we needed to recognize that positive change could arise from disasters.[5]

This is typically a point where the optimist-plus and the pessimist-plus come together. They have a common concern *not to be in denial*, to see the problems and to act accordingly. One is more focused on the bad news than the other, but both are well anchored in reality. Moreover, if you add a little kindness to this clear-sightedness, you get the ideal collapsological approach: to inform people of the bad news as gently and objectively as possible, so that each and every one manages to give of their best.

The awkward postures are really those of the pessimists-minus (the disaster-mongers, 'Everything is done for!') and the optimists-minus (the ostriches, 'We don't need all this depressing news!'). The first group have opened up to reality but they have not (yet) been able to recreate a positive future prospect, perhaps because they are trapped in their emotions and their shadows. The second, in their denial and fear, seem not yet ready for what the shadows of the world may show them of their own shadows.

Gabriele Oettingen, professor of psychology at the Universities of New York and Hamburg, has devoted her professional life to studying what drives people to achieve their goals (including the limitations of so-called 'positive thinking').[6] In one of her experiments, she recruited two groups of students and asked the first group to imagine that the week ahead was going to be fantastic: good grades, parties and other enjoyable activities. She asked the students in the second group to write down all their thoughts and dreams about the coming week, good or bad. Surprisingly, the students in the first group felt less energy than the group that was asked to dream in a neutral way. In another similar experiment, she asked a first group of students to imagine that they would receive a substantial reward if they completed an assignment successfully. She asked the second group to think about the reward but also the behaviours that could prevent them from completing the work. Result? The second group performed better than the first.[7]

Fantasizing about something positive lowers one's blood pressure. In contrast, if we wish for the same thing but also bear in mind that we might fail to get it, our blood pressure goes up. So we feel better when our desires are not restrained by worries, but also less energized and less prepared to act. Blind optimism does not motivate us, because it leads to complacency and relaxation. We need to add a good dose of clear-sightedness about the situation, including the things that might slow us down and the obstacles that might get in the way.[8] 'Positive thinking' alone deprives us of what we need to respond to challenges, and significantly reduces the chances of overcoming them as well as possible.

We should also say something about the vision of the future, more specifically about the openness of possibilities. We feel that claiming, like the psychologists Steven Pinker[9] and our friend Jacques Lecomte,[10] or the hyperoptimistic pro-capitalist historian Johan Norberg,[11] that times have never been better and that we should stop listening to prophets of doom, is rather confused, not to say counterproductive. It's like the speech of the famous 'inductivist turkey',[12] who, confident that the living conditions of the farm where she grew up are stable (they treat her well and feed her daily), and being a good statistician, is able to tell her fellow turkeys on Christmas Eve that there is no need to worry about the future.

Collapsologists do not deny that some aspects of the world are improving and that there are some beautiful 'young shoots' coming up. They simply introduce the possibility that there are also 'black swans', large unpredictable events, and 'grey swans', events which are considered unlikely but possible, which may disrupt our expectations of smooth onward progress. This is not at all incompatible with the good news or the fact that some situations may improve. Black swans can also be positive. The good news does not wipe out the bad news, and the possibility of better futures coexist with the possibility of much worse futures. What is new and worrying today is that many factors have come together that potentially could make the future, on a global scale, very dark.

People vary in their tendency to optimism or pessimism. Our only warning is not to let either of them lead you into denial, cowardice or ignorance.

Our personal belief that the thermo-industrial civilization will collapse over the coming years is not related to our optimistic or pessimistic character. We are often asked whether we are optimistic or pessimistic about the future. We are neither one nor the other. The collapsonaut in us tends to reply that it depends on how tired we are feeling . . . As for the collapsologist, he never sees the glass half empty or half full; he sees it completely full: half water and half air . . . and with lots of cracks!

Mistrusting hope

If we agree that hope is to expect with confidence that something will happen, we have to admit that hope suffers from a serious problem: passivity (*esperar* in Spanish means both 'to hope' and 'to wait'). Derrick Jensen, a writer and environmental activist who is known not to mince words, claims that 'hope is, in fact, a curse, a bane'.[13] It 'keeps us chained to the system, the conglomerate of individuals, ideas and ideals that is destroying the planet'. It makes us believe that:

> suddenly somehow the system may inexplicably change. Or technology will save us. Or the Great Mother. Or beings from Alpha Centauri. Or Jesus Christ. Or Santa Claus. All of these false hopes – all of this rendering of our power – leads to inaction, or at least to ineffectiveness. . . . One reason my mother stayed with my father was that there were no battered women's shelters in the fifties and sixties, but another was because of the false hope that he would change.[14]

Less angry than Jensen, but equally clear, is the ecopsychologist and Buddhist Joanna Macy. Macy admitted, after having published the book *Active Hope* with the psychologist

Chris Johnstone,[15] that she would never have imagined writing a book with the word 'hope' in the title, because for her, hope puts people to sleep. 'In the Buddhist tradition, there's hardly a word for hope. Hope takes you out of the present moment.'[16] There is a Buddhist saying that 'hope and fear chase each other's tails'.[17]

To counteract hope's demobilizing nature, Macy and Johnstone distinguished in their book between two types of hope: the passive type that we usually hear about, and what they called 'active hope'. Thus, *passive hope* is summed up by: 'I hope she'll come back some day', but active hope answers: 'Then go and find her!'

Active hope is just a question of realizing what is important to us, what we hope to happen. 'There is no need for optimism,' says Joanna Macy, 'we can apply active hope even when we feel hopeless.' As a daily practice, like tai chi or gardening, active hope 'is something we *do* rather than something we *have*'. There is no need to be obsessed with futures that seem likely; we just have to focus on what we really want. Then, and only then, should we take specific steps in that direction, and give the best of ourselves 'so that we may even be surprised by what we bring'. Everything is in the intention of the present moment or, as Seneca said, 'when you have unlearned hope, I will teach you to want to act'.[18]

Active hope is essential in order not to sink into despair or discouragement. 'Hope comes from within', notes the writer and journalist Michel Maxime Egger. 'This aspiration to accomplish what is not yet accomplished in one's being, this drive to bring about what has not yet happened in history, springs from deep in the heart. In this, hope is intimately connected to the inner life of people who grow in their humanity and who realize their potential, cosmic, human and divine.'[19]

In reality, hope is a subject to which science has given very little attention. This is a shame, because there are precious lessons to be learned here. For example, a study conducted in Sweden, on a thousand adolescents and young adults who answered a questionnaire, showed that hope was positively correlated with action *only* among individuals highly concerned about global disasters. For young people who didn't care much, having hope was inversely correlated with action.[20] Lesson No. 1: informing oneself as well as possible is vital. Lesson No. 2: as with optimism, beware of hope when it is connected to denial.

Other researchers have even shown that while the fact of being concerned seems to motivate the search for information, 'positive' people do not find out much, they even avoid the truth.[21] Thus a positive attitude often hides some degree of denial.

This denial and the refusal to plunge into the shadows can be expressed through a refusal to know, but also through a refusal to feel emotions. 'Many people are afraid to feel despair', says Derrick Jensen. 'They fear that if they allow themselves to perceive how desperate is our situation, they must then be perpetually miserable. They forget it is possible to feel many things at once. I am full of rage, sorrow, joy, love, hate, despair, happiness, satisfaction, dissatisfaction, and a thousand other feelings.'[22]

Getting out of denial pushes us out of our comfort zone. It's true that our generation's pathway has some unpleasant moments. But avoiding them is no solution, because 'the truth that many people never understand, until it is too late, is that the more you try to avoid suffering, the more you suffer'.[23]

As Derrick Jensen says,

A wonderful thing happens when you give up on [passive] hope, which is that you realize you never needed it in the first place. You realize that giving up on hope didn't kill you, nor did it make you less effective. In fact it made you more effective, because you ceased relying on someone or something else to solve your problems [. . .] You become like those Jews who participated in the Warsaw Ghetto uprising.[24]

What we need for the storms that will come is therefore not the certainty that everything will be better tomorrow, but the *courage* that opens up possibilities and gets us moving again.

Imagine being shown with certainty that there will never be a collapse and that there is absolutely no concern for the future. What would you do to change your life? Nothing. Imagine that you have been told that the human species will definitely disappear in 2042 because of a giant meteorite. What would you do? Spend the end of your life at the pub, thinking, 'What's the point?' What keeps us moving, Joanna Macy remarks, is precisely this radical uncertainty. And we find ourselves in balance, on this thin edge between the radical uncertainty of future events and the conviction that it is physically impossible to continue our way of life.

Ultimately, nobody knows if 'it will work'. But that's not really the question. In the words of the playwright and statesman Václav Havel, 'hope is not the same thing as optimism. It is not the conviction that something will turn out well, but the certainty that something makes sense, regardless of how it turns out.'[25]

This connects up with the psychologist William James' proposal (the 'Jamesian bet'): when a problem is insurmountable, we must invent a solution and bet on it, doing everything in our power to see it happen.

And if our path comes to a sudden end, we can say that we will have lived fully, in accordance with our convictions and by having done what seemed right to us. It is this momentum, this alignment, that opens a path of possibilities ... through a small gap already opened up by radical uncertainty. As the author Margaret Wheatley sums it up: 'The cure for despair is not hope. It's discovering what we want to do about something we care about.'[26]

What about the children?

You are irresponsible, bigoted, stuck in the past, you've sacrificed the planet, reduced the third world to starvation! In eighty years, you have done away with almost all living species, you have exhausted all the resources, stuffed yourselves with all the fish! There are fifty billion chickens raised in battery farms every year in the world, and people are dying from hunger! You are the worst generation in the history of humanity! And one misfortune never arrives alone, you live super old!

Sophie, pregnant, addressing a stunned group of senior citizens[27]

One question often comes up among people who are discovering the likelihood of collapse or going through a phase of despair: how can we bring children into this devastated world? Can we reconcile the collapse with a future for our children? We are aware that we are treading delicately here, because these issues directly affect us in the heart and the guts, and can bring up real fear and distress. We don't intend to give conclusive advice (our own ideas will certainly evolve further), and we don't want to deliberately provoke distress, but it can be helpful to bring these questions and reactions into the light.

More and more couples are consciously deciding not to

have children so as not to overload the Earth, or because of climate change.[28] From some points of view, for some people, to raise a child in this society can seem like an absurd act, even a selfish and immoral act, leading to an increase in suffering. It would be more of the same bad behaviour we are already committing, even without a child, by consuming and wasting 'more than one planet' through our excessive use of resources. But from another point of view, having a child can be seen as a gift, an act of love and an act of responsibility in a world where there *might* be room for eight billion moderate human beings, aware and sensitive to all living things.

We don't intend to start a discussion, however tempting, about the possible motivations for having or not having children. In any case, we feel that individual choices cannot be meaningfully discussed without thinking about collective choices. As long as we are not dealing with the birth rate at the collective level (an extremely complex issue, and a dangerous one perhaps in the current political and cultural context),[29] the choice to give birth will remain entirely relegated to the individual and private sphere. However, it seems equally inappropriate to put the choice of whether to have children, perhaps the most important choice of one's life, in the same basket as questions concerning depoliticized individual 'solutions' and 'eco-responsible' behaviour, such as whether one should stop the tap running while washing one's teeth.

In the absence of real debate, we can talk about our own experience. As it happens, we are all three young fathers. Three of our youngest sons are 'children of collapse': they were consciously desired *after* the coming to awareness of likely collapse that has coloured our lives.

We have chosen to transmit onwards the love of life that brought us ourselves into being, and to have confidence in the capacity of humans, as living beings, to go through the storms of sorrow and joy, to adapt to coming situations and to create a culture that supports life. These decisions were at that time the right ones for us, that is, based on active hope – not just the hope that tomorrow will be better, or on naive optimism. It was an impulse of life itself, the same impulse that prevents us from, or gives us no desire to, kill ourselves. The love we have (and will have) for our children is immense, as is the pain that we would feel if they were to suffer or if they were to die before us.

The other question that keeps coming up is, what should we say to them? This is how we have dealt with it. When they are very young, not much. This is the time when they are becoming rooted in the world through wonder. When questions come, just answer them, frankly and following your heart, and without going beyond the question. And then, as they reach the age of reason, gently draw their attention towards what seems important to us, but without bringing out the slideshow and the microphone (a difficult exercise for us!). Simply share what touches us, what moves us, being as genuine as possible. Show them a little more about who we are as adults, what we can do and how we are vulnerable. Without showing off, but without hiding either. And let them go their own way, let them develop their perception of the world in contact with a growing number of other humans and as many other-than-humans as possible.

The collapse and all its numbers are cold concepts. But for them, our words are warm, and they will hear stories that they will believe, passionately, a little, or not at all. We will help them build meaning. What counts is the way we tell the story, the emotions, the grounding, our truth, and especially letting them imagine their own stories around the kernels they will keep from ours. We must give them the means to be creative, taking care not to close off any possibility of a future.

Today some of our children are almost young adults; they have seen us writing, heard us talking to others, they have read our books and seen the effect those books have had on others. The process of collapse and metamorphosis is part of their mental landscape, as it is of a growing number of their friends and other young people of their generation. Some are afraid of the future, others less so and others not at all.

Their future choices will obviously depend on the choices we make today (as individuals, but also as a society). As long as they have kept enough self-confidence and enough love from their childhood, though, they will be able to chart their course whatever happens, with or without us. And when we have become old fools disoriented by the times we are living through (or wise grandpas with long white beards), they will manage much better than us!

But what touches us is less what we can teach them as what we are discovering through them: a wide range of emotions, the exploration of our interiority, being grounded, present and alive, commitment and taking on responsibility. It is well known that in the face of death and suffering, children are often far wiser than many adults.[30] In hindsight, we realize that we have received from them a pretty strong dose of common sense and some deep connections, precisely what has led us to write this book.

To end what we have to say about children, we cannot help quoting a few words by the novelist Ursula Le Guin:

> [Every child needs] protection and shelter. But he also needs the truth. And it seems to me that the way you can speak absolutely honestly and factually to a child about both good and evil is to talk about himself. Himself, his inner self, the deep, the deepest Self. That is something he can cope with; indeed, his job in growing up is to become himself. He can't do this if he feels the task is hopeless, nor can he if he's led

to think there isn't any task. A child's growth will be stunted
and perverted if he is forced to despair or if he is encouraged
in false hope, if he is terrified or if he is coddled. What he
needs to grow up is reality, the wholeness which exceeds all
our virtue and all our vice. He needs knowledge; he needs
self-knowledge. He needs to see himself and the shadow he
casts. That is something he can face, his own shadow; and he
can learn to control it and to be guided by it. So that, when
he grows up into his strength and responsibility as an adult
in society, he will be less inclined, perhaps, either to give up
in despair or to deny what he sees, when he must face the
evil that is done in the world, and the injustices and grief
and suffering that we all must bear, and the final shadow at
the end of all.[31]

Part Two

New Horizons

We do not see things as they are, we see them as we are.
Ancient Talmudic proverb quoted by Anais Nin, *Seduction of the Minotaur* (Chicago: Swallow Press, 1962), p. 124

When you want to build a boat, do not start by gathering wood, cutting boards and distributing work, but by awaking in men the desire for the great and beautiful sea.
Antoine de Saint-Exupéry, *The Wisdom of the Sands* (Chicago, IL: University of Chicago Press, 1979)

4

Integrating other ways of knowing

Here we step back a little. The aim is to break out from our established ways of thinking and open up some new horizons. A first step is to realize there are other ways of thinking that are worth taking seriously, and a second is to agree to question our own certainties. Given these, it's worth trying to give ourselves a wider perspective on our global predicament, one that might take us out of our usual frame of reference, help us from being strangled by taken-for-granted assumptions and open up some new paths.

We are not looking for 'solutions' here. We are exploring new ways to open up possibilities. These attempts should be taken for what they are: just attempts, thought experiments that may perhaps resonate with something within you that you may not have even known was there.

This part of the book offers ideas for creating meaning in unfamiliar ways, so as to transform our way of being in the world, and therefore our society. This can provide people who want radical change with some valuable room for manoeuvre.

We will explore ways of seeing the world which differ from our own, as well as narratives of future collapse. To begin, we will try to give some flexibility to the noble but rigid institution of science, so that it can become our ally, rather than just continuing to feed the destruction.

New scientific (in)disciplines

In your opinion, who should determine the acceptable amount of greenhouse gas emissions that we could emit by 2050? Should it be the climatologists? If so, which ones? Or the risk and disaster specialists? The insurance companies? The NGO experts? Heads of State? Oil companies? The populations whose territory will soon be engulfed or turned into desert? You? The species which are threatened? And what role should science and scientific institutions play in this decision making?

Problems which are too complex

There is no satisfactory answer to such a question; the implications are so complex and involve so many different groups. Such problems are referred to as 'hyperobjects',[1] 'divergent problems'[2] (as opposed to convergent problems whose solution approaches closer at each attempt at resolution) or 'wicked problems'.[3] They are effectively insoluble; each attempt to try to solve one aspect of the problem generates other new aspects.

The climate issue is a question of this kind. Once we get beyond an increase of 2°C in average global temperature, unpredictable qualitative changes begin to appear. We enter a world that the climate specialist Joachim Schellnhuber has called 'terra quasi-incognita'.[4] There we are faced with two major challenges: first, the limitations of science in dealing with the complexity of the systems involved, and second, the immensity and the mutually conflicting nature of the stakes, which concern the life and health of so many people.[5]

Wicked problems occur in so-called highly complex systems. These contain a great deal of irreducible uncertainty and unpredictability. For example, we will never be able to do a full-scale experiment on the effects of the disappearance of Amazonia, nor accurately predict the weather for longer than a week, nor fully assess the impacts of genetically modified organisms (GMOs) or of nuclear power over a hundred thousand years, or even over a century, because there are too many parameters involved and it would require a degree of computing power that it is impossible to achieve.[6]

How does science react when dealing with a specific problem? Schematically, there are several kinds of approach, related to the level of uncertainty and the size of the issues. In *basic* science (both theoretical work and laboratory research), uncertainty can be effectively reduced to very low levels. The stakes involved in decisions about the research are also relatively minor, generally only involving the researchers. When an invention or a discovery comes out of the laboratories, we enter the field of *applied* science. The uncertainty and the stakes increase but remain minor and/or controllable, most often by statistics and engineers. An example might be a surgical operation or putting a satellite into orbit. When the stakes and the uncertainty increase further, we call on *professional expertise*, and more precisely *expert judgement* (an example might be a psychiatric diagnosis).

But for wicked problems involving entire populations and major stakes, when everything turns grey and significant controversies emerge, then applied science and experts are not enough. It can even be risky or counter-productive to use the so-called 'normal' scientific approaches, which are focused on finding technical solutions and use reductionist modes of analysis which are localized within specific disciplines.

The collapse of our civilization and of our world involves many such wicked problems. We have to learn how to understand and manage them. And for that, we must continue to enrich the practices of science. So, how can we produce useful knowledge to help us navigate in this fog?

Seeing further, thanks to the complexity sciences

During the second half of the twentieth century, several remarkable new branches started to grow out of the great tree of science. We can group them under the general label of complexity science[7] (complexus meaning 'what is woven together'); the Colombian anthropologist Arturo Escobar calls them 'sciences of interrelation'.[8] These disciplines came along to critique and shake up the quantitative and deterministic conceptions of other sciences which had traditionally focused on the study of object-elements rather than interactions.

So, for example, we have seen the emergence of approaches such as chaos theory and the theory of self-organization, which describe the emergence of nonlinear and unpredictable phenomena. These were brought into existence by the Nobel Prize winner Ilya Prigogine (1917–2003), the mathematician Benoît Mandelbrot (1924–2010) and the biologist Stuart Kauffmann (b.1939) among others. Then there is ecology, which is really just the study of the relations and the interdependence between living beings (among each other and with their environment). We can also think of the cybernetics of Norbert Wiener (1894–1964) and the dynamic systems theory developed by Karl Ludwig von Bertalanffy (1901–1972), Gregory Bateson (1904–1980) or Jay Forrester (1918–2016); of the very beautiful theory of autopoiesis developed by Humberto Maturana (b.1928) and Francisco Varela (1946–2001) which describes how a living system constructs itself in interaction with its environment, self-regulates and can be transformed while keeping its main functions; and of the Gaia theory established by James Lovelock (b.1919) and Lynn Margulis (1938–2011), which describes the processes of self-regulation of the biosphere. There is also the very young and dynamic theory of networks, which is a kind of applied science of complexity.[9]

These various disciplines have led to tremendous advances in our understanding of societies, of living organisms, of ecosystems and even of the Earth system. For example, do you know what there is in common between the functioning of the microbiota in our gut, the dissemination of 'fake news' on social networks, the formation of terrorist cells in the Middle East, the remarkable fragility of international finance, and the thresholds of collapse for animal populations? All these phenomena (and many others), seen and analysed as networks of interactions, the formation and integration of which we are only beginning to understand, show an astonishing universality of structure.[10]

The fields of application of these forms of knowledge seem limitless: the dynamics of traffic jams on the roads, the transmission of diseases, the effect of terrorist attacks on the internet or on a city, the reaction of living cells to a change of environment, the control of social networks, the stability of finance during the next major crisis or the disappearance of animal populations or species. The power of the new approaches is impressive, and they excite many people in political circles. They can also be very worrying for those who see the maintenance or expansion of a society of governance, management, technocratic power and generalized surveillance as one of the causes of our ills, and lead them to fear the worst.

Since the end of the twentieth century and its series of cat-astrophic announcements about the state of the biosphere, many scientists have been racing against the clock. They are desperately trying to understand how our 'Frankenstein' society works. What is this gigantic monster born of globali-zation over which it seems we no longer have control? The complexity sciences have provided us with means to under-stand better how it functions, but, paradoxically, they also give us ways to see its vulnerability, in other words its pos-sible collapse.

Reality cannot be described only through quantities and algorithms. Health, for example, is an emergent property of living organisms. You can consider it as a function of a set of quantitative variables such as blood pressure, temperature and so on, but it also involves qualitative characteristics such as well-being, awareness or pain, qualities for which there are no *objective* measuring instruments. Yet scientists in the disciplines we have traditionally regarded as basic have dif-ficulty or are reluctant to deal with these qualitative aspects because they are difficult to objectify.

However powerful they may be, our computers have limi-tations. 'The sciences of complexity suggest why we cannot control the processes that underlie the health of organ-isms, ecosystems, organizations, and communities', writes Canadian mathematician and biologist Brian Goodwin. 'They are governed by subtle principles in which causality is not linear but cyclic, cause and effect are not separable and therefore manipulable. Those systems are the causes and effects of themselves, involving ever-increasing loops of mutual dependence.'[11]

At the end of the 1990s, Brian Goodwin suggested expanding the conceptual framework of science in order to better navigate these paradoxes, through the development of a 'holistic science'[12] that would integrate 'aspects of reductionism and traditional science while developing other ways of observing and building knowledge'.[13] Influenced by phenomenology,[14] 'holistic science' aims to 'tackl[e] challenges related to physics, earth system science, ecology, biology, organisational development and health studies'[15] while using rigorous qualitative methodologies,[16] for example, in the assessment of ecosystem health[17] or of animal welfare.[18] Holistic science is about exploring the real 'through direct and subjective experience, and [making] use of intersubjective consensus as a way of distinguishing the aspects of experience and knowledge that are common to the group and those that are specific to individuals'.[19]

This requires a substantial epistemological effort in order to upset the traditional divisions of disciplines and the established practices of researchers. The humanities and social sciences have been using qualitative methodologies for a long time. Testing them in the natural sciences too, for example, might be an opportunity to bring about a vital rapprochement between nature and culture.

We, as scientists, haven't been used to dealing with a reality which is random, erratic, fuzzy and unpredictable. But, as Carolyn Baker remarks, 'if collapse is anything, it is a planetary immersion in the maelstrom of paradox. Unless we understand and honour paradox, we will end up, like all of the mainstream media on earth, asking all of the wrong questions.'[20] Could a more complex science help us to ask better ones?

We need intuition so we can act urgently

In the 1970s, the ecological (or environmentalist) issue gradually began to make cracks in the granite base of the French economy's so-called Thirty Glorious Years.[21] It brought awareness of the interdependence and fragility of the systems on which we depend, and of the possibility of future shortages. It asked the question no one wanted to hear, about the limits of the world which everyone thought had no limits. It was a major conceptual revolution, and we still have not finished digesting it fifty years on.

At the time, a sense of urgency began growing in the scientific community, and scientists from several disciplines began to work specifically on ecological disasters. We needed to understand as quickly as possible, so as to give society the tools and also the reasons to act. The American conservation biologist Michael Soulé calls these disciplines the 'crisis disciplines', and they fit into the general category of 'survival science': ecology, conservation biology, climatology, geology, oceanography, meteorology and so on.[22] All of them are synthesizing, systemic, complex and multidisciplinary disciplines that draw as they need from basic science, applied science and professional expertise, but also go beyond them.

These crisis disciplines reveal a central problem of our time. Through studies of complex adaptive systems (climate, biodiversity, globalized economy, etc.), they show: 1. that these systems are incredibly complex; 2. that it is already too late to prevent major irreversible changes or breakdowns; and therefore 3. that we will not have time to get to know everything we need. The coming time will definitely be a *time of uncertainty*.

By 1985, seeing the mismatch between the rapid growth of disasters and the slow pace of scientific progress, Soulé raised a fundamental epistemological[23] question. 'In crisis disciplines,' he wrote, 'one must act before knowing all the facts; crisis disciplines are thus a mixture of science and *art*, and their pursuit requires *intuition* as well as information.'[24]

In other words, if we wait until we know everything with rigorous objectivity before we take action, we will be condemned to watch helplessly as the Anthropocene unfolds outside the windows of our peaceful laboratories.

Recourse to intuition is quite disturbing for a society which prides itself on making decisions based on rational, quantified, objective knowledge, devoid of any kind of emotion. Are we to act before we understand? Can this still be regarded as a scientific approach?

A problem here is that intuition has been a bundle of conceptual tangles for centuries. The French philosopher Henri Bergson (1859–1941), for example, wrote extensively on the difference between two cognitive modes which he referred to as *reason* and *intuition*. The first uses concepts and analyses them, which fragments objects and presents reality in a static manner, while the second apprehends phenomena in a more global and dynamic way.

More recently, the psychologist Daniel Kahneman (b.1934), who was awarded the 2002 Nobel Prize for economics, gave credibility to the study of 'irrational' behaviour. Taking up the intuitive-rational dichotomy, he described two contrasting cognitive modes that shape our behaviour. 'System 1' is experiential, *intuitive*, preconscious, fast, automatic, holistic, mainly non-verbal and connected to our emotions. 'System 2' is conscious, analytical, slow, *rational*, mostly verbal and not connected to our feelings.

When you learn to drive, for example, your (rational) system 2 gets in motion, it works so you can manage to coordinate the movement of your hands and your feet, while paying attention to the rules of the road. It's difficult, slow and exhausting. But through practice, the brain transfers these skills to the (intuitive) system 1. This makes driving progressively more automatic and comfortable, so the driver can have a conversation with the passengers while driving at speed and anticipating the next junction.

In everyday life, we prefer to use system 1 (the intuitive and spontaneous one), out of comfort and laziness. From time to time, when an unusual or dangerous situation appears, system 2 gets turned on to analyse the potential threat. This preference for automatic mode makes life smoother but also regularly generates errors in everyday life, which Kahneman called 'judgmental heuristics'.[25] Intuition is a double-edged sword.

Today, intuition is no longer seen just as a philosophical topic, or as a kind of magical 'Eureka!' moment. In global terms, we could define it as 'thought produced in part by unconscious processes', but in reality there are several definitions, since it has been treated simultaneously by the sciences of management and decision making, by cognitive science and by psychology.

In 2005, researchers in management science further refined our understanding of intuition by distinguishing two types: automated expertise and holistic intuition.[26] The first is what allows us to drive a car without consciously thinking about it, what speeds up the processing of tasks in a familiar situation. Its limitation is that it is not adapted to unknown, strange or unpredictable situations, such as one finds in a world of wicked problems.

The second type, holistic intuition, is a judgement or choice made from an *unconscious synthesis* of information taken from various kinds of experience (and from all the senses). Unlike automated experience, it is generally very useful in the exploratory phases of research, or when faced by unpredictable or urgent situations, because it allows one to speed up the processing of too much information coming from ambiguous sources. In particular, it brings into play what we call 'creativity', so leading to the emergence of adaptive strategies which are genuinely innovative.

Holistic intuition can prove particularly useful for navigating an uncertain and chaotic world subject to frequent catastrophic events. It is not a magic wand that lets one do whatever one wants, or lets one escape classical scientific objectivity (when one has the time and the means for it). It is, however, another cognitive tool that we can use to adapt to our new world.

In the case of wicked problems, the number of variables and of interactions between variables is so large that we cannot get a realistic and complete picture of what is happening. It is hard to believe that we will be able to fully understand these problems (let alone control them) before they cause global disruptions in our societies or destabilize our Earth system to the extent that doing science at all becomes impossible. So we have no choice: we have to start running through the fog, and make intuition our ally.

The sciences certainly appear to us to be still necessary as a common language through which we can make ourselves understood. But during the twenty-first century, those whose minds persist in achieving objectivity and certainty at all costs before they start acting will be more likely than others to die with a book in their hand, or sitting in front of a screen.

We need resilience to find our way through uncertainty

The field of study that deals with the resilience of socio-ecological ecosystems is a kind of side branch of ecology. It uses complex thinking, it has understood well that the human and nature cannot be thought of independently from each other, and it provides vital information on how ecosystems and communities recover after experiencing different kinds of crisis. This means that it gives us ways of understanding present collapses and those which are to come, and also allows us to see (and perhaps to anticipate) processes of recovery.

For ecologists, resilience refers to the 'capacity of a system to absorb disturbance; to undergo change and still retain essentially the same function, structure, and feedbacks', and therefore also the same identity.[27] This is not a question of the system resisting change or of necessarily wanting to get back to the same state, but of bouncing back *by opening itself to the possibility of transforming itself* so as not to lose some of its functions.

Some ideas from this discipline seem to us particularly helpful in changing the perception that we have of disturbances. We begin with the *adaptive cycle*, which describes the cyclical transformation of highly complex and adaptive systems (systems, that is, that evolve). In other words, living systems. These are not stable. They are in a *dynamic non-equilibrium*, which goes through four phases.

There is the *growth* phase, which gives birth to a so-called pioneer system. This is the case, for example, during the first stages of appearance of a forest on open ground (in other words, of an ecosystem). Then, during the stage of solidification or *maturation*, the system becomes more complex as it goes along, through the arrival of new species, and it 'stores' matter and energy, as in the growth of a forest. In this specific case, for the same amount of incoming energy (the solar flux), the forest becomes able to shelter more and more species and to accumulate a maximum of biomass. The third phase is called 'relaxation', simplification or simply *collapse*, and it frees again the accumulated matter and energy. In the case of the forest, this takes place through fire. The fourth phase, called renewal or *reorganization*, sees the remaining elements come together to resume the cycle through a new phase of growth. After a cycle, the forest has been more or less transformed, but it has retained its identity and structure.

It can happen on occasion that, during the phases of destruction and reorganization, the system takes another way of reorganization, towards a new identity. A forest, for example, which does not grow back and becomes a steppe or a desert. This kind of bifurcation (sometimes desirable) is almost impossible to predict and appears when the external conditions change beyond a certain threshold. This can help to illuminate the possible dynamics of collapse and metamorphosis of our world.

Another interesting aspect of this model is that it allows us to think of the way in which these living systems nest within each other (as they do in real life), and so to appreciate that every system consists of nesting subsystems. The whole forms a dynamic structure called a 'panarchy'). It is the synchronization of the 'micro-collapses' of the subsystems that eventually brings down the larger system that they make up.

Resilience thinking helps to construct a conceptual framework which sees collapse as the creative destruction of a large global adaptive system (composed of an infinity of intertwined natural and human subsystems). Every system and subsystem eventually collapses, and often is also reborn. What is interesting for us is to see the collapse of thermo-industrial civilization as a whirlwind of micro- and macro-collapses, themselves interdependent through a variety of natural systems, some of which are already in the course of collapse. A disintegration followed by a reorganization may or may not offer the opportunity to switch to another form of social organization, perhaps not a civilization, and in any case not dependent on fossil fuels, and if possible compatible with living beings.

Or, more simply, as summarized by Edgar Morin: 'This is what history is: emergences and collapses, calm periods and cataclysms, bifurcations, whirlpools, the emergence of the unexpected. And sometimes, even in dark times, seeds of hope arise. To learn to think in that way: that is the spirit of complexity.'[28]

Outside the ivory tower

In addition to being complex, wicked problems include areas where the stakes are particularly high (the survival of humanity, of other species, increased incidence of cancers, population health, etc.). Consequently, they generate complex ethical problems, into which can enter irreconcilable conflicts of values between different cultural, social or political groups.

For example, how do we choose between the welfare of one generation and another, or between one region of the globe and another? How do we choose between making one living species suffer or disappear, or another one? How far should we pollute a river, or allow it to dry up, if it is considered to be a living being by another culture? In all of these cases, it would be absurd today if we were still to expect laboratory research to provide a 'unique truth'.

We need to cross academic disciplines, open up and break down walls

Scholars in various scientific disciplines have realized the critical situation in which we are immersed, and each group – climatologists, agronomists, engineers, architects, economists, sociologists, etc. – have their own proposals. But just adding together the various 'mono-disciplinary' proposals for understanding and action cannot constitute a global strategy.

Many scientists realize this, and even worry about it. But they cannot say it too loudly, any more 'than parents can argue in front of their children',[29] to quote the philosopher of science Isabelle Stengers. If the public were confronted by such a cacophony of views, they might lose confidence in science: scientific authority is at stake. Starting from this

situation, which can be overwhelming and even paralysing, the philosopher Tom Dedeurwaerdere, of the Catholic
University of Louvain in Belgium, suggests three ways in
which we can open up scientific practice.[30]

The first is to take the interdisciplinary approach further.
Interdisciplinarity involves having researchers from different scientific disciplines work together and so forcing them
to create a new common language. For example, GDP is a
simple measure of economic activity from a single discipline.
But we have known for quite a while that this index does
not measure the happiness of a society, nor its quality of life.
Far from it. Other indices have been created, as a result of
bringing together several social science disciplines, though
regrettably they have not yet been put into effect.

To open up the ivory tower to society, Tom
Dedeurwaerdere proposes to move from interdisciplinarity
to *transdisciplinarity*. This involves two further ingredients:
opening up scientific practice to non-scientific circles, and
including an ethical dimension. This is not just a matter of
no longer seeing science as 'neutral'. It involves formulating
research questions *with the actors within society* (the political
world, voluntary sector, activists, etc.), collecting and analysing data with these same actors, and finally applying the
conclusions with and for the social group. The more a problem is contested (or 'wicked'), the more transdisciplinarity is
needed.[31]

The biomedical sciences have already used this approach
to set up ways to manage ethical complexity.[32] Significant
decisions involve an 'extended peer community', including
legitimate non-scientific actors, as well as stakeholder rep-
resentatives. Logically, it is society *as a whole* which should
decide why and how to bring out scientific findings, not the
scientists alone, or politicians or other interest groups.

These propositions are in line with Isabelle Stengers'

approach in her book *Another Science is Possible*. She develops the notion of 'public intelligence of the sciences' to dissolve the opposition between science and opinion. This will require a drastic cultural shift: 'Here the scientific ethos itself is at stake, and in particular scientists' mistrust of everything that runs the risk of "mixing up" what they consider to be "facts" and "values"'.[33]

To move forward, we also need to build bridges quickly between research organizations, between researchers and ordinary citizens, and particularly between different types of knowledge. In recent decades, this type of approach has begun to be recognized. In Bruno Latour's words:

> It is not a matter of learning how to repair cognitive deficiencies, but rather of how to live in the same world, share the same culture, face up to the same stakes, perceive a landscape that can be explored in concert. Here we find the habitual vice of epistemology, which consists in attributing to intellectual deficits something that is quite simply a deficit in shared practice.[34]

Such a development would be a great help to the survival sciences, and especially to the field of collapse.

Include indigenous knowledges

During the second half of the twentieth century, some people realized that the great techno-scientific adventures such as the Green Revolution had failed to make a sustainable improvement to the living conditions of the majority of the world's peasant population. While most scientists saw traditional forms of knowledge as ineffective, inferior, or as a barrier to 'development',[35] anthropologists who worked with (often oppressed) indigenous peoples came to realize that these forms of knowledge conveyed a wisdom that 'emphasized the symbiotic character of man and nature'.[36]

As a prerequisite for their survival, indigenous peoples around the world have always observed their environment with great care. This has led them to develop knowledge, based on empirical observations adapted to local conditions, that has allowed them to evolve as the environment has changed. These 'traditional ecological knowledges'[37] encompass the worldviews of indigenous peoples, bringing together ways of knowing that we might classify within ecology, within spirituality, within human–animal relationships, and in yet other fields.

Some researchers began to think that combining this indigenous knowledge with classical Western science might promote respectful and equitable ways of generating knowledge. Better still, it might help us solve some of the complex crises,[38] such as the connection between climate and deforestation,[39] or the maintenance of biodiversity, especially since, according to the Right and Resources Initiative,[40] the lands where indigenous peoples live host less than 4 per cent of the world's population but about 80 per cent of the planet's biodiversity.

A group of researchers open to this complementarity between traditional ecological knowledge and classical sciences devised a 'multiple evidence based' (MEB)[41] approach. One advantage of this innovative framework[42] is that it recognizes that the interpretation and validation of knowledge takes place simultaneously.[43]

For example, during the 1989 Exxon Valdez disaster in Alaska, US federal agencies used local traditional knowledge to enhance the success of restoration efforts. The Aboriginal community was able to provide crucial detailed information on the biology and historical distribution of many species affected by the oil spill.[44]

In Europe too, the idea that non-scientists hold some keys to resilience is gaining ground. In 2015, the Brussels-Capital Region launched a research programme, Co-Create for Urban Resilience, intended to support innovation through a process of co-creation between the research world and Brussels' own indigenous population. More specifically, the programme plans to launch 'projects that propose societal innovations in the context of potential disruptions in the interdependent services on which our urban society is based (particularly limitations on mineral and energy resources)'.[45]

This 'participatory action research' programme contains both the essence of collapsology but also of the approach that we have just described. Its aim is to create not citizens, but knowledge-'users', in tune with their time. The idea is to 'involve the people concerned directly, so that they benefit from the results (user empowerment); go beyond disciplinary boundaries and integrate non-academic or non-formal knowledge (transdisciplinarity); break the barriers between the citizen, the industrial sector, the voluntary sector and the academic sector (trans-sectoriality); and finally, to change the attitude and practice of the academic researcher (participatory action research)'.[46]

Today, traditional and local ways of knowing and 'participatory action research' are fertilizing an increasing number of scientific disciplines on topics as diverse as climate change adaptation,[47] biodiversity conservation,[48] the development of appropriate technologies,[49] health,[50] education,[51] fisheries[52] and forest[53] management, agriculture,[54] psychology,[55] etc. But all this has its difficulties, especially within an institution which struggles to tolerate other ways of knowing.

Towards a post-normal science

For the writer and environmental science professor David Orr, '[t]he crisis of sustainability [. . .] has occurred [. . .] when and where [the] union between knowledge, livelihood, and living has been broken and knowledge is used for the single purpose of increasing productivity'.[56] It is high time to repair these broken connections and to use the power of science for less destructive purposes. Our aim is not to abandon Science and enter a world of darkness, but to enrich the practices of sciences through a process of opening and transforming these practices.

The critique of 'normal' science is not new. It was formulated in the 1970s by the philosopher of science Jerome Ravetz,[57] who criticized the industrial and 'techno-scientist' turn of science, linking up with such authors as Jacques Ellul and Ivan Illich. These critiques culminated in the 1990s with the birth of the concept of 'post-normal' science (see figure 1),[58] a strategy for solving scientific problems when 'facts are uncertain, values are in dispute, stakes are high and decisions urgent'.[59]

In other words, it is no longer enough to ask scientists to look for 'optimal solutions' (substantive rationality); we need to create a 'process aimed at finding shared and "satisfying" solutions' (procedural rationality).[60]

All this requires that stakeholders participate in the process of formulating scientific objectives, of determining the criteria for evaluating the methodology, of returning information for analysis, and finally of making decisions. This isn't easy, especially since this expert community 'must include a plurality of knowledge (scientific, indigenous, local, traditional), values (social, economic, ecological, ethical) and beliefs (material, spiritual) that, added to the traditional

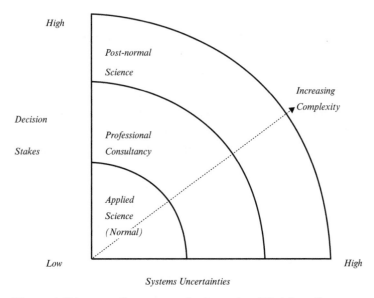

Figure 1 Diagram of post-normal science (modified from Jerome R. Ravetz, 'The post-normal science of precaution', *Futures* 36(3), 2004: 347–57)

'scientific facts', illuminates the analysis of the problem at stake'.[61]

Ravetz was also proposing a science directed towards the qualitative rather than the quantitative. He speaks of a 'quality assurance' not because this methodology manages uncertainty better, but because it is a process of social construction capable of answering the concerns of all the actors, and of taking into account the multiple narratives behind the problem in question.

The rationalists are likely to say, 'Stop there!,' seeing in this approach an attack against scientific objectivity, a new 'cultural relativism', an 'ideological control of the sciences', or an 'unbearable religious or spiritual regression that would bring us back to the Middle Ages'.

We agree, rather, with Bruno Latour (in his *Down to*

Earth) that 'it is not necessary . . . to shun rationality in order to add feelings to cold knowledge. It is essential to acquire as much cold-blooded knowledge as possible about the *heated* activity *of an Earth* finally grasped *from up close.*'[62] We need to find the conceptual tools – and post-normal science is one of them – to get closer and *experience* what the sociologist calls the 'critical zone', 'a minuscule zone a few kilometers thick between the atmosphere and bedrock. A biofilm, a varnish, a skin, a few infinitely folded layers',[63] where all living organisms, including ourselves, are born and die.

Post-normal science is not an anti-science. Quite the contrary. By breathing democracy into these processes of knowledge production about issues that concern us all, it becomes a protection that can save science (and the world) from the danger of scientism and technoscience.[64] It works to enrich scientific practice and to bring it out of its ivory tower. Better still, to bring it down to earth.

5

Opening to other visions of the world

Many human beings have become deaf. 'Centuries of hubris block our ears like wax plugs; we cannot hear the message which reality is screaming at us.'[1]

According to David Abram's argument in his book *The Spell of the Sensuous*,[2] the key step in this disconnect between humans and nature was the invention of abstract language, which gave abstract meaning to sounds and written symbols independent of the context in which they were spoken, in other words the actual environment, feelings and interpretation of the people there at the time. Through equipping ourselves with this powerful tool for theorizing – language – we humans entered into the cold world of abstraction, and broke the dialogue with nature. Through losing the direct connection with the senses, humans prevented nature from speaking to us, and it entered into what Dominique Bourg calls *le grand mutisme* (the 'great silence').[3]

Modern physics continued this 'banishing of sensory qualities to the benefit of figures and numbers', leading to an 'autistic civilization'[4] whose connections of reciprocity and empathy with other-than-humans (both living and non-living) have been lost, or, even worse, to a psychopathic civilization that has feelings only for itself. 'All emotion is brought back [to humans] in one way or another. Other beings are only objects for the satisfaction of human desires. This lack of empathy explains why humans have no moral sense and so why there is no limit to the harm they can do to others physically and morally.'[5]

This great disconnect became stronger after the Renaissance, with the increasing emphasis on technical progress and on the enslavement of the Earth to human material needs. Modern society was constructed by 'working' on nature as mere matter (Descartes), and by making other living beings 'work' as humans wished. Thus, 'a certain conception of "nature" has allowed the Moderns to occupy the Earth in such a way that it forbids others to occupy their own territories differently'.[6]

From the universe to the pluriverse

But human beings, even with technology to protect them, are not independent of the environment in which they live. In the Anthropocene, we can no longer suppose that there are two orders of reality, the history of human beings and the evolution of the Earth, each possessing its own dynamic.[7] To come back down to earth, and to listen again to what the world has to say to us, involves discovering and meeting the earth's nonhuman beings.

This is not a simple theoretical exercise. Its aim is radically practical: to promote, as the anthropologist Philippe Descola puts it, a 'less conflictual coexistence with non-humans, and so to try to erase the devastating effects of our lack of concern and our voracity for the global environment, for which we are mainly responsible'.[8]

Today, the boundaries are being redrawn. A series of truly innovative anthropological works is allowing us to explore this possibility of coexistence, as are the multiplicity of real-life experiences from collectives (most often in states of conflict) all around the globe.

Even Pope Francis has stated, in his encyclical *Laudato si'*,[9] that an 'inadequate presentation of Christian anthropology gave rise to a wrong understanding of the relationship between human beings and the world'. He puts the blame on a 'Promethean vision of mastery over the world', and warns against anthropocentrism, the idea that human beings are at the centre of the universe and that everything relates to them.[10] 'Once the human being declares independence from reality and behaves with absolute dominion, the very foundations of our life begin to crumble.'[11]

We Moderns barely know how to start exploring this truly confusing and exciting direction. There are a few theoretical studies that can help, if only to remove some of our inhibitions, but the essential component is practical. We are very poorly equipped for that, however, because we have forgotten. How many of you have spoken to a tree? When you go for a walk, which of you thinks about what to say to the woodlands? Do you know what the wolves think when they come back to repopulate a particular region? It can be quite complicated, even clumsy, to explore such questions, and to rediscover, or perhaps even to discover for the first time, unfamiliar ways of entering into dialogue with other-than-humans. That is to be expected, however. This chapter is an invitation to relax our inhibitions.

Other ways to see the world

Bruno Latour's works have made some major cracks in the edifice of modernity. In his books, including *We Have Never been Modern*, *An Inquiry into Modes of Existence*, and *Down to Earth*,[12] he shows that science is not the pure and disinterested activity that it claims to be. There is a gap between what people (including, notably, scientists) do, and how they report it. We Moderns officially claim to separate facts and values, but unofficially we mix them up all the time.

> One of the oddities of the modern age is that we have had a definition of matter that is hardly material, hardly terrestrial at all. The Moderns take pride in a realism that they have never been able to put to work. How can one qualify as materialists people who are capable of inadvertently letting the temperature of their planet rise by 3.5°C on average, or who inflict on their fellow-citizens the role of agents of the sixth extinction without anyone even noticing?[13]

But if we Moderns have never really been modern, we have equally not accepted other ways of being. The word 'ontology' refers to the representation of the world that each culture constructs for itself, in other words, its relationship to the practical, implicit and daily world of reality. Ontologies are not beliefs or ideologies; they are generative schemes that take shape during childhood and give meaning to the world. They are ways of being in the world.

Since they believe that they hold the keys of truth (thanks to science), the Moderns have convinced themselves that they can do without other ontologies. But the idea that any one ontology is more 'true' than the others goes against the work of Philippe Descola and many other anthropologists. Descola's explorations of cultures different from ours show the various ways which humans have of viewing other living beings as partners capable of intentionality, with whom they interact fully in everyday life. He has classified ontologies into four broad categories.

Naturalism is the ontology of Western modernity, since the end of the Middle Ages.[14] It is the only ontology to have invented the concept of nature and so the duality between human and nature. Naturalism supposes that on the physical plane, all living beings share the same kind of bodies (and descend from the same ancestors), but that in terms of their interiority, human beings are different from all other natural beings. In other words, it denies any form of interiority to what is not human.[15]

Animism occurs among the indigenous peoples of South and North America and parts of Asia. It is an inverse ontology to naturalism, since it sees similarities between beings from the point of view of interiority (all beings have a 'spirit' of the same nature) but sees differences in external form (all these 'spirits' incarnate in bodies of different species). Consequently, animists do not make a clear distinction between themselves and non-human beings, and still live in dialogue with them.

Totemism is found in Australia and North America and recognizes a similarity both of interiority and of externality. The various different types of beings are therefore classified by their physical, psychic and moral characteristics ('round', 'dark', etc.).

Analogy is a system of representation found among some Central American, Latin American and West African people. It presupposes differences both of interiority and of externality. All beings are singular. The comparison between distinct beings is therefore made through analogy.

These four great ontologies can be considered as cardinal points, because cultures and individuals are not confined to a single category. There is no typical representative of one or another ontology (for example, how many of you talk to your pet, your plants or your car?).

Naturalism has the problem of being based on separation. For the anthropologist Arturo Escobar, the pillars of the Modern ontology are: 'individualism, the belief in science, economics and reality, embodied in an expansionist drive for development on a global scale'.[16] From Descartes to Marx, this Modern ontology separates emotions and reason, and demands a radical break, or even a repudiation, of earlier forms of thought and practice.

Conversely, the other ontologies are relational. For them, no entity pre-exists the relations that constitute it. As Arturo Escobar explains, 'there are no individuals, there are only persons who are in continuous relationship with the entire human and non-human world'.[17] Arne Næss's ecosophy, following on from the achievements of complexity science, similarly rejects the dualistic vision of human beings in an 'environment'. For Næss, organisms are 'knots in the biospherical net or field of intrinsic relations'.[18]

Diplomatic relations between modes of existence

The Modern world has sought to extricate itself from the Earth system, but, with the changes now happening globally, the Earth is coming back to confront it full on: the rise in the oceans, the melting glaciers, storms, heat waves, etc. We believed ourselves beyond the earth, free from any biological contingencies and touching the celestial light of the pure spirit. Now we find ourselves alone, entangled in a muddy marsh as the fog around us becomes denser and denser. It's all beyond us.

Obviously, we are not outside Nature. Our connections with the world and with other forms of life are real, complex, sometimes mysterious, and above all indestructible. Ignore these connections and your feet will get caught in them.

Arturo Escobar was able to study several non-Western ontologies during his career, and he worked tirelessly to 'decolonize' Western influence. His work is a radical critique of 'development', nourished by his contacts with the campaigns of indigenous people and descendants of Africans in Colombia.

In this sense his work connects with the 'detachment' (*desprendimiento*) approach, advocated by many Latin American intellectuals who had realized that, two centuries after the wars of independence, the colonial system was still central to their political, cultural, social and economic practices. This 'detachment' or 'disengagement' approach consists, in Valeria Wagner's words, 'not in opposing or attempting to avoid the whole matrix, but in detaching yourself from the values that hold its elements together (an emotional process of disengagement) and separating and dissociating the elements (an intellectual process of disengagement)'.[19] The aim is to regain some autonomy, along with a capacity to act that goes beyond Western modernity.

Escobar invites us to enter into dialogue with non-Western peoples (often caught up in conflict), with non-Modern cosmologies, and even with other-than-humans, in order to learn to live consciously what he calls the 'pluriverse' (as opposed to the universal Modern). The idea is not to choose the best ontology from a menu that is offered to us by the anthropologists, but to discover the diversity of the approaches that are already present, to devise new ones, and to learn how they can coexist.[20]

But those of us who have not studied anthropology, are pressed by time and entangled in our Western modes of representation, what are we supposed to do? Should we spend some time living among peoples who have actively main-

tained, adapted and reinvented their knowledge, in phase
with their environment, so as to learn from the philosophies
that they have accumulated in contact with other-than-
humans over thousands of years? It wouldn't be a bad idea.
Although some of these peoples too have lost their bearings
through the impact of global changes, if we have to come
back down to earth, in Bruno Latour's words,[21] it's probable
that the earth on which we land will look 'rather more like
their terrain than ours'.[22] Moreover, as Descola reminds us,
'the considerable difference between non-Modern political
systems and our institutions is that they are able to integrate
non-humans into their groups, or to see in non-humans
political subjects acting within their own groups'.[23]

Another option (to avoid too many journeys by air) would
be to rediscover the non-Modern European traditions. We
are thinking of Celtic rituals, with their conscious relationships with other species, of Russian popular beliefs and
folklore of the 'spirits of place', of the knowledge of the
witches who were burned on the scaffolds of the Renaissance,
of the Luddites (the 'machine breakers' of the early nine-
teenth century) who refused to allow their communities to
be destroyed by industry), of the popular knowledge on the
virtues (medicinal effects) of local plants that has been suppressed by the pharmaceutical industry, or of the rich and
complex practices of the 'commons' before they were privat-
ized by the enclosure movement.

In addition to these inspirations from the past (which we
shouldn't idealize, but from which we can draw to re-seed
the future), it is also essential to go and experience contemporary conflicts. 'The projects in defence of the Earth
and of their own territory which are being undertaken by
indigenous, Afro-descendants, environmentalists, peasant,
and women activists should not be dismissed as relics of the
past or of a romanticism no longer relevant in a world of

scientific and technical rationality. On the contrary, they are a genuine vanguard within contemporary thought.'[24]

These conflicts have led to concrete results, especially in the field of law, which are making cracks in the granite base of Western representations. As the essayist and jurist Valérie Cabanes, a specialist in international law, has noted, major advances have been made in the recognition of the rights of non-human entities to exist.[25] Rivers, mountains, forests, oceans are considered by the first peoples as specific entities, as *persons*.

In Bolivia, Mother Earth received legal recognition in 2010.[26] In the United States, the Keystone XL pipeline crossing into North Dakota was denounced as threatening water *seen as a fundamental entity*. 'Water is sacred, water is life and must be protected for all', chanted the Innu of Quebec and the Sarayaku of Ecuador, who had come to support the Sioux, Apaches, Cherokee and Navajo people. Rights of nature are included in the constitutions of Ecuador (2008), Bolivia (2009) and Mexico (2017). The year 2017 was notable in other ways too. It saw the first granting of specific rights to the Whanganui River by the New Zealand Parliament. A few days later, the High Court of Uttarakhand, a state in northern India, recognized the Ganges river and its main tributary, the Yamuna, as well as the Himalayan eco-systems within its territory (lakes, glaciers, forests, etc.), as legal persons. Colombia granted rights to the Atrato River to protect it from pollution related to mining. It was also in this year that, at the first World Conference on Oceans (in New York), New Caledonia proposed to recognize the rights of the Pacific Ocean.[27]

These various explorations lead us to realize that there is a diversity of 'modes of existence', making up the world with all its beings, and that it is time to adopt an 'ontological pluralism' that even the Moderns, as we have seen, never completely abandoned. For Latour, the first step towards this coexistence is to delineate the fundamental values of the Moderns and, starting from there, to discover the other modes of existence. 'Our method thus does not imply asserting that "everything is true", "that everything is equal to everything else", that all the versions of existence [. . .] ought to cohabit without our worrying any longer about sorting them out [. . .]. It implies only that the sorting out will have to take place, from now on, on a level playing field, contingent on precise tests.'[28]

We are witnessing a true Copernican revolution, and a project of society (of our civilization?) that envisages the reconciliation of different views of the world. It leads towards what Arturo Escobar calls a 'politics of ontology' and to the radical idea that the political domain extends not only to non-Moderns, but also to non-humans. This obviously implies creating an immense 'diplomatic' machinery which can set up a framework for negotiations between modes of existence, within this pluriverse of ontologies of equal dignity.

Diplomatic ability will not be a luxury in this project of 'symmetrical' dialogues. For Bruno Latour, 'a large proportion of the tensions [. . .] stem from the fact that the *veracity* of one mode [of existence] is judged in terms of the conditions of veridiction of a different mode'.[29] In this respect, the proposal for diplomatic relations connects with that of postnormal science: 'We must instead choose an ethical-political position that cannot be demonstrated as true, but rather has to be experienced and lived in its practical and political implications.'[30]

It is by no means certain, however, that the dominant ontology of the world – the 'Modern' – will allow itself to be dismissed so easily! Some elite groups will pursue the 'modernization' of the Earth at the risk of its collapse. They have in a sense seceded, by denying climate change (or its significance for the human and non-human masses) despite being well aware of its nature. They openly declare their refusal of solidarity, of any world that they share with the lower classes, and have abandoned the fantasy of a modernization that would benefit everyone. These elites 'shatter the very idea of modernity, of universality'.[31] They themselves are smashing the ideological base of industrial modernity, of 'development' and 'growth'.

In this context of conflict, neither the state, nor the multinationals, are reliable allies in our search for non-oppressive forms of society. And, for the present, 'science cannot even enter into dialogue with other forms of knowledge, since it grants itself the monopoly of knowledge, compassion and ethics'.[32]

The historian Christophe Bonneuil suggests that we are living through a 'radicalization of a war of the worlds'. This war is between Moderns and Earth-Dwellers, between those who think that the land is their property to make Modern, and those who know how to belong to the Earth and who are building new connections between humans and with other-than-humans within the territories where the conflict is taking place.[33] In opposing projects of extractivism or land-grabbing by states or multinationals, local indigenous, peasant or activist communities are opposing a global project. They are leading what is in fact an ontological conflict, through defending, living and building other ways of 'feeling-thinking' the world, to use Arturo Escobar's expression.[34]

There are already conflicts within and between these worlds, and it is certain that there will be more in the future. Worse, 'that war, at once civic and moral, divides each of us from within'.[35] But these conflicts will reveal cracks, from which new ontologies may perhaps emerge, weeds that will create the forests of tomorrow. We must be ready to see them emerge and ready to form new alliances.

To change your ontology, to put yourself in the place of the others, to understand them, to try to feel as they do – all these explorations will enrich the possible relations of reciprocity between humans and other living beings. Can an Indian who cannot slaughter a sacred cow put himself in the shoes of a trapper from the far north? Can a Native American who converses intimately with plants (through poems called *anents*[36]) help a farmer from Beauce[37] manage his crops? What will the arguments of the bulldozers who are used to extract minerals be worth, at the UN General Assembly in 2046, against the wisdom of the salamanders? Such reflections can stimulate the imagination, as evidenced by Alessandro Pignocchi's splendid comics,[38] which imagine the Jivaro Indians studying the inhabitants of our own regions using the tools of Lévi-Strauss's structural anthropology, and demonstrate the practical (and hilarious) consequences if our political leaders were to convert to animism.

The emergence of a pluriversal mycelium

What are we going to do about the huge chaos left behind by modernity and capitalism? How can we recover from the end of the world (Danowski),[39] that is to say the collapse, even partial, of the way in which most people see the world?

Rebuilding over the ruins of capitalism

How will we live among the remains of capitalism? In her answer to this haunting question, the American anthropologist Anna Tsing[40] refers to an aromatic mushroom prized by the Japanese, the *matsutake*, which has the specific feature of growing in forest soils devastated by over-exploitation. Following, among others, the precarious communities of Asian gatherers in the United States who survive through selling the mushroom, she shows how capitalism continues to develop over its own ruins until its final fall. She invites us to prepare for the emergence of a much more organic world, with which we will have to come to terms. When the chainsaws go quiet, life will begin again, but in what way?

The mushroom is a beautiful metaphor for the organic emergence of unexpected life within a devastated territory. Even after it has been cut down, the forest often finds ways to come back, to persist, in what Tsing calls a movement of 'resurgence', as preferable to the rather technical term 'resilience'.

People who remained in the territories (the 'grey areas') of Fukushima and Chernobyl gradually came to terms with the danger by learning to manage it, by developing radioactivity measures, and by exchanging knowledge and experiences. The documentary film *Tchernobyl, Fukushima: vivre avec* (*Chernobyl, Fukushima: Living with it*)[41] 'not only tells us how a liveable situation can be made out of a post-disaster world, but also, above all, how helping each other is the way it is done'.[42] These practices all arise from common problems which lead to *ad hoc* solutions. They amount to what the collective Dingdingdong called a true *entraidologie* or science of mutual aid, and they make it possible to recreate a future in these territories.

Mushrooms serve as a symbol of opportunistic associations between species, mutual dependences, hybridizations, cross-breedings, mutual support between living beings and between species, and especially of lateral, decentralized operation. As Tsing notes, in contrast to the vertical, sharp-edged logic of the plantation, they represent the logic of the forest, of the weeds that grow on the margins or gradually appear after the destruction comes to an end.

One lesson we can draw from this metaphor is that a redeployment takes place in abandoned areas, *without resources*, once the insatiable ogre of the plantation has gone. In these newly free areas, pioneering non-humans may re-emerge, preparing the land for the arrival of humans (also pioneers) who are coming back to earth. 'The Earth-Dwellers', explains Christophe Bonneuil,

> are unsubdued non-human forces and beings of the 'third nature' [the feral one, which emerges after the devastation], to use the anthropologist Anna Tsing's expression. They are also countless human collectives and their low-tech creation, who have abandoned the Modern myth of uprooting oneself from the earth to experience relationship with it: indigenous groups who have rejected 'development', alternative groups opposed to growth, or inhabitants of territories in resistance.[43]

Defended zones, fungal territories

Such experiences are often mocked, attacked, ignored or misunderstood, but they distribute their spores throughout the ruins of the world. They create footholds within a specific territory. Liberated zones, particularly 'defended zones' (*Zone à defender* or ZAD) created to defend land against development projects, mean many things to different people because they carry the hope of these young shoots.[44] We project our fantasies of a better life onto them, but also our fears of giving up the familiar comforts that insulate us from the world.

All of these experiences come out of this History of resistance, in response to the unprecedented violence of industrialization, which destroyed social classes, women, craft communities, communal practices, and entire indigenous territories, cultures and species.

This resistance to modern 'progress' and 'comfort', which is woven through the huts, the stone farmhouses, the fields and woodlands, is part of a long tradition: it draws on the common stock of resourcefulness and of peasant activity in many styles over many centuries, on the free anarchist communes of the early twentieth century, the communes of the 1970s, and the eco-communities and rural alternatives that have flourished since the 2000s, hiding behind protective ferns, forests and villages.[45]

Both in South America and in the French countryside, these zones where people come back to the earth are trying out a different relationship to land: 'neither Cartesian nor Euclidean, even less liberal'.[46] They do not see a space with clear limits, or a property in the classical sense, but a 'practical adaptation through cultural, agricultural, ecological, economic, ritual practices, etc.'.[47]

Anchoring oneself in the land in such a way generates powerful feelings of belonging and identity, an intimate attachment. This return to the Earth (the repolitization of belonging to a piece of land) should not be confused with the 'back-to-the-land' movement of unhappy memory which took place during the Vichy regime.[48] We are not just talking about simply protecting 'nature', but defending a living territory, an environment, even an extension of our own being, as in the famous words of the Australian activist John Seed when he defended the rainforest by chaining himself to trees, taken up again as a slogan at Notre-Dame-des-Landes:[49] '*Nous ne défendons pas la forêt, nous sommes la forêt qui se défend*' ('We are not defending the forest, we are the forest defending itself').[50]

Every human community has sacred, non-negotiable, values, alongside more utilitarian and negotiable values. If the community's relations to its territory change, these values can change as well. But what has become sacred for the people living there is seen as profane (and negotiable) by the outside world. Therefore, it makes sense that some people will defend their territory with passion and courage, even (if the attraction of death becomes strong enough) preferring to die rather than change. The impact of a disruption of ontological values can still surprise us. 'To say: "We are dwellers on the earth[51] among other earth-dwellers" does not lead to the same politics as saying "We are humans in nature".'[52]

It is also important to be aware that 'the indigenous and Afro-descendant struggles in the South, like the anti-productivist and autonomous alternatives and movements in the North, are inventing advanced forms of democratic emancipation and self-management'.[53] These are places of experimentation. They therefore need isolation to 'escape this zone of death',[54] which is the capitalist modernization front. This implies learning to fight, in self-defence, against the assaults of the 'militants of the extreme Modern'.[55] And, the Hollywood film *Avatar* provides us with an appropriate imaginary: 'if the armored vehicles and the bulldozers of the gendarmes are meant to serve development, then, to find new models of life, we have to oppose those who control these machines'.[56]

Fortunately, alliances are being formed between humans and non-humans within the liberated zone, between the zone and the outside . . . and also between different struggles. The mycelium is connecting up. As is evidenced by this sympathetic advice from the Indian physicist and activist Vandana Shiva: 'Instead of sending in its Robocops, the French government should send its youth to the ZAD, to teach them to live in dignity, at peace with the land. To become people who are the creators of their own existence, not consumers or disposable persons.'[57]

Alliances of Earth-Dwellers

For the philosophers Léna Balaud and Antoine Chopot, 'in the Anthropocene era, injustice is not only local, human or social, but planetary, transversal to all beings – from oil, soil and genetically modified seeds, through climate refugees, proletarianized workers and indigenous populations expelled from the places where they live'.[58]

We need to consider politics therefore not as oppositions between human groups (classes, countries, etc.), but as conflicts between assemblages of humans and non-humans;[59] and the fight against capitalism also needs to add the refusal to exploit other species to the refusal to exploit particular classes of humans.

We are not talking here about a few scattered, insignificant conflicts. Movements fighting for greater social and environmental justice are very numerous. In his 2007 book *Blessed Unrest*, the US activist Paul Hawken wrote: 'I soon realized that my initial estimate of 100,000 organizations was off by at least a factor of ten, and I now believe that there are over one – and maybe even two – million organizations working toward ecological sustainability and social justice.'[60] A decade later, what he calls the awakening of the Earth's 'immune system' has certainly grown further.

There are also alliances to be made with other-than-humans. '"Nature" is no longer a set of simple objects and passive mechanisms, devoid of interiority, but a vibrating, wild, multispecies weave of powers that feel, act and react.'[61] Other-than-humans people the world, they have their own intelligence, and they constitute – and even contribute to and make use of – what we call the commons.

Some people fear that in focusing our efforts on this expansion of modes of existence and devoting time to relationships with other species, we may lose the sense of struggle, and lose the specific 'intra-human' political power that we need to restrain the industrial imbalance. Without this power, they fear, we may be reduced to the roles of 'observers, victims, and survivors'.[62]

But, along with Léna Balaud and Antoine Chopot, we can also make the opposite bet, and bet on Earth-Dwellers as a whole. We can hope that it may be precisely the alliance with the other-than-humans that will give back power and opportunities to our struggles and our efforts at resurgence.[63] One example comes from Argentina and Paraguay, where a battle against transgenic soybeans has been won thanks to wild amaranth, a fertile, edible, protein-rich plant which has become resistant to Monsanto's Roundup. Finding motivated allies among the struggling peasants, amaranth dispersed itself in the form of 'seed bombs', nullifying the plans of one of the world's largest future transgenic seed production centres![64]

But if politics is the art of 'opposing each other without slaughtering each other' (Marcel Mauss), we will not only need to find allies but also ways of managing conflicts between us and particular species. The philosopher Baptiste Morizot's work of exploration (and even diplomacy) is notable.[65] Working from the assumption that animals maintain social and political relations among themselves, comprising territories, alliances, signs, negotiations, collective decisions and forms of conflict resolution, he tried to interact with the political behaviour of the wolf, which is a social animal par excellence. The war against the wolf has lasted for centuries, perhaps it is time to try diplomacy?

The latest work in ethology or in plant intelligence shows that this is only the beginning. Understanding the languages of other species and how they relate to each other opens up avenues for political relationships with them. This is a major conceptual reversal, which involves recognizing that groups of non-humans have a point of view based on their situation, just like we do, if different from ours, and that historically they have been in relation with each other, and with us, on the basis of these same points of view. To bring non-humans into politics would then paradoxically bring us into the purely ecological intelligence and rationality of the more than human world and into the perspectivist geopolitics of life forms.[66]

The political contract with other-than-humans is not something we need to invent; we first have to discover it among them!

What might a huge inter-species parliament look like? How could we get to the point of understanding and inter-acting with all this incredible complexity without falling into the pitfall (very risky) of a gigantic pluriversal governance, like the Parliament of the Republic in *Star Wars*?

Animals, trees, mushrooms and microbes are not pas-sive beings, they are effective politicians. They are even landscapers, and even activists, because they have been trans-forming the earth for millions of years, helping to form and maintain the *critical zone*, the tiny common life space on which we live, and from which we draw ceaselessly. In other words, they *give* to us. Our incredible qualities of empa-thy and reciprocity (which we use spontaneously among ourselves) can therefore easily be applied to them, and can help to support an immense act of counter-gift, of what the anthropologist Marcel Mauss calls an 'obligation' of return. We are infinitely indebted to them.

Finally, this *obligation* can be read according to the other meaning of the word: if we do not do this, it is quite possible that the mushrooms at the end of the world will grow back without us.

6

Telling other stories

'The system is collapsing all around us just at the time when most people have lost the ability to imagine that anything else could exist.'[1] David Graeber's words remind us that what we have just explored in the previous chapter – realizing that other worlds exist and trying to fit into them – is above all an invitation to stimulate our imagination: to shift our point of view, to feel differently, to have encounters that may change our lives, to be touched, to build a new foundation for our ethics.

We have seen that our Modern ontology sets the framework for our relationship to the world. It permeates our unconscious, it structures our myths, and makes stories arise that affect us. But how can we tell which of those stories are toxic? How can we create other ones? How can we be sure that they will move us towards a better world? What story (or stories) can we set going to help us get through these storms? How can we make meaning out of what is happening to us?

The challenge of changing the narrative of our time is immense – it implies setting off an earthquake. It also demands of art-'users' that they drop their inhibitions and engage in fields usually reserved for science, and requires science-'users' to let themselves undergo experiences that push them beyond their areas of competence.

'Zombie' stories

There are stories that have been told for so long that they no longer resemble stories but indisputable truths. They have become part of the landscape, they give meaning to our world and to our existence, they constitute the unconscious basis of our thoughts and actions.

One of these is the story of *progress*, which tells us that our society can keep on growing without end. Knowledge, technology, the individual, freedom, the economy, our social systems are all capable of improving indefinitely, for century upon century, because there is no limit to progress. This story generates others, such as 'technocratic solutionism',[2] the belief that any problem will have a technical solution: hybrid cars and wind turbines to 'solve' global warming and the end of fossil fuels; drones, big data, smart meters and intelligent smart grids to implement the energy transition; a circular and collaborative economy to abolish the production of waste, inequalities and social tensions; the colonization of Mars to escape the ecological disaster, etc.

There is also a strange belief that there is only one law of the jungle – *competition* – and that it can be translated into the 'law of the strongest'. And a magical and tragic tale that begins with: 'There was once a population of human beings, which separated itself from Nature through its intelligence.' And all these tales intertwine, with a certain logic. 'The myth of progress is founded on the myth of nature. The first tells us that we are destined for greatness; the second tells us that greatness is cost-free.'[3]

In contrast to this vision, the priest, historian and ecologist Thomas Berry (1914–2009), one of the pioneers of the relationship between religion and ecology, saw no *objects* in the world, but only *subjects*. This wise old man was convinced that we had to change our narrative and saw our time as caught 'in-between stories', suspended in a kind of transition where old and new stories clash, the new fighting to emerge while the old refuse to die and wander around the world, infecting the newcomers.[4]

Lev Grossman, a columnist for *Time* magazine, sees the zombie as the 'official monster of the recession'.[5] Zombies are devoid of soul, they move without aim, they are unable to reason. The zombie is the 'modern fiction par excellence: that of absolute autonomy, of a being who does not need connections with others'.[6] These beings have no relationship with their peers, have no strategic goals and feel no fear. All they have is the strength of numbers. They keep going a world without meaning, which refuses to die.

As in the case of Modern ontologies, in the previous chapter, the first stage in plunging into the workshop of alternative narratives is to highlight the stories that already inhabit us. This is what Cyril Dion proposed in his *Little Manual of Contemporary Resistance*.[7] 'We are unable to think outside of our narrative', he says, 'because we confuse it with reality',[8] and he suggests embarking on a cartography of the locks and barriers that run through our society. These he calls 'invisible architectures', borrowing an expression from the specialist in 'collective intelligence', Jean-François Noubel.

An example is air travel. Tell someone that there will soon be no planes in the sky because of the Anthropocene. He will be dubious and reply, 'Maybe, but I cannot give up going on long-distance journeys.' This answer is based on an invisible belief that long-distance journeys are only made by air, and this is connected to another architecture, on which our relationship to time is based, which assumes that journeys must be fast.

Today the transition to a new story seems impossible, since we are continually kept in line by the rhythm of life around us, the people around us, media, advertising, the release of new consumer items, bills to pay, and so on. 'Radically changing the trajectory of our societies requires building new stories, but also modifying these notorious architectures.'[9] It's a much more complicated task than just writing a new story on a blank piece of paper.

Stories as weapons for large-scale subversion

The fundamental need for stories

Humans need stories because it's how we make sense of our world and our existence. They shape our beliefs, our values, our hopes. They permeate us from an early age. We are structured by the stories of our parents, of our time. 'People easily understand that "primitives"' – our ancestors – 'cement their social order by believing in ghosts and spirits, and gathering each full moon to dance together around the campfire', notes historian Yuval Noah Harari. 'What we fail to appreciate is that our modern institutions function on exactly the same basis.'[10]

Myths are stories that come from the unconscious. According to Mircea Eliade (1907–1986), Romanian philosopher and specialist on myth, myth 'supplies models for human behaviour and, by that very fact, gives meaning and value to life'.[11] For Joseph Campbell (1904–1987), who taught mythology at Sarah Lawrence University, the myth offers us 'an experience of being alive, so that our life experiences on the purely physical plane will have resonances within our own innermost being and reality, so that we actually feel the rapture of being alive'.[12] Such myths draw on the collective unconscious. 'Any large-scale human cooperation – whether a modern state, a medieval church, an ancient city or an archaic tribe – is rooted in common myths that exist only in people's collective imagination.'[13]

All these (unconscious) myths and (conscious) stories constitute the 'means by which the emotional brain makes sense of the information collected by the rational brain'.[14] And when a situation is beyond us, finding meaning becomes vital. Our obsession with the 'why', says writer Nancy Huston, comes from the fact that we are aware of the entire 'arc' of our life – from birth to death – and that only the creation of meaning allows us to support this existential state.[15]

Viktor Frankl (1905–1997), a psychiatrist and neurologist, experienced the horror of concentration camps during the Second World War. As a result of his experience, Frankl founded a psychotherapeutic approach which he called 'logotherapy', believing that when people find meaning in their lives, suffering diminished and mental health improved.[16] In the camps, the longevity of a prisoner was directly affected by the way he imagined his future. 'What was really needed was a fundamental change in our attitude toward life', he writes. 'We had to learn ourselves and, furthermore, we had to teach the despairing men, that it did not really matter what we expected from life, but rather what life expected from us. We needed to stop asking about the meaning of life, and instead to think of ourselves as those who were being questioned by life – daily and hourly.'[17]

Reconquering the future: the importance of science fiction

For the American environmental activist Starhawk, our habit of contrasting reality and fiction has an unfortunate consequence; it depoliticizes the imaginary and relegates it to a sphere of life which is seen as harmless, childish and entertaining. This is misleading. In order to upset the culture (this 'set of stories that we tell ourselves relentlessly'), she argues that we have to find the subversive force of stories, and set about 'making stories which are uncomfortable and disturbing for the dominant imaginary'.[18]

If we look at the situation like this, we can both invent our own stories and also dig up others whose existence has been forgotten. For example, in our schools, why don't we present modernity as the period that allowed the great disconnect with other species to reach its climax. Wasn't the Renaissance also the time of the crushing of the feminine (the massacre of witches) and of the destruction of the bonds of mutual aid that welded together the communities of the Middle Ages?[19] Those Thirty Glorious Years from 1945 to 1975[20] (we could rename them the 'Thirty Dreadful Years'), were they not the greatest period of waste in history? Why don't we see transhumanism, with its creation of hybrid beings, irreversibly dependent on a socio-politico-technical system (the transnationals) addicted to oil and rare earths, as the point of no return of this break with the rest of the world?

Making up stories is not just for writers; anyone can do it. We must become again future-'users', creators of our stories. Transition initiatives help a lot by making it possible to do this in groups and in a more sympathetic atmosphere. People can imagine their locality in twenty or thirty years undergoing the familiar catastrophes of the Anthropocene, but with the underlying theme that life will be better than

today. At first people make timid and theoretical sugges-
tions, but they gradually become more refined and extend
themselves. The more precise and practical the visions, the
more believable and potentially motivating they will be.
This act of imagination and collective creativity involves
intuition as much as objective knowledge. It welds groups
together by building a common vision and inviting people
to share their joy (joy, according to Spinoza, is the increase
of the power to act). It gives a sense of direction, sketches
paths into the future and gets us moving. To imagine ourselves in thirty years, with our neighbours, to add new
people, imagine how their lives might evolve in the streets
that we know, whether the atmosphere is pleasant or less
so, a time of conflict or rebuilding . . . For the political scientist Luc Semal, 'this work on the collective imagination
helps reinforce local resilience, because it gradually accus-
toms people to an inevitably more frugal post-petroleum
and post-growth future'.[21]

Novels have the same power. According to Ursula Le
Guin – the great science-fiction novelist who wrote the novel
on which the film *Avatar* was based, an emblematic story of a
clash between Earth-Dwellers and Moderns – they can build
crucial connections between readers.

> The only way to the truly collective, to the image that is
> alive and meaningful in all of us, seems to be through the
> truly personal. Not the impersonality of pure reason; not the
> impersonality of 'the masses'; but the irreducibly personal;
> the self. To reach the others, the artist goes into himself.
> Using reason, he deliberately enters the irrational. The fur-
> ther he goes into himself, *the closer he comes to the other.*[22]

Science fiction is a way of exploring the future. Through
a skilful mixture of unconscious material (myths) and

intelligence (so as not to get carried away by easy myths), it can give us the tools to understand uncertain technoscientific futures. Science fiction constructs thought experiments, and helps us test the future.

The physical sciences often use thought experiments when experimental devices are impossible or too expensive to carry out (e.g. to imagine how time would pass on a spacecraft travelling at the speed of light). For scientific purposes, however, these experiments take place in a very simple world, with defined parameters, so that the results are as convincing as possible. What would happen if scientists used thought experiments to test complex systems like societies or political systems? The social sciences have refused to try, leaving the field open to science fiction (SF).[23]

What SF stories do, at least the good ones, isn't to make us believe things, but to get us to experiment with our abilities to transform ourselves. As the philosopher Isabelle Stengers says, in this sense SF writers are realists, because they are trying to 'uncover what is real within a larger reality',[24] which is, as Ursula Le Guin emphasizes, 'in process of construction'. Alain Damasio moves on to practice: 'For example, transhumanism directs people's thoughts to a certain type of future. As an SF writer, my job is to construct imaginary worlds that make something else desirable.'[25] As Le Guin notes,

The fantasist, whether he uses the ancient archetype of myth and legend or the younger ones of science and technology, may be talking as seriously as any sociologist – and a great deal more directly – about human life as it is lived, and as it might be lived, and as it ought to be lived. For after all, as great scientists have said and as all children know, it is above all by the imagination that we achieve perception, and compassion, and hope.[26]

The idea then is the same as with the announcement of an incurable disease: a story should not close doors or flatten the future, but instead open up possibilities and provide a multiplicity of ways to take the situation in hand. Isabelle Stengers, who participated in the reflections on Huntington's disease, is a witness to this: 'The Dingdingdong collective and SF have helped me not to despair, by encouraging the possibility of a democracy that is disobedient and imaginative. And this possibility is nourished by the joy associated with the imagination.'[27] A utopia represents a world which is ideal but closed. As for dystopias, they reflect the anxieties of the time. But we can open up these fields by describing what have been called 'possitopias'. A possitopia is 'an improvement over the current reality and realistically achievable, but only if appropriate measures are taken'.[28]

For an example, we can turn to the globally successful *MaddAddam* trilogy, in which the Canadian author Margaret Atwood recounts the adventures of four teenagers living before, during and after a great collapse.[29] The story takes place in the United States in the (dystopian) near future where companies have taken control of everything. After the virtual annihilation of the population, the main concern of the four heroes becomes survival and the creation of a new community (so post-apocalyptic but 'possitopic'). The interest of this series of novels lies in what is eventually revealed about the emerging new world and in the characters who have found meaning in their battle for the future of humanity.

This *MaddAddam* trilogy can be understood as an alternative to how we usually think of the apocalypse. It leads to revelation rather than extinction. It opens up new possibilities, rather than the end of all possibilities.[30] In exploring themes such as love, hope, freedom and autonomy, Margaret Atwood shows us how a community could be reborn. In

Andrew Sean Greer's words, her trilogy is 'an epic not only of an imagined future but of our own past, an exposition of how oral storytelling traditions led to written ones and ultimately to our sense of origin'.[31]

Stories of times to come

The French writer, film director and activist Cyril Dion, author of the Afterword to this book, has invited people to 'create structural contexts that will awaken our creativity, stimulate our capacity for empathy, nourish our understanding and inspire our enthusiasm'.[32] We are happy to accept his invitation. Let's get going! We are not talking here about writing novels anticipating the collapse that open up new possibilities – though that would be exciting and quite welcome, because such novels are rare – but of exploring stories which might enrich the way in which we imagine the collapse.

The collapse as opening up possibilities

Telling a story of collapse of our society, the kind of story we *expect*, always calls on the same apocalyptic themes. For the most part these are ultra-violent and male-dominated (apart from a few exceptions, such as Jean Hegland's novel *Into the Forest*),[33] and they follow the adventures of a few survivors of a ruined world. The real challenge is to get out of this unhappy rut, which is made up of a mixture of old myth (the apocalypse) and new (materialism, competition, the break with nature, etc.). This challenge doesn't just apply to novels or film scripts, it's just as relevant to everyday life: how we talk within the family, public lectures, newspaper articles, and the like.

If there is some meaning to be found in collapse, isn't it in seizing the opportunity for a radical rethink of how our society operates? Or in the joy of seeing the mega-machine's destruction of life slow down? Or the beginning of rebirth? What could the prospect be that would get us moving again?

To open up what is possible, it's important to give our imagined future a complex texture: to evoke specific collapses, carefully describing the connections between collapses of the ecosystem and of human society; not to present things in a homogeneous way where everything has been determined in advance; to point out that some collapses are desirable and others are not; to describe catastrophic moments, slow degradations, but also long periods of waiting; also to dwell on personal, interior collapses, and on collapses of illusions, of systems of thought and of representations of the world, and so on.

To open up what is possible above all involves imagining past what we are losing to anticipate what might emerge. In this context, the myth of the hero can obviously unfold, as can the stories of mutual aid (the individualists will find it more difficult to survive), and of alliances with other-than-humans fighting, for example, against the capitalist forces of industrial appropriation.

The prospect of radical upheaval also makes it possible to turn our values upside down. For example, the American collapsologist Chris Martenson, in his famous *Crash Course*,[34] points out that our current society gives little value to basic products (water, wood, food, etc.), a little more to processed products (craft and industry), and a great deal to virtual products (money, digital). Imagining a post-collapse world makes it easy to turn this scale on its head, a move which has a significant heuristic power when it comes to preparation: water, wood and food will be invaluable, while no one will want to drink money (even if it is liquid) or eat credit cards or dream about a new smartphone app.

For the three of us, the development of this story took place first of all through a rational stage (making connections between various scientific disciplines), then we began sharing our images of the future. This stimulated both an inner transformation (in our emotions and our relationship to the world) and an external transformation (in our lifestyle, our political commitment and collective organization). This allowed us to restore meaning to our lives, to feel less lost, to wake up and to enter into a new kind of resonance with our times. We feel that we are living in a decisive moment in history, but are also aware of our vulnerability and fragility in the face of that moment. We are brought back in touch, at the same time, both with something greater than us, and with our own mortality.

A mobilization – as in time of war?

'In the North this summer, a devastating offensive is underway. Enemy forces have seized huge swaths of territory; with each passing week, another 22,000 square miles of Arctic ice disappears. Experts dispatched to the battlefield in July saw little cause for hope, especially since this siege is one of the oldest fronts in the war. [. . .] World War III is well and truly underway. And we are losing.'[35] So wrote the journalist and environmentalist Bill McKibben in 2016 about the efforts needed to combat climate change.

There is a real urgency and the size of the issue is immense. Our home, our territory, our health, our life and our future are at stake. We risk losing everything. So why shouldn't we set going a gigantic war effort, as when the Allies and the USSR defeated the Nazis? We could launch great new Manhattan projects,[36] but in the form of thousands of small, low-tech projects, and for the purposes of disarmament. We could organize vast invasions, like D-day in Normandy in 1944, to stop desertification by massive reforestation. With the huge power still available to us through fossil fuels, it would surely still be possible to bring about a rapid and coordinated transition.

This story is quite effective in many of our countries because it echoes our experience of the Second World War, the military victories and the rapid large-scale reconstruction which followed.[37] All this thrills us, it awakens our sense of sacrifice, of heroism, of the defence of sacred values, identity, territory and the like.

In general, there are three main ways to weld individuals into a group, or even to create a simple sense of brotherhood: a common enemy (a big bad wolf), a hostile environment (a natural disaster) or a very specific common objective, limited in time.[38]

Mark Diesendorf, professor at the University of New South Wales in Australia, and his colleague Laurence Delina, now at Hong Kong University of Science and Technology, asked some years ago whether this type of mobilization might work against climate change 'without major threats to democracy'.[39] While not dismissing this approach, they point to some potential problems.

The first is that building up the military imagery and warlike rhetoric could make it easy to forget the inner and ideally peaceful dimension (emotional, ontological, spiritual, etc.) of such a mobilization. As a result, this story could give disproportionate power to the governments and multinationals who would lead this gigantic war effort with 'solutions' like geo-engineering. Not to mention that the mechanisms which allow rapid and effective mobilization (the machines and the oil) are also the enemies we are fighting.

Nor is it certain that a military-style mobilization would

be effective at countering slow-moving and intangible threats, or vague and undefined 'enemies' (such as climate change, the loss of biodiversity, greenhouse gases, the fossil fuel industry, capitalism, government inaction), where the need is for sacrifices spread over generations.[40] During the Second World War, there was a sudden break in the situation (for example, the Pearl Harbor attack for the USA) and the enemy was clearly identifiable.

Despite all of this, we believe that the image of a war could be of some help, if it is focused on large-scale plans for general mobilization, as at the time of the Victory Gardens in the United Kingdom and the United States (vegetable gardens in support of the war effort), fair rationing policies, and post-war reconstruction efforts (such as the Marshall Plan). It could also contribute to the emergence of a decentralized resistance network that might undermine the morale of the destructive powers, and organize incursions into the 'occupied zone', while defending the liberated areas of the 'free zone'. Though if we indeed create both a new National Council of Resistance (CNR)[41] and a Natural Council of Resilience,[42] we should not forget that the border between the free zone and the occupied zone also lies within each of us.

Whether our motivation is strong enough for us to give our lives for the cause of reducing material consumption by 80 per cent is not so certain. But building a sense of a general mobilization could help us in growing something which has been largely missing from the transition movements: effective coordination. Aligning ourselves, even temporarily, with a common story like this could give a huge boost to all those people who strongly desire to change the world but are not so inspired when told to carry out small everyday actions at an individual level.

The 'Great Turning' . . . To get ourselves moving

One approach that has been gaining momentum over the past ten years is that of a voluntary ecological transition, beginning with citizen initiatives and aiming to make our societies once more compatible with the biosphere and resilient to future disasters. Examples include Alternatiba[43] and the Décroissance ('degrowth') movement,[44] as well as the international Transition Network.[45] The latter, founded by the permaculturist Rob Hopkins in 2006, and popularized in France by the film *Demain* ('Tomorrow'),[46] connects thousands of projects all around the world. The Transition Network has close connections with the work of Joanna Macy and her 'story', which she calls 'The Great Turning'.[47]

For Macy, three great stories are currently fighting with each other. These are the 'Business as usual' story, according to which skilfully devised technological innovations will bring 'solutions' to our 'problems'; the 'Great Shipwreck' (Great Unravelling) story, which envisages the virtual extinction of our species and life on Earth (an archetypal version of apocalyptic collapse); and finally Macy's suggestion, the story of the 'Great Turning', which involves reorienting ourselves collectively towards a 'society that supports Life'.

Macy asks us to think of the time in which we are living as the beginning of a third great revolution, after the agricultural and industrial revolutions. Those revolutions took many decades (even many centuries for the first). The new revolution will involve a more rapid transformation than previous revolutions, and in some ways a deeper change. It will involve not just choosing the techniques and institutions we want but also rethinking who we are, what we really need, and how we interact among ourselves and with the totality of life.

This story makes us the actors of our own generation, and also responsible for generations to come. The first two stories could come true if we choose *not to act* (either 'because it's all too late' or because we allow others to do it for us). The story of the Great Turning involves a conscious choice that appeals to creativity and imagination. It is a narrative that can give meaning to our lives, and can help connect together the growing number of people aware of global issues.

However, the Great Turning cannot guarantee that we will avoid suffering. It's not for nothing that of late Joanna Macy has been encouraging us to work on good relationships between humans, in anticipation of 'difficult times'. In so doing, she helps us realize that the Great Turning is certain to include a period of collapses. That prospect may also help liberate the creativity necessary for the emergence of new worlds.

What we take from this narrative is its assumption of a break with the linear model of history (the story is rather one of destruction and reorganization), the possibility of taking an active role in revolutionary change and the sense of being part of a vast movement. But others have taken a further step.

'Uncivilisation': let our imagination loose

The writer Paul Kingsnorth was deputy editor of the famous English magazine *The Ecologist* for fifteen years: 'I did all the things that environmentalists do. But after a while, I stopped believing it.'[48] Despite all the efforts of the environmentalist movements, the situation just continued to get worse. As Kingsnorth puts it,

> The environmentalists . . . were not being honest with themselves. It was increasingly obvious that climate change could

not be stopped, that modern life was not consistent with the needs of the global ecosystem, that economic growth was part of the problem, and that the future was not going to be bright, green, comfy and 'sustainable' for ten billion people but was more likely to offer decline, depletion, chaos and hardship for all of us.[49]

So, while Paul's colleagues continued to organize actions and awareness campaigns on the assumption that the impossible would somehow happen, Paul and his friend, the writer Dougald Hine, decided to move off on a tangent, betting on writing, art and music to move us 'beyond the self-satisfied stories we tell ourselves about our ability to manage the future'.[50] The two friends then published a splendid pamphlet, *Uncivilisation: The Dark Mountain Manifesto*,[51] as a call 'for a clear-sighted view of humanity's true place in the world'.[52]

So, in 2009 was born the Dark Mountain Project, a 'cultural movement for an era of global upheaval', animated by a network of writers, artists and thinkers who have by today linked up around the world thousands of enthusiastic people expressing a real sense of relief. All have in common that they have stopped hoping to 'save the planet' and instead want to forge a new way of imagining the future. In hindsight, Kingsnorth comments that 'accepting this reality brings about not despair, as some have suggested, but a great sense of hope. Once we stop pretending that [the collapse cannot] happen, we are free to think seriously about the future'.[53]

As he recognizes, this posture would have seemed heretical a few years ago, but it is so no longer. He also notes a real growth in the awareness that society is incapable of responding to the 'crises' it has created. 'Together, we are able to say it loud and clear: we are not going to "save the planet" ... the planet is not dying, but our civilization might be, and neither green technology nor ethical shopping is going to prevent a serious crash.'[54]

The manifesto is based on the observation that a 'human civilisation is an intensely fragile construction'.[55] It is supported by shared beliefs: 'belief in the rightness of its values, belief in the strength of its system of law and order, belief in its currency; above all, perhaps, belief in its future'.[56] Once these shared beliefs start to crumble, the edifice can collapse very quickly. History has plenty of examples.

We have lived since our birth in this bubble, in this 'delusion of isolation under which we have laboured for so long',[57] and we are accustomed not to see beyond these beliefs, to the distant and obscure territories that lie outside. The invitation of the Dark Mountain movement is to start exploring them at last, through writing and through publishing 'uncivilized' writings.

We are the generation born in the age of ecocide. And 'Ecocide demands a response. That response is too important to be left to politicians, economists, conceptual thinkers, number crunchers; too all-pervasive to be left to activists or campaigners. Artists are needed. So far, though, the artistic response has been muted. In between traditional nature poetry and agitprop, what is there?'[58]

We have presented some sketches of stories that have moved us. They will gain power or wither, other stories will emerge, from everywhere, old and new, unconscious and conscious, crossing and pollinating each other. You would have to be pretty smart to guess which ones will form the foundations of tomorrow's communities.

Interlude:
Entry to collapsosophy

So far, we have explored psychological and subjective aspects of collapse that we felt needed to be considered for the times ahead. This was mostly on the basis of scientific work and some notable writings that already border on 'collapsosophy'.

It's now time to get out of our comfort zone (articles published in scientific journals can never quite do this), and to enter fully into the central point of this book: how do we make a connection with, how do we give meaning to, our lives and our times?

At the threshold of this third part, we close our eyes, take a breath, and plunge into the depths through the only possible entrance, our personal experience and commitment. We will speak here about issues that we think are essential, that we have lived from the inside for years, but that we do not generally discuss in public, and even less in gatherings of professional people from science or politics.

We have decided to risk this step because engaging with these issues has given us a vital boost of energy, and also because we know that they touch many people. The connections that we have made, for example, through Work that Reconnects workshops (see chapter 7), through rituals of initiation to masculinity (see chapter 8) or through seminars at Schumacher College, have been so intense that they have given us the strength to continue. Probably only connections such as these have this kind of power.

Some people perhaps may find all this clumsy, laughable, confusing or trivial. This may even place our scientific work in disrepute, through some strange and absurd process typical of our times. We are prepared to take on these risks because they are themselves trivial in comparison with the tsunami of hard knocks that await us in the decades to come. To engage with this changing and unpredictable world will require exploring, getting out of our ruts, discovering, experimenting, clearing the ground, making mistakes, transgressing, risking, building bridges. This is the nature of the mycelium from which mushrooms grow.

Two specific keys have been important for us. These are ecopsychology and ecofeminism. We first discovered them through experience, then, to find words for our experience, through reading. We introduce them very briefly here because they give a particular colour to the next two chapters.

Rediscovering connections through ecopsychology

Our disconnect with Nature may well be the biggest cause of our problems. It seems to lead to serious psychological and pathological disorders among us Moderns, which in turn bring about our systematic destruction of our habitat.

Ecopsychology clears up the relationship between the human psyche and nature.[1] The crisis that threatens our planet, says Joanna Macy, stems from our pathological sense of self: our disconnect with nature is accompanied by a deep disconnect with ourselves.

In other words, the threats that weigh on our survival can be put down to our psychological and social immaturity, to our lack of authenticity, in other words our lack of psychological and spiritual awareness, our inability to cultivate the true self that lies beyond the ego's limits. Ecopsychology aims to help us understand the psychological roots of collapse, and encourages us to undertake deep interior and spiritual work.

Our discovery of Joanna Macy's work was a decisive event for us. This tireless activist, now nearly ninety years old, has combined her practice of Buddhism under Tibetan and other Asian masters with a militant commitment to peace. A former professor of systems theory, she is also one of the pioneers of deep ecology. From the 1980s, in the field of antinuclear campaigns, she became aware that, without introspection, activists (who want to change the world) are very often trapped in the habits and beliefs of their subconscious and that of the public, something which can easily lead to ineffective strategies, intolerance, conflicts between egos, emotional disorders, cynicism and exhaustion.

She has created a practical methodology inspired by many traditions of the world which aims to reconnect activists who are in pain with their own emotions. This transforms them both internally and collectively, relieves their feelings, makes them more resilient and more alive, and restores inspiration and meaning to their struggle. Put differently, it offers an accelerated course for experimenting with mutual trust, developing empathy between humans and with other-than-humans, and learning what is genuine support. It is a real work of mutual reliance, involving body, soul and emotions.

The methodology, developed in hundreds of workshops,

and involving thousands of participants and facilitators from around the world, is now called the 'Work that Reconnects'.[2] It was established in France, Belgium and Switzerland some ten years ago through groups such as Roseaux Dansants[3] and Terr'Eveille,[4] and has continued to develop there.

One of us was able to spend quite a long time with Joanna Macy when she visited Europe in 2013. Seeing her overflowing energy, a participant asked her what motivated her to keep on leading workshops at her age. Her answer was clear: 'If I still do all this, it's to create as much chance for us as possible to avoid violence when everything changes. That requires two ingredients', she added, 'wisdom and compassion.' And that does not mean passivity. Her long, militant commitment, which made her 'get the measure of the feelings of denial, helplessness, and despair that we feel when faced by the ecological crisis',[5] has never been weakened, quite the contrary.

Thinking back, these workshops were an important transition for us, in part for the connections we have woven and still weave with the participants. We have learned to see with the heart and with new eyes, and, most moving for us, to reconnect with inner selves and emotions which some of us thought had been buried forever. The effect is still with us: an intense feeling of clarity, peace, wholeness and courage. Today, sitting at our computers, we scientific rationalists are surprised to find ourselves writing these lines.

Accepting our feminine side through ecofeminism

The existential break with nature, which is ecophilosophy's central concern, led to a loss of sensitivity, opening the way to a society which dominated, exploited and destroyed nature. The ecofeminist movement goes a step further in showing that this society has the same relationship with women. For ecofeminists, the degradation of nature and the degradation of women's condition have the same origin. We will develop this idea in chapter 8.

The ecofeminist movement has many different forms and today still has a strong presence in the English-speaking industrial nations and in some emerging countries. It appeared during the 1980s, when the Cold War was still at its height, to ward off the fear of the nuclear apocalypse. 'Faced with the nuclear threat, the fear or even terror of a future destroyed by nuclear radiation, and the distress of leaving behind them a world in ruins, these women resisted despair through joy and through the sense of agency that grew out of their political action.'[6]

This movement was original in that it based itself in creative and experimental practice, rather than in the university. They *took action*, without asking anyone, without theorizing, without spiritual leaders and without hierarchies, always aiming at the transformation of the world. They brought into the political field the importance of the body (not just of ideas), of aesthetics (not just technical efficiency), of the imagination and emotions (not just reason), and also of magic (not just cobblestones and tear gas).

They built bridges with the labour movement as well as with the non-human worlds. 'They all shared the same vital need to fight in a living, instinctual, intelligent and aware way, in a non-dualist mode which healed and transformed.'[7]

As Émilie Hache sums it up in the ecofeminist reader *Reclaim*, when we face disasters and the threat of collapse,

it is not a question of turning to ecofeminism to give us the solution to today's problems, but to remind us that we can respond collectively to a catastrophic situation, and that such a response has power; to remind us of the importance in such situations, as crucial as it is counter-intuitive, of reconnecting with ourselves and of creating new visions; and finally to incite us to ask ourselves what we want, what makes us powerful, and to invent it.[8]

When we returned to this ecofeminist literature, we also discovered a way of writing and sharing very different from that of classic academic writing. Much more poetic and organic, less rigid, these writings emphasize relations between beings, or between histories, and constantly emphasize the interdependence that the sciences that grew out of patriarchy neglected for so long. Mixing science, politics, emotions, fiction and spirituality into a single pot has been a real relief for us and has helped free us up to adopt our systemic, lateral and transdisciplinary way of approaching things, as well as in the path of our own lives.

Part Three

Collapsosophy

No tree, it is said, can grow to heaven unless its roots reach down to hell.
Carl Gustav Jung, *Aion: Researches into the Phenomenology of the Self*,
trans. R.F.C. Hull (New York: Pantheon Books, 1959), p. 43

7

Weaving connections

Our society is thirsty for connections and for meaning. This is because it has dried up the sources. Science, technology and capitalism have taken the sacred out of everything[1] and left us isolated, drowning in an ever-vaster quantity of things of all kinds. Is there any meaning in all this? What's happened to everyone else?

The philosopher Abdennour Bidar uses the term 'weavers' (*tisserands*) for people who are working to 'repair the torn fabric of the world'.[2] There are many of them. For him, there are three main forms of connection to rediscover: the connection with yourself, the connection with other people and the connection with nature. This is the same as what Joanna Macy has been suggesting for forty years through the Work that Reconnects workshops. In the process, these two authors (and other 'weavers') touch on a fourth fundamental connection that needs to be rebuilt: being in harmony with what lies beyond us.

We have discussed the first kind of connection (with

yourself, your emotions and your internal state) in previous chapters. In this chapter, we propose to explore the other connections: reconnecting with other humans, through the ability to help each other, which is deeply embedded within us; coming together again with non-human beings, who are also aware in their own way of the 'deep time' of life's history on Earth; and finally getting back into contact with what we could call the 'sacred'.

What we have learned through our experience over the last few years is something that our ancestors and other peoples already knew, that it is possible to be connected without social networks, new technologies, indium, cobalt or palladium.[3]

Between humans

It's worth recalling that, though humanity's problems have innumerable causes, there are still three ways, which feed off each other, of dying *en masse*: wars, diseases and famines. They can still occur locally and sporadically, but when they take place on a large scale, they inevitably lead to what historians or archaeologists of the future will call a collapse.

The coming years bring with them the very real possibility of armed conflict. Our previous book, *Mutual Aid: The Other Law of the Jungle* (*Entraide: L'autre loi de la jungle*),[4] aimed to provide some ideas and tools to prevent these conflicts, or at least to avoid their happening as rapidly and on so large a scale. Though if that were to occur, these ideas about mutual aid would simply be the everyday character of life of the groups and communities that would survive in the rubble.

A future of mutual aid?

The lessons we drew from exploring what we call *mutual aid*, and which includes all the ways in which living things associate with each other, can be summed up in a few key points.

First, there is the evidence that mutual aid and competition have been everywhere, between individuals and between species, since the dawn of time. Helping each other is deeply rooted in us as humans, both in our biological heritage and in the cultural practices which are interwoven with our biology, and it comes naturally to us. As recent studies have shown, cooperation has been a central theme in popular narratives around the whole world for tens of thousands of years.[5] But the problem of our society is that it has fallen under the influence of a powerful culture that only allows for individuals and competition.

Next, although it may seem counterintuitive for competition-ridden society, it is shortages, crises and hostile environments that make mutual aid emerge. We find this principle on two different time scales. First in our own lives when we encounter a very stressful situation or when we have to react to a disaster. In an emergency, people self-organize without panic and help each other in remarkably effective ways. All that is left in them is the acute awareness of being human, of needing security, of needing to help the other. Self-help and altruism emerge spontaneously, as happened on 11 September 2001 in New York, or at Bataclan in Paris in 2015. All this happens very quickly, in a few hours or a few days. Then, on the long time scale of biological evolution, a hostile environment brings out mutual aid between organisms, simply because those which adopt solitary or selfish strategies are much less likely to survive. As the evolutionary theorists Edward O. Wilson and David S. Wilson stated in a recent survey of the subject: 'Selfishness beats altruism within single groups. Altruistic groups beat selfish groups.' Everything else is commentary.[6]

Thus, a collapse perspective leads us to envisage not so much a rose-tinted future paradise of mutual aid and altruism, but rather a situation where human groups who do not help each other will have less chance of survival. The standard of living of an average European is equivalent to 400 'energy slaves', meaning that each European consumes on a daily basis an amount of energy equivalent to a workforce of 400 healthy people. If these 'energy slaves' (fossil fuels) diminish or disappear, we will have to start working much harder, while also accepting that our standard of living will fall substantially. We will then rediscover the effectiveness of working in a group, and realize that it was precisely wealth and abundance that allowed the emergence of selfish and individualistic behaviours. In other words, in our present environment the help of the other is not necessary, and competitiveness does not involve real risks.

We also saw that mutual help in a group, however spontaneous and powerful at first, can quickly collapse if is not reinforced by social norms such as rewarding altruistic people, punishing cheats, and good and bad reputation, as well as the basic need to feel security, fairness and trust within the group.[7] Consequently we can suppose, and we observe in fact, that while occasional serious disasters lead to the emergence of prosocial acts (solidarity, altruism, mutual help), over time, if a basic institutional structure doesn't form between the reconstituted individuals, social chaos can easily come back and degenerate into deadly conflict.

The challenge for the next few years, then, is to demonstrate the toxicity of our competitive culture, to denounce it and to transform it. We need to appreciate that a culture of mutual aid can be fragile and hard to sustain. It requires a lot of practice and willingness until effective 'invisible architectures' have been put in place to support it. But the result is worth the effort: mutual help is powerful, and can move mountains. 'We are not saints, but we are sometimes good team players',[8] says the psychologist Jonathan Haidt.

Which groups?

Every group of individuals (family, nation, company, association, religion or whatever) has a kind of skin or membrane – a self – that defines it, that protects it from the world outside and filters what it agrees to let in or out. Sometimes the membrane becomes watertight and the group 'closes in on itself', considering what is external to it as foreign, even hostile, or simply non-existent. Individuals within the group then lose their reciprocal relationships with individuals outside, whose subject status becomes transformed into that of an object, in relation to which anything is permitted. This is what happens between supporters of football teams, between religions, between countries at war, or between humans and animals.

How can we rebuild the connections with those and with what is around us, so that they are mutual, trustworthy, secure and equitable? That is the big undertaking of our time. It's in our interest to do whatever is needed to strengthen our relationships with others, both humans and non-humans. To do this, we need to examine the various membranes that constitute us, learn how to make them porous (stop them from becoming exclusive) and discover more extensive ones, so transforming beings who seem distant into subjects within our enlarged community.

The challenge will be to juggle with this interweaving of identities so that we can get through the storms ahead without allowing our feelings of sadness, fear or anger to transform into forms of aggression. During a major upheaval of the social order, and consequently of the norms that structure that order, we can always count on the very solid 'membranes' of small groups, which we can form relatively easily (family, neighbourhood, village, even associations and so on). However, we should also be aware that even if a reference group such as the nation contracts or disappears, it doesn't stop us from feeling, and bringing to life, much more extensive 'membranes' that include all of humanity and everything that lives. We can feel compassion and empathy freely for whoever it may be.

This question of the membrane and its radical enlargement occurs in a very practical way in relation to refugees and migrations. The spontaneous rejection of some outside the 'nation' membrane, as long as this membrane is still meaningful, can be understood (among others reasons) by fear of scarcity ('There won't be enough for everybody, we'll end up fighting each other') or the anxiety of losing one's identity ('Do they share my values? I'm not willing to compromise them').

It is normal for accepting a stranger to cause fear at times. Opening one of our protective membranes (family, city, nation, etc.) to strangers is always a risk. But openness and welcome can be cultivated and it is possible to become 'competent' through learning how to manage these membranes. Also, you only need to spend an evening with some Sudanese refugees to discover people 'like us', with the same concerns, emotions and needs.

Governments call this great phenomenon of migration a 'crisis', but what has happened since 2015 is only the small beginning of a great movement that will become much larger in the course of the century.[9] Projections for 2050 suggest a figure of 200 million displaced persons because of climatic factors (floods, droughts, etc.) and many more if one considers all the other reasons (wars, epidemics, etc.). The political apparatus seems to have no way of preparing for the long term, showing the extent to which it was not designed for such purposes. We are not only talking here of the Global South. Global warming or nuclear accidents may force people in the UK or France to seek refuge in Scandinavia or Russia, Californians or New Yorkers to flee to Canada. If we look at today's African refugees, we see the human condition as it may be for most people in the twenty-first century.

Migrations have been characteristic of humanity for hundreds of thousands of years. If we were not so powerfully wired for empathy and mutual assistance, we, beardless, immature little monkeys, totally vulnerable at birth, would have been dead long ago. Our ability to cooperate, to make groups and societies, has made us one of the most widespread species on Earth.

However, there is a serious obstacle to the implementation of mutual aid in a group. This is hierarchy. Many animals are able to coordinate and divide tasks, but only humans (or, more accurately, some human cultures) have developed social structures in the form of vast *hierarchical pyramids*. While this recent mode of organization[10] has proved effective in stable and predictable situations – such as the military, or building cathedrals or railways – it is both inadequate and ineffective when the situation becomes complex and the environment changes.

As Marc Halévy,[11] a physicist, philosopher and business consultant, points out: 'By definition, a hierarchical pyramid structure is the easiest way to connect x points to each other. The simplest, so the stupidest. How do you expect information originating from thousands of actors to be handled, at the required level of complexity, by the ten people on the board of directors?' With the bewildering level of complexity of our huge societies, we seriously need to question the appropriateness of such architectures of power. They not only make us far more vulnerable and less resilient in the event of major disruptions, such as those in the electricity grid, or prolonged strikes affecting supply chains, but their rigidity makes them themselves become factors in aggravating disasters.

The occasional attempts to build 'team spirit' in companies has no real effect; the hierarchical pyramid structure encourages 'everyone for themselves'. Our obligation is always to become more successful and find ways to climb up the ladder. Sébastien Faure, an early twentieth-century anarchist teacher, already noted more than a hundred years ago: 'So, what one sets in motion, with a system of ranking, is: among the people at the top, vanity, presumption, contempt of the inferior, and in any case careerism; among the people at the bottom, envy, discouragement, unwillingness to make an effort, resignation.'[12]

In addition, 'top-down' decisions regularly generate a feeling of unfairness – for example, on the issue of differences in how people are treated in relation to salaries. A feeling of fairness, however, is one of the three ingredients (along with security and trust) necessary for the emergence and maintenance of mutual aid. Consequently, even if mutual aid manages to keep going in such pyramidal structures, it is systematically inhibited by the decision making and power mechanisms inherent to this type of structure.

In recent years, as noted by management specialist Frederic Laloux, new organic and decentralized organizational methods have been developed. In a striking convergence with colony-based living organisms (such as ants or mushrooms), these organizations rely on both local and interconnected intelligence, making for resilience and cooperation.[13] Our society is progressively moving (and it is high time that it did so) from 'power over' to 'power with'.[14]

Empathy, compassion, reciprocity, trust and the subtleties of group dynamics cannot be felt through a book, they have to be experienced. We have all felt significant moments of mutual help at a difficult time, received a helping hand, felt a hand on our shoulder, a look of gratitude or the thrill of being part of a group. For Carolyn Baker, 'It is important to know our neighbours, not only for security purposes, but to know what they might need from us that they may be too proud to reveal. Are you sure that your neighbours have enough to eat?'[15]

We need each other, and appreciating this leads us to admit and express our vulnerability, both as individuals and as social groups of whatever kind. We saw in chapter 2 that the capacity for resilience came from the bonds that people had woven with those around them. This is 'social capital'. When bad news comes, it is important not to feel alone, and not to feel that the people around you don't know how to react as a group. We need to learn, experience and teach the art of being together, from now on and as quickly as possible.

With 'other-than-humans'

Many Westerners are barely aware of the wild species that live on Earth, particularly those that live in their immediate neighbourhood. Sometimes we may know more about elephants, giraffes and tigers than the insects, rodents or birds in nearby woodlands. The same is true for the vegetable kingdom: alders or mosses may be less familiar to us than redwoods or baobabs.

In addition to missing out on experiencing these treasures, we have allowed ourselves to be persuaded that animals are 'inferior' and less intelligent beings. Even worse, biologists, people who have been spontaneously attracted to the living world, find that access to their field of science specifically requires a loss of sensitivity to living species, in order not to bias the objectivity of the research.

Consequently, it seems to us that making or remaking a connection with other-than-human beings is a major issue, and it will be all the more crucial in a collapse situation, when we will need them to recreate the conditions of our material and spiritual life. Our need will not be so much for resources as for new partners.

Learning from other species

Each day the current situation brings us closer to an inevitable conclusion: while humans imagine themselves to be intelligent, most are quite hopeless when it comes to sustainability. The biosphere, however, has an incredible 3.8 billion years of experience of resilience and of problem-solving. The keys of sustainability are there, under our eyes. This is the central idea of Janine Benyus, the founder of modern biomimicry:[16] to draw inspiration from the principles of life which ensure the functioning of ecosystems and of other species so as to improve our own 'design flaws'. Early peoples often made good use of this approach, in many different circumstances. Today, in their turn, biologists, permaculturists, agroecologists and engineers are discovering and using these principles.

Let's mention some of these principles. The most obvious is 'circularity'. In ecosystems, for example in a forest, there is no waste. What some species reject is used as resources by others, and the rare toxic molecules are always biodegradable. All living molecules combine, fall apart and come together again in a constant flow. As for non-renewable mineral elements (such as pebbles from beaver dams), they return at the end of their life to their environment of origin, in an unmodified form, and again usable by other living beings. And it is this circularity that makes *death* another principle of life. We are alive because others are dead; and in dying, we allow yet others to live. Death, which is of course associated with reproduction and so with rebirth, is also the best way to constantly create novelty, so as to adapt to the changing environment.

All or almost all of the energy of living beings comes from the sun. In other words, it is made available for the biosphere by plants through photosynthesis. It is harvested and consumed locally by other organisms, and not centrally produced and redistributed over long distances, as we do as a result of our dependence on fossil fuels or on uranium.

The principle of mutual aid (yet again), that power-ful mechanism that we have just examined among human beings, is the great generator of innovations among living beings. It is, for example, the symbiosis with fungi, at the level of the roots, which has allowed the plants to develop so luxuriantly on the land, and to build up our soils. This association teaches us a lot about mutual aid: by allowing trees to connect up with each other and to exchange nutri-ents (going from the strongest to the weakest), fungi form an immense and very effective network of redistribution which looks strikingly like our principles of family allowances and social security. They got there 400 million years before us. The icing on the cake is that they achieve this solidarity between species on a vast scale without a Board of Directors or a Secretary of State, that is to say without a hierarchical pyramid.

Our aim here is not so much to appropriate these prin-ciples as to realize, as we suggested in chapter 5, that they could form the foundation, the hidden and still to be discovered architecture, of a great political treaty with other-than-humans. All this could be negotiated on a case-by-case

basis and, some day, human beings will sign the first trea-
ties of which they are not entirely the authors. If we don't
agree to work within the limits posed by these principles of
life, how else can we get back to living in harmony with the
biosphere, and build a genuine post-petroleum economy? As
the ecologist and philosopher Aldo Leopold said, in words
which outline the basis for a common ethic of our shared
'critical zone' of life on earth: 'A thing is right when it tends
to preserve the integrity, stability and beauty of the biotic
community. It is wrong when it tends otherwise.'[17]

Meeting other species

One advantage of no longer feeling alone on Earth, and
surrounded by subjects rather than objects, is that you can
ask for help. How can we regenerate ecosystems? Ask the
plants, fungi and animals that are repopulating the tem-
ples of Angkor[18] in Cambodia. How can we build places to
live without metal or fossil fuels? Ask bamboo, hemp, flax
or nettle. How can we make our mineral-based cities more
liveable? Ask the plants, who know how to regulate the temperature, smooth out the unevenness of rainfall, make good
use of our excess carbon dioxide, all the while providing a
habitat for many animal, plant and fungal species, which give
generously of their fruit and flowers in return.[19]

How can we calm our existential anxiety? Ask the trees
again, because they spread around volatile substances that
reduce stress in those who breathe them,[20] speed up the
recovery from illness for patients who see them from a hos-
pital window,[21] and significantly reduce the crime rates in
neighbourhoods where they are cultivated.[22]

For those of us who are wary of having too much to do
with these other earthly beings, perhaps it's time to reconnect
with our inner child, who knows how to play spontaneously

with pigeons, ladybirds, butterflies, ants, snails, lizards, woodlice or spiders. This powerful feeling of affection, this atavistic tropism, called 'biophilia' by the great naturalist Edward O. Wilson, is still present in all of us, if sometimes well hidden. It can bring a lot of joy and can be called on easily if we give it the opportunity.

> Stop and smell the roses – as those plant volatile chemicals enter your nose, the cross-cultural dialogue is opened.[23]

The more we become aware of our vulnerability as individuals and species, and of our radical interdependence with the web of life, the more we become sensitive to the presence of 'other-than-humans', our cousins, our neighbours . . . In the ZAD of Notre-Dame-des-Landes, humans had an opportunity to let these connections reappear, as witnessed by Camille, a long-time ZAD activist:

> To live somewhere isn't just to stay there. [. . .] It's an interlacing of connections. We belong to places as much as they belong to us. It's to stop being indifferent to our surroundings, it's to be attached: to people, environments, fields, hedges, to woodlands, houses. To a particular plant that keeps appearing in the same place, to a particular animal that you get used to seeing there. It is to be sensitive to, empowered within the spaces around us.[24]

At present, a global change of perception is taking place within our society. We can see this in the dramatic increase in the number of vegetarians and vegans, and the growth of associations fighting for animal welfare and 'animal rights'.[25] This opening towards the other animals comes partly from the scientific world, with such charismatic ambassadors as the biologist Marc Bekoff, the philosopher and ethologist of ethologists Vinciane Despret or the primatologists Jane Goodall and Frans de Waal. All encourage us to get off of our cultural pedestal. On the edges of science, or a little beyond, we find attempts emerging to get closer with animals, such as 'intuitive communication' (somewhat like telepathy but with a less politically incorrect name). Although classical science is still largely refractory, an increasing number of people around the globe teach and practise this activity, including in the veterinary world.[26] Whether one 'believes' or not, this movement is growing, and it connects with the cosmogonies of many indigenous peoples, among whom there is nothing unusual about addressing brothers and sisters who are other-than-human.

The movement towards plants is even more striking, with its astonishing popularity, as well as the number of scientific experiments showing sensitivity, intelligence and what one would be tempted to call the 'consciousness' among plants. The Dutch agronomist Maja Kooistra, who in the 2000s moved back and forth between learning to communicate with trees and working at the Ministry of Agriculture, notes:

> Thanks to the extreme longevity and richness of experience of the oldest among them, trees have established extensive communication networks that convey treasures of natural wisdom. Everyone, humans included [by communicating directly with them], can draw without reserve on these huge archives of the history of life on earth, this colossal memory with which we are connected without even knowing.[27]

Among the most iconic figures of this trend are the Italian professor Stefano Mancuso, founder of 'plant neurobiology', and the Australian botanist Monica Gagliano. The latter has demonstrated the existence of Pavlov reflexes in peas. Their research and that of their colleagues as a whole show that plants are endowed in their own way with five senses (vision, smell, taste, hearing and touch, and yet others);[28] that they communicate with each other or with insect predators to protect themselves from herbivores; that they have memory, which enables them to improve their reactions to environmental changes; and even that they are able to recognize their relatives (in a broad sense) so as to help them better.[29] This sensitivity and intelligence has its physical base in the 'diffuse brain' of millions of root tips, so there is a close similarity between neurons (in animals) and plant cells.[30] Monica Gagliano sees a revolution as underway: 'Emerging scientific research has revealed that plants show all the traditional indicators of sentience [the ability to feel]. This casts doubt on the utility of the traditional rigid division made between plants and animals.'[31]

To imagine that these memories and intelligences can be found in millennia-old trees makes you dizzy: 'Because of their ability to live for millennia – in the case of some root systems of the Quaking Aspen, more than 100,000 years – their neural networks can, certainly in many cases, go far beyond ours. Quaking Aspen root systems can spread over up to 40 hectares of soil, creating a network of neurons that is considerably larger than any that a human has experienced.'[32]

The Canadian botanist Suzanne Simard, the researcher who discovered the mutual aid relationships that took place between trees through mycorrhizae, recently took a new direction through showing the close similarity between the architecture of our neural networks and that of the mycorrhizal networks connecting trees and plants in forests.[33] She concludes: 'Viewing this evidence through the lens of tree cognition, microbiome collaborations, and forest intelligence may contribute to a more holistic approach to studying ecosystems and a greater human empathy and caring for the health of our forests.'[34]

All these discoveries have comforted our three scientific souls and also our intuition (which school and the university did not totally destroy) and our feelings. When we attended Work that Reconnects workshops, we were able to experience in practice the degree to which this connection (or reconnection) could be mobilized by many of the participants, ourselves included. When we 'feel-think' (in Escobar's phrase) ourselves as a species among other species, it can have a dramatic effect on our relationship to time, our humility, our rationality, our dreams or our intuition.

Since 2015, we have taken a further step within the Terr'Eveille association,[35] through experimenting directly with one-on-one meetings with beings of different species, even if to start with we mostly pretend to do it as a kind of game.[36] The idea is to speak directly and clearly, take time to hear their reactions, and then give as much trust as possible to the response-sensations, rather than just dismissing them as autosuggestion. If nothing else, this is an opportunity to feel how far our civilization has instilled in us a culture that forbids us to do such things in 'normal' life. If you keep doing these practices, they become deeper, and you gradually become able to perceive each being with new eyes, not just as an element of the scenery, but as a possible partner.

With deep time

Let's continue to expand our membrane. A characteristic feature of our epoch is its much reduced time horizon. We have allowed economism to reduce everything to the short term, and become almost blind to what exists beyond our small existence and, even worse, beyond our individual interests. By being separated in this way from the distant past and the distant future, we lose connection with them and therefore of important possibilities of finding meaning in our lives. Ram Dass's famous injunction to 'be here now'[37] is absolutely not an excuse to dispense with this connection with deep time. On the contrary, they are intimately connected.

Just one second

To rediscover the soil, the earth, also means to discover the history we share with the other inhabitants of the planet. In her workshops, Joanna Macy invites us to take a dizzying dive into 'deep time'. According to the astrophysicists, our universe was born 15 thousand million years ago. For much of that time, elements scattered in various parts of the cosmos were gradually clustering together until they formed our solar system, a small tribe of planets swirling around a star, among which was the one that saw us being born (you, us, the cellar spider and the elder bush outside the window). The Earth was formed 4.5 thousand million years ago.

To trace the story of the appearance of life, let us reduce these 4.5 thousand million years to a calendar year. If the Earth was formed on 1 January, life did not appear until 26 February. Bacteria started the show, beginning to reproduce, to eat each other, to collaborate, to differentiate themselves into innumerable species, in short to invent everything needed to colonize different environments. These are the same bacteria that gradually establish alliances with *all* species of plants, animals, protists and fungi, and still remain the dominant form of life today, 3.8 thousand million years later (something which, contrary to popular belief, is largely to our advantage).[38]

On 3 April, something decisive happens: photosynthesis appears. This extraordinary ability to use sunlight to assemble the basic building blocks of life from water and carbon dioxide will supply a vast source of energy for everyone, and will transform the face of the Earth. The oxygen released will then become the fuel for respiration, another bacterial innovation, which makes it possible to profit from the solar energy stored by plants.

We have to wait until 24 September to see the first multicellular organisms appear.[39] On 22 November, almost two months later, the first plants appear on earth.[40] The first forests begin to grow on 1 December,[41] and this speeds up the diversification of animals. On 6 December,[42] the first reptiles appear, and on 14 December,[43] the first mammals. The primates emerge on 25 December,[44] followed by *Homo sapiens* at one minute to midnight on 31 December.[45]

The industrial revolution, which matters so much to us, and which gave birth to the culture within which most of us grew up, corresponds to the very last second of this cosmic year. This second, even if it is the one that saw us born, only has meaning in the light of all that came before it, of all our common history with Earth and with all the beings and ancestors since the first molecules came together.

This story allows us to completely rethink our very anthropocentric way of presenting History (which has a capital H but only lasts for a small second). It also helps to bring down the wall between culture and nature, which we have erected between us and the others-than-human. We can now start to see the history of our membership in a large family on whom we are dependent and with whom we have become mutually *interdependent*. When we see these family photos, and this short film in accelerated time, it can cause wonder and humility, homesickness and healing, and it can help expand our membrane, our sense of identity, and so contribute to changing our view of the world.

We can also focus down on the last 315,000 years of our young species (the last minute), and remember that without those thousands of generations of humans who have survived through time, ice ages, migrations, etc., we would not be here.

It is time to realize fully that this long succession of hunter-gatherers had their own wisdom and created important forms of knowledge, which allowed them not to stray too far from life as a whole, even if it sometimes impacted on its environment. There is still time to extract ourselves from the straitjacket of our present-day culture and get back in touch with the art of living well on Earth. Remember Francis Weller's fourth gate of sorrow (see chapter 2). It is not just that we are able to remember what has been passed on to us. Our bodies, our guts, our heart are begging us to do it.

The day after tomorrow, our great-grandchildren's great-grandchildren will arrive. Our descendants are counting on us. When the leaders of the Six Nations League met at the Grand Council, says Iroquois author Doug George-Kanentiio, they began by reciting 'a prayer to the Creator through which the Iroquois gave thanks collectively and were reminded of their responsibilities towards the next generation and the natural world'.[46] Gratitude and humility. In their public and private decisions, they were expected to take into account their successors of the seventh generation. 'This means that our leadership was required to enact laws that would protect the rights of our descendants two hundred years into the future.'[47]

To feel the wisdom of our human and non-human ancestors resonate within us, we should get in touch with our inner wildness ... Go and look for them, so as to be able to connect them with what is alive within us, here on the threshold of this tormented century. Enter into deep time. It can help us to relativize this little second that was the thermo-industrial civilization, this tiny period of disconnection and forgetfulness of who we are, and to see our descendants dancing around the fire that was passed on from our forefathers.

With what is beyond us

Astronauts, with their scientific and military training, have the reputation of being rather serious and pragmatic people. Yet, some of them speak about undergoing an overwhelming experience, a kind of cognitive shock which they willingly called 'mystical', during their stay in space. They were irresistibly attracted by the peaceful view of the Earth through the portholes, and speak, between long moments of contemplation, of having been moved by the fragility and beauty of our tiny, unique cosmic vessel. They returned to Earth profoundly transformed, newly aware people, humanists, and determined to protect this jewel we share.[48]

The oceanic sentiment and the sacred

In two documentaries depicting this phenomenon, *Overview* (2012), and its successor, *Planetary* (2015),[49] the film director Guy Reid shows that those on earth can also feel this overwhelming sense of ecstasy through undergoing powerful spiritual experiences. What all these people felt was what Romain Rolland (1866–1944), Nobel Prize winner in literature, called the 'oceanic feeling', a feeling of unity with the universe, of fusion with the 'Great All', of a connection with something that goes beyond us. Despite our training, which was scientific and rather antireligious, we experienced a similar feeling during our encounters with the 'wild'; a deep sense of humility and respect, feelings of fullness, serenity, trust, openness, of an obvious simplicity that we had rediscovered, and the like.

Above all, we felt the gentle warmth of joy, despite the immensity of our surroundings, this joy of feeling our deep interdependence with the web of life, from the primordial bacteria, down to us and our children, passing through our human and non-human ancestors, the mountains and rivers ... We were part of a single community, with an 'amplified sense of our identity' (something Arne Næss also speaks of). We felt ourselves to be at once our own personal selves and part of a whole that went beyond us.

This is also a reason for the cultivation of beauty. This is not a luxury reserved for artists. Paradoxically, it's even a necessity for the times to come, a pledge of connection, a compass. The writer Alain Damasio, known for his science-fiction novels,[50] says something similar, criticizing the neoliberal equation of individualism with freedom: 'I think the neoliberal system is extremely ugly. I believe in connections, I believe that it is connections that give us power. I believe that it is the links we weave with what is outside us, with animals, with the forest, with others that really increase our freedom.'[51]

In the experience of encountering such extended time scales, and such extraordinary organisms, at once so different and so close to us, living through phenomena that we cannot grasp, there is a moment when reason disengages and the body lets go. This feeling of being in touch with something greater is what we venture to call the 'sacred'.

The sacred, as we understand it here, is not a dogma or a religious sentiment. It is this connection to our fundamental values, to what really matters deep within us, and to the invisible, to what exists beyond us.

We are aware that we are discussing concepts that go beyond our expertise and that other peoples often connect to 'global' entities that they consider sacred (such as Pachamama, Mother Earth or Gaia). Are we talking about the same thing that was felt by the astronauts, or is felt by thinkers such as the deep ecologist, Arne Næss? Perhaps. For now, this is where we are: 'For the ecopsychologists, the sacred is a hazy notion that translates an experience of communion with and within nature that goes beyond the beliefs of any specific religion.'[52]

We are not talking about an idyllic vision of the world. 'What goes beyond us' can manifest as lethal changes on a global scale, unable to be grasped by scientific thought at the time, provoking strong emotions and irrational behaviours. The damage done to the biosphere has become immeasurable, disproportionate, 'transcendental', as Dominique Bourg notes. To imagine a world at +5°C in 2050, as Shell and BP's internal reports suggest, is beyond our ability, and perhaps also beyond our strength.

When everything is turned upside down, however, when we are overwhelmed and no longer understand the world, it may be useful to understand that what is being played out is of a different order. To have been able to prepare for it is certainly not unimportant. 'It is this apocalyptic perspective,' says the philosopher of disasters Jean-Pierre Dupuy, 'which makes it at the same time possible, urgent and necessary to allow ourselves to accept the idea that we are constituted by the sacred.'[53] Then it becomes a question of entering into another kind of relationship with what appears strange to us, what we cannot understand rationally. Death, for example, is beyond us. Perhaps contemplating a collapse invites us to imagine rituals, practices and techniques like those which human beings use in contact with death?

If we consider that everything that we have received – the earth, life, knowledge, and so on – is a gift, it brings feelings of wonder, gratitude, joy and recognition. How can we not feel some obligation of a counter-gift, of an indebtedness? The philosopher Corine Pelluchon calls it *considération*, this responsibility that arises from no longer feeling alone in the world, but connected to a shared world, a world that has welcomed us and which will survive us.[54] As is the case in many cultures, we may well feel that all the resources that have been given to us are, in a sense, sacred.

Feeling our interdependence with other beings and the world, along with our extreme vulnerability as an individual, society and species, also leads to a feeling of gratitude. This is a powerful feeling because it 'implies two things: relationship and humility'.[55] It helps us to find stability, to bring ourselves back into the present moment and to create empathy towards whatever we are in contact with. It also allows us to recognize that we cannot control everything, and that, for example, faced with situations that seem to be lost in advance, other living beings can also prove to be valuable allies.

> Gratitude enhances our resilience, strengthening us to face disturbing information. [. . .] [Gratitude] is a social emotion. It points our warmth and goodwill out towards others. [It] builds trust and generosity.[56]

It is significant that Work that Reconnects workshops begin with a lengthy anchoring in gratitude. 'In the most dire scenarios', notes Carolyn Baker, 'being able to find one small thing every day for which one is grateful enhances resilience and the potential to survive.'[57] It may be the best gift we can offer to our world. Fortunately, as Joanna Macy says, 'that our world is in crisis – to the point where survival of conscious life on Earth is in question – in no way diminishes the wonder of this present moment'.[58] For the great secret is that gratitude does not depend on our external circumstances. It is a skill that is learned and improved by practice.

To feel all this, and to understand that humility is fundamental to all spiritualities, forces us to ask the following question: is it really possible to approach the *end of a world* without spirituality? We do not think so. But the tragedy is that our rational society has given us absolutely no preparation. By rejecting the (spiritual) baby with the (religious) bathwater, it has deprived itself of the basic tools we will need in the long term.

Spirituality is a 'more fundamental and universal reality than the religions'.[59] The phenomenon that conditions its emergence is primordial, and remains just as essential for society *even in the absence of a religious system*. There are non-religious, secular, even atheistic spiritualities, and conversely religions that reject the spiritual by reducing their practice to a list of rituals to be followed to the letter (like Salafism). To put it differently, religion could be considered as a childish and highly rule-bound form of spirituality. At the same time, scientism, with its belief that science is capable of solving all the problems of the world, is a particularly dangerous religion of our time.

Dominique Bourg attributes two interdependent functions to spirituality, found in all societies. The first is the establishment of a relationship with what surrounds us (nature), the connection that each society weaves with the environment in which it is immersed, and from which it develops. This is a question of giving a meaning to *what is given*, to what we have received, to what we have not produced. Spirituality 'comes from the relationship between the system and what it is not, what is external to it',[60] in other words the sacred.

The second function is that which 'leads societies to suggest models of self-realization to individuals'.[61] This is what gives a prospect of going beyond oneself, a model to imitate, a state to attain. In our societies of personal enrichment, as Bourg continues by way of an example, 'consumerism is [. . .]

the spirituality corresponding to the religion of growth'.[62]
Facing the prospect of collapse, a rich, consciously adopted
spirituality will undoubtedly bring resilience and be a source
of joy. It will give us reasons to choose to live, rather than
just to survive.

8

Growing up and settling down

There is a huge and incredible disconnect between the beauty and power of the collective intelligence of our time, and our glaring lack of collective wisdom and of respect for life. It is this disconnect that drives us to write these last chapters, in which we leave our usual social roles (such as agronomist, scientist, specialist in biomimicry, collapsologist).

In this chapter we present some ideas about themes we find important, particularly in regard to the attitude we all might adopt towards possible collapse. We have aimed to balance contemplation and action, both in the outside world and also within each of us. Take what we say as points for reflection, themes on which to work, or beginnings of lines of exploration. There is no dogma here and no obligation. These mutually related topics slowly made their way into us, and have been nourished by some remarkable writings and by equally remarkable experiences, mostly in group contexts.

Emerging from patho-adolescence

Have you felt a certain arrogance and danger in the air, which has been growing stronger over the last two decades? A sense that reciprocity, humility, service to others, has become less common. It makes one think of a narcissistic child having a crisis. As if we are not succeeding, as a society, in growing up.

This unhealthy state of our collective psyche is what the research psychologist and psychotherapist Bill Plotkin (he refers to himself as a depth psychologist) calls 'patho-adolescence':

> In today's Western societies, besides the scarcity of true maturity, many adult people suffer from various adolescent pathologies – disabling social insecurity, confusion of identity, extremely low self-esteem, few or no social skills, narcissism, relentless greed, arrested moral development, recurrent physical violence, materialistic obsessions, little or no capacity for intimacy or empathy.[1]

Patho-adolescence

Normal adolescence is by definition a transient phase. In 'patho-adolescence', the characteristic features of normal adolescence are so exaggerated and persistent that they become pathological, and therefore harmful to the whole of life. First of all, there is the demand for 'everything straightaway', the need for the immediate satisfaction of an unlimited material appetite without any awareness of the consequences for others. Since the Rio Conference in 1992, we have used as much metal as all the generations that preceded us.[2] This attitude of systematically grabbing whatever we want doubtless results from a repressed fear of death and finiteness.[3]

Adolescents have by definition the strength of youth, and the future is before them. Everything is action and nothing can stop them. As the psychiatrist Christophe Fauré observes, when something hurts them or causes them pain, '[they] do not speak their distress, their loss, they act it out'. He continues: 'to act may seem to the adolescent less "dangerous" than to risk becoming vulnerable through opening one's heart'.[4] And if they cannot see any meaning or future prospect, they will behave violently. We cannot help thinking of the young people who left to join the Islamic State to satisfy their anger, desperately searching for some meaning, something sacred.

On the global scale, the flight is into the future: transhumanism and the cyborg represent the ultimate climax of this momentum, emerging from a Californian valley filled with super-wealthy adolescents playing at who will be first to destroy death. Psychologists have long felt that one of the most important signs of maturity is the ability to confront the fear of one's own death.[5] An adult *knows* that there is death, and that there will always be hard times to get through. A patho-adolescent does not want to hear about it. For Carolyn Baker, the moment of realizing one's mortality causes a great shock to the ego. 'I believe this is precisely the underlying reason millions of people refuse to look honestly at collapse. The ego under all the "yes-buts" has way too much to lose.'[6]

Among other defects of patho-adolescence, there is the desire for amnesia, to reject the past, history and the ancients ('all idiots') and, consequently, lack of thought for the future. It is the patho-adolescents who lie to themselves, claiming that infinite growth is possible, or that technology will save the world, and so on. There is also an irresistible need to behave like everyone else, as a source of reassurance, even if this degenerates into a deadly monoculture. Worse still, this Panurge-like behaviour has been exploited by the big corporations, flattering our narcissism by offering us 'power' (immediacy, speed, widespread popularity, and the like), at the cost of our personal ability to act. 'There is an impulse towards devitalization, towards making life simple, which ends up destroying the dignity of the human being',[7] remarks the writer Alain Damasio.

The consequences are of course tragic: such impulses lead to a society which is materialistic, depressive, addictive, greedy, competitive up to the point of hostility, violent, ugly and, finally, self-destructive.

The passage to adulthood

What could lead us to the next level of maturity?[8] What do we do to get moving again? Bill Plotkin, who has guided thousands of women and men through initiatory passages since the 1980s, suggests a model of personal evolution rooted in the cycles of nature. He explores it in detail in his monumental *Nature and the Human Soul*.[9] Plotkin's model, largely inspired by the work of Carl Gustav Jung, is divided into four main stages – childhood, adolescence, adulthood and elderhood – each of which is divided into two parts, giving eight stages in all. The passage that interests us here is the one that takes the adolescent to adulthood.

At the end of adolescence comes a period of withdrawal from social life. It is time to leave behind your beliefs about yourself and the world. This is when you start looking for your 'soul talent', what it is that you have to offer to your community. Adolescence thus ends with a decisive passage, a difficult and demanding phase of transition, an *initiation*. First there is a call of the 'mission of life', then the decision to accept it fully, and finally the commitment to live this particular gift that we have just discovered. 'The newly initiated adult apprentices herself to the creative process itself and to a discipline through which she can learn the particular magic to which her soul has summoned her.'[10]

In our society, this initiation does not usually happen; and if it does, it happens very late, well beyond the twentieth year. The 'first' steps of the initiate in her or his new world are hesitant and risky, because they involve a transformation of the whole being, so there is a vital need for trust and approval from the 'real' adults, the old people. But where are they nowadays?

Such initiations as are currently available therefore tend to be collective, like those of Bill Plotkin and his friends in Colorado, or those in Switzerland and Belgium, organized by the philosopher, pedagogue and writer Pierre-Yves Albrecht (in which we have not participated). Similarly, the initiatory networks of the ManKind Project[11] (for men) and Woman Within (for women), which have grown all around the world for some thirty years, are bringing men and women to an emotional and spiritual maturity that enables them to develop richer and more genuine relationships with those around them: children, partners, friends and so on, but also with the whole line of women and men who preceded them and who will follow them.

The adults who have thus been initiated become more present in the world, learn to take on and manage overt conflict, to trust each other, to express their feelings. As with any initiation, there is no turning back, you come out deeply transformed. Initiation is a moment of great vulnerability that allows you to draw on the strength within yourself and also from the other initiates. It creates deep and powerful bonds with the deep self and with those who will become 'brothers' and 'sisters'.

What initiation also does is to force us to get to what is essential, just as the experience of a serious illness, an accident or the proximity of death, does, in a more violent way. We discover peace in ourselves, a deep calm. We begin our second life.

One of the main benefits of an initiation is to confront what Jung called the *shadow*, which is made up of all the aspects of our lives which we find unacceptable, which we repress or deny. To make oneself see them, *to bring them into the light*, is difficult, but it is necessary so that they don't invade us in a repressed form, which is much more difficult to cope with.

The purpose of this work, though, is not to destroy our shadows, but to learn to live with them, to dance with them. 'What we're talking about', says the Buddhist teacher Pema Chödrön, 'is getting to know fear, becoming familiar with fear, looking it right in the eye – not as a way to solve problems, but as a complete undoing of old ways of seeing, hearing, smelling, tasting, and thinking. The truth is that when we really begin to do this, we're going to be continually humbled.'[12] Courage here is not needed to fight others, but to tame your own shadow. In men, this is the characteristic of the *new warrior*, the new initiate. 'If he only learns to deal with his own shadow', said Jung, 'he has done something real for the world. He has succeeded in shouldering at least an infinitesimal part of the gigantic, unsolved social problems of our day.'[13]

With experience and the passing of years, there comes a time when one has gone far enough along this path of maturation. Then comes the feeling of being 'fulfilled to over-flowing', says Bill Kauth, one of the founders of the ManKind Project movement. From there, says Kauth, when the mission of life seems totally natural, 'there is nothing to do but give'.[14]

To respond to the coming collapses we are going to have to grow up, to emerge from the eternal adolescence in which our civilization is happily basking. Can we take up the course of our collective development again, consciously and wisely? Do we have to wait for sudden collapses to make us do it? Or, on the contrary, do we need to do it now, so we will be better prepared when the storms come?

Reconciling our masculine and feminine sides

This question burst in on our lives during a Work that Reconnects workshop: the connection between the sufferings that we, as men, inflict on women, and those humanity has inflicted on the planet as a whole for many thousands of years.

Too much of the masculine

'The ecofeminists realized the vital need of telling other stories before anyone else did.'[15] Several of them developed a radical critique of patriarchal monotheistic religions precisely through an analysis of the stories pervading these religions: stories involving hatred of women, of a male God, of separation from nature and so on. They began to rewrite their own history, incorporating the destruction of women and of the feminine in our societies.

Patriarchy originated almost five thousand years ago, at the end of the Neolithic and the beginning of the Bronze Age, the time of the first civilizations that had writing. As man discovered his potential as a farmer and as a procreator, both at around the same time, he took over power and turned the situation to his advantage. 'Once man had taken control of the earth, and so of agricultural production (and later industry), and women's wombs (and so human fertility), it was logical that man's over-exploitation of each would lead eventually to this menacing double danger: overpopulation, through too many births, and destruction of the environment, through too much production.'[16]

Thus, the philosopher Jeanne Burgart Goutal explains, 'It was at this time that human societies (at least most of them) would have shifted from their original gynocentric, peaceful and ecological way of life, which placed women and nature, both respected, and seen as active and independent, at the heart of culture and religion, to a patriarchal military organization, structured around manhood and the cult of transcendence.'[17]

Everyone knows the story of the witch hunts, and most of us associate them with the Middle Ages or the Inquisition, during a somewhat vague period when they still burned people in public. However, the climax of the persecution of women for witchcraft (200,000 women accused of witchcraft, of whom at least 100,000 were executed or lynched[18]) took place precisely during the Renaissance, between the fifteenth and eighteenth century, at the time when light and reason were supposedly also at their peak.

The height of this paroxysm was doubtless reached in the seventeenth century, where it can be seen in the writings of the philosopher Francis Bacon, one of the pioneers of modern scientific thought. Carolyn Merchant, an ecofeminist philosopher and historian of science, shows that Bacon uses the vocabulary of violence, coercion and even torture to describe the scientific method: 'nature exhibits herself more clearly under the trials and vexations of art than when left to herself'.[19] To this must be added the sexual metaphors. Thus, 'As woman's womb had symbolically yielded to the forceps, so nature's womb harboured secrets that through technology could be wrested from her grasp for use in the improvement of the human condition.'[20] Nature, he implied, is a public woman. We must subdue her, penetrate her secrets and chain her according to our desires.[21] The scientific approach, for Bacon, is therefore like interrogating a witch: she (nature or the witch) must be forced to give up her secrets to us.[22] There is a terrible shadow over modern science, about which they were careful not to teach us when we studied philosophy.

This fierceness against women is also linked to the rise of capitalism. In her book *Caliban and the Witch*, Silvia Federici recalls that the 'the witch-hunt occurred simultaneously with the colonization and extermination of the populations of the New World, the English enclosures, the beginning of the slave trade, the enactment of "bloody laws" against vagabonds and beggars'.[23] To be able to develop smoothly, capitalism needed several conditions: it had to get rid of a vision of nature which was too anthropomorphic (after all, how could you kill or rape the mother who had nourished you as a baby?), it had to destroy the autonomy of village communities (old women were often the healers who helped with deliveries and abortions), it had to take over the land from the peasants (through enclosures, and the abolition of customary rights of management of the commons among peasants), and it had to develop a cold and calculating style of thinking that refused to tolerate thinking in any other way.

The US eco-feminist activist Starhawk notes that:

> the persecutions of the Witches shattered the peasants' connection with the land, drove women out of the work of healing, and imposed the mechanist view of the world as a dead machine. That rupture underlies the entwined oppressions of race, sex, class, and ecological destruction.[24]

So all these oppressions can seen as originating in male domination!

It's possible that this reading of history is too exaggerated. For example, we know that in some regions at least, there were also plenty of male witches and ladies of high society also burned at the stake. The work of future historians will doubtless refine the ecofeminist hypothesis, but that hardly detracts from this story's power to shine light on the dark places of our society.

In any case, the great historical imbalance between the sexes is still part of our society. How, then, can we make these relations between men and women more equitable and peaceful, both in view of coming breakdowns of the social order, but also to provide a better basis for possible societies of the future?

The power of reconciliation

The secret wound of patriarchy is not only carried by women. Men also suffer, as descendants of all those – fathers, sons, brothers, husbands and lovers – who felt helpless, ashamed, guilty or cowards when their daughters, mothers, sisters, wives and lovers were abducted, accused, imprisoned, dominated, tortured and executed. Nowadays, there are many men who feel uncomfortable at having to hide their emotions and appear tough and unmoved, all the while feeling shame at the violence that some of their peers continue to inflict on women (and by the way, thanks to Harvey Weinstein for reminding us that 'some' was a euphemism).[25]

In more serious cases, we find what a recent study termed the 'masculine depressive syndrome'.[26] It is difficult to diagnose because men do not report depression as much as women, instead preferring to break out in anger, abuse drugs and alcohol, or take life-threatening risks.

What do ecofeminists do to heal themselves from these wounds from the past? They *reclaim* their power by reviving the memory of the witches, in other words by recalling the crucial role of peasant women, seed-keepers, healers, grandmothers, of magical rituals celebrating connection to the land, of the unpaid *productive and reproductive* activities of the sustainable economies of pre-capitalist societies. For the philosopher Émilie Hache,

> calling ourselves 'witches' is [. . .] a way to reconnect with ourselves and the world, by reconnecting with our history, with the historical defeat of women in the war that capitalism declared on them, but also with our fears – fear of rejection, assault, being devalued, etc. – a way of reconnecting with our emotions, our own judgment, our own experience, and ultimately our own power.[27]

In 2016, the Navajo woman and activist artist Pat McCabe, accompanied by other 'elders' from all the continents, organized a European tour of ceremonies to heal the collective wounds passed down from the witch hunts.[28] These rituals gave many women the opportunity to experience 'reconciliation and remembrance, an opportunity for meeting between the masculine and the feminine, between the nation of men and the nation of women, and between indigenous and Europeans'.[29]

On this theme of men and women, it's important to add a further aspect: the masculine–feminine dimension. Here feminine and masculine are archetypes, in the sense defined by Jung, in other words primitive, universal symbols, belonging to the collective unconscious, pre-existing representations that structure the psyche. You can find them, for example, in children's stories, where the archetype of the hero, the warrior, the king and the queen, the witch, the magician, etc., are standard characters who live and express themselves (to a greater or lesser degree) in each of us, female or male.

Thus, masculine and feminine, like Yin and Yang in Chinese thought, are two polarities which group together qualities that we *all* carry within us, men and women. This idea may seem strange at first because the patriarchal order makes us think of the feminine as the exclusive prerogative of women, so that the emotions, caring or the interior life, for example, aren't part of a 'real' man. Similarly, women weren't supposed to display qualities thought of as masculine (and so belonging to their own masculine aspect), such as reasoning, action, defending one's territory, aggressivity and such.

Schematically, on our *feminine* side we find intuition, mystery, opening up, interior life (emotion), inclusion, the ability to take care, to make connections and synthesize, to accept (in excess, this becomes complete fusion), cooperation, sharing of territory and the like. The central theme of creation for the feminine is interdependence. Reality is alive and can be apprehended in many different ways. We are guardians of the earth and of all forms of life.

On our *masculine* side, we find: reason, words, boundaries, external life (activity), exclusion, the ability to protect, to give meaning, to decide, to analyse, to separate when needed (in excess, this becomes aggression and violence), competition and defence of one's territory. The central theme of creation is separation. The logical mind is the only way to know reality, which is mechanistic. Nature is separate from us, and we can use it as we wish.

Thus, in everyday life, a woman who can make decisions, speak in front of her colleagues, and who can compete effectively always remains a woman, if one with a highly developed masculine side. Conversely, a man who cares for others, expresses his feelings, trusts his intuition and has an intense inner life, simply has a strong feminine aspect.

This archetypal dimension, far from essentializing masculine and feminine, makes full sense when we realize that these polarities *are not opposed to each other*. In our previous examples, the professional woman may also have a rich spiritual life, be able to express her emotions and be a great mother; and his strong feminine aspect does not prevent a sensitive man from being a rugby player with a powerful masculine side.

To strengthen one's masculine side does not imply the automatic reduction of the feminine. On the contrary. For Jacques Ferber,[30] it is not a question of a linear axis:

> We should see these two polarities as two orthogonal axes, where masculine and feminine could grow independently of one another, leading to the growth of a two-dimensional surface representing the extent of our soul, whether woman or man. What matters is not so much to choose one or the other, but to *cultivate both*.

In other words, and we have experienced this, the feminine part within us gives power to our male part, and vice versa. The worst is obviously not to cultivate either.

In the face of the storms to come, many fear the return of men's default behaviour of domination and violence, especially towards women. This is a justifiable fear, because these archetypes can easily re-emerge, especially if our wounds have not been recognized and healed collectively, and we continue to hide these shadows under the carpet. It is up to all of us, then, men and women, to grow up, individually and collectively, so we can see these outbreaks of our shadows coming, and weaken their harmful effects.

What we suggest, in addition to doing personal work on our shadows and on developing our masculine and feminine aspects, is to aim at a new balance between the two polarities *within society*. For our feminine aspects, schematically, this would mean working on *making connections*, as with mutual aid, breaking down walls, 'power with', interdependence, alliance with other-than-humans and the like, and on *culti-vating our interiority* (our emotions, intuition, spirituality and so on). The connections we make will be of great value in living with shortages and hostile environments, and cultivating our interiority will make our actions more mature. All this can give another dimension to the long awaited 'politics of collapse', or what others simply call 'transition'.

Initiations, particularly those into our masculine and feminine aspects, can help greatly on this path. For men (we speak from our point of view, as male authors), to work on these two archetypes is to participate in a transformation based on the essential values of authenticity, coherence, commitment, integrity. We men can also live and experience all of these values in our relations with women. For the co-founder of the ManKind Project (MKP), Bill Kauth, this is simply the 'beginning of the healing of a five thousand-year-old wound between men and women'.[31]

Groups and networks for women's initiations are much more numerous and diverse than those for men. For men, apart from the MKP movement, which brings together more than 70,000 men around the globe, we know of the Men's Networks (Réseaux Hommes). These were launched by the Quebec psychoanalyst Guy Corneau, who died in 2017. None of us have taken part in them, but they seem to be more mutual aid groups. Then there are the men's Tantra groups developed in France by Jacques Lucas, alongside the women's Tantra developed by Marisa Ortolan. Finally Work that Reconnects workshops have been organized in single-sex groups, although this is less common, so as to explore the relations between the feminine (or the masculine) and nature more deeply.

For us, the main strength of these networks and mutual aid groups is that they provide contexts where people can express and share emotions, in a safe container, while feeling safe to do so with real authenticity. Seeing other men and women on these paths, with so much diversity, restores courage and confidence in the future. That men are able to speak publicly about their intuitions, emotions and interiority is, from the point of view of reconciliation, a significant political act.

The reconciliation of men and women, and the work of balancing the masculine and feminine aspects within each of us, will contribute to the many alliances we will need to create and strengthen for the times to come. The networks we have just mentioned have already begun to invent and experiment with rituals of reconciliation between men and women on the basis of their various approaches. This brings them closer to the intense, magical, powerful and beautiful rituals of neopagan witches. To start with, working in this way can be confusing, curious, maybe embarrassing, but it gradually becomes quite natural. You just have to get started. There is nothing esoteric about it, especially when one realizes the acute awareness of those involved about present and future disasters.

Restoring the wild

Does the wild still exist? Hasn't the steamroller of civilization already swallowed up and ravaged it all? Over the centuries-long taming of the wild world, plants, animals, microbes, landscapes, cultures have all been brought into line, framed, locked up, measured, *processed*. So have our own psyches, drastically impoverished and themselves domesticated, up to the point of madness.

This business of domestication is not just a minor branch of agronomy, it has come to define our world. Consider, for example, that the biomass of human beings in total represents 36 per cent of the biomass of all the mammals in the world. And that 60 per cent of the biomass of mammals on the planet consists of domestic animals. Only 4 per cent are wild species, and that includes the elephants and the blue whales.[32] The proportion is similar for the world's birds, 70 per cent of which are chickens, turkeys, geese and ducks.

Wilderness areas have declined sharply, particularly over the last twenty years, despite efforts to protect them (twice as much has been lost as has been placed under protection since the 1990s).[33] Only 13 per cent of wilderness areas (areas not frequented by humans) remain in the oceans,[34] and 23 per cent on the continents.[35]

If we look at our psychic life, there is also a massive lack of connection. In 2003, Europeans spent 90 per cent of their time indoors,[36] and according to a recent survey, Britons spend less than two hours a day outdoors – mainly to shop or when driving their cars.[37] Three-quarters of UK children spend less time playing outside than we allow to the inmates in our prisons.[38]

How many people know the names of the plants growing on the pavement across the street, or can say when the moon will start to wane? How many can locate five species of mushrooms that grow in their neighbourhood? What species of migratory birds have you seen this year? When was the last time you talked to a tree? Immersed your body in non-chlorinated water? Taken an insect in your hand? Slept under the stars?

If, like many people, you do not know how to answer most of these questions, you are perhaps living what ecologist and writer Robert M. Pyle named in 1993 the 'extinction of experience'; the loss of direct, regular connections with the living world.[39] But the loss of these connections is not only a philosophical issue; it is also a question of health.

Depriving ourselves of these connections leads to what the

journalist Richard Louv, in his best-seller *Last Child in the Wood*,[40] calls 'nature-deficit disorder': obesity, hyper-activity, increase of diabetes and heart disease, and, more generally, decreased life span. Among our children, we are seeing a decline in visits to nature parks, in time spent outside, in participation in outdoor activities and so on, and the resulting symptoms are just as bad: an increase in obesity, myopia, psychological disorders such as anxiety and depression (the consumption of anti-depressants in children has exploded in recent years), lack of attention and creativity, declining academic performance and learning ability, schizophrenia and behavioural problems.

Conversely, there are plenty of studies showing the benefits of time spent in the woods or of closer contact with non-human animals.[41] Spending part of the day outdoors reduces inflammation and high blood pressure, relieves pain, reduces fatigue and stress, helps fight depression and anxiety, improves short-term memory, boosts self-esteem and mood, protects vision, increases concentration and creativity, stimulates the immune system and the production of anti-cancer proteins and so on.

Is it too late to slow down, or even stop, the advance of domestication? Perhaps it's time to consider going on the offensive with an effective, deliberate mass movement to 'rewild' the planet?

The wild around us

The idea of 'rewilding' emerged in the 1990s,[42] in response to the disappearance of the undomesticated areas of North America, the progressive loss of wilderness and of the 'wild' character of nature. Rewilding is a large-scale conservation strategy directed towards maintaining large open spaces and reintroducing key species such as wolves and bison.[43] The late US environmentalist Paul Shepard even went a step further by proposing a Pleistocene-type rewilding, named after the last but one geological epoch. This would involve reintroducing a much richer megafauna, similar to what was around in that period, and would rely on our dormant biology, still well adapted to the world of the hunter-gatherers which preceded the Neolithic, and which Shepard assumed would willingly reappear if given the opportunity.[44]

Whatever the specific way in which it is implemented, it seems essential to give space back to these uncontrolled ecosystems, providing for minimal human intervention, or even none at all. The biologist and naturalist Edward O. Wilson recently calculated that the only way for humanity to avert a mass extinction crisis as devastating as the one that killed the dinosaurs 65 million years ago, would be to reserve *half* of the planet for the wild, as a permanent secure area for the several million other species that populate our planet.[45]

Without asking if this is possible or not (a useless question typical of the attitude of 'passive hope'), this proposal already offers a prospect for Earth-Dwellers and shows where the front line might be.

Other-than-human beings do not represent an abstract and hostile collectivity called 'nature' against which we have to fight, but a concrete network of beings with whom it is possible to build short-term or lasting alliances, and with whom we share our habitats. Seeing things in this way also allows us to realize that the wild can become a source of life and abundance, once we become thoroughly disconnected from the industrial world (whether we willingly anticipate that disconnection, or simply submit to it).

Courses on 'living wild' or 'soft survival', which can be found these days in many parts of the world, don't just offer a useful list of wild edible plants that we can use in emergencies, they change the way in which we see wild places and wild beings. The 'uninhabited places' full of brambles and nettles are transformed over a few days into a territory thickly populated by inhabitants with whom we can create many different kinds of connections (and not just by eating them!). Above all, this kind of stay allows us to see our civilization, in its absurdities, its fragility, its lack of moderation, and its destructive impact on our soul, from another angle.

The wild in us

Fortunately, we may be 'uprooted' but we are not beyond cure, even adults. Just a few days of really intense experience with the wild world is enough to have deep beneficial effects. In an experiment in the United States, people who had taken part in recreational activities in a forest subsequently gave more to conservation organizations, ate more responsibly, voted more for parties with ecological programmes, and so on.[46] It works in the opposite direction as well: young Spaniards who took part in collective recycling or water- and energy-saving actions later visited wild places more often than the young people who had not participated in these activities.[47]

Spending time in the wild goes beyond the small ecological gestures of everyday life. The wild is a place of healing for our sick psyches and bodies, and it's easier there to get in touch with the things that matter: inner peace, the meaning of life, increased awareness of the self, others and the environment, better perception of one's physical abilities and so on. What psychiatrists and psychologists call *wilderness therapy*[48] began in the 1990s, mainly for adolescents to start with, and it has grown considerably. When will 'doses of the wild' start to be reimbursed by Social Security?

Rewilding our souls means first of all de-domestication, that is to say, an experience of being without the harmful effects of modern industrial society, such as pollution, stress, virtual reality and so on, then re-learning awareness of other sensory worlds, using our dormant cognitive functions. Most of the skills that allowed us to live in balance with the biosphere and with the cycles of nature have been buried for centuries, but they are still there. Recontacting them is a way of reconnecting with our roots and with our deep soul.

It's also an excellent way to get out of our heads (our rationality), and to recontact our bodies, and our intuition. 'Ask any mountain-climber,' notes Carolyn Baker,

> if what she knows and thinks about will keep her safe thousands of feet above level ground. She will tell you that being present in the body, being supremely attentive to every move, every intuitive hunch, every physical sensation, is nothing less than a matter of life and death.[49]

Our personal well-being is closely tied to the discovery of what Bill Plotkin calls our 'wild soul'. 'Every human being has a unique and mystical relationship to the wild world', he wrote. 'The conscious discovery and culture of this relationship is at the heart of true adult life.'[50]

To experience our wild self does not mean to leave our humanity, or to risk losing it. On the contrary, it is a way of expressing a deeply buried part of ourselves, a feeling from far back but very familiar, which we feel we have been missing for too long. It is like discovering a huge interior continent, becoming present in it and connecting to it with our senses, with deep authenticity and joy. It is a transformation, and a call to find again the magic and the mystery of life.

Constituting 'rough-weather networks'

If we follow on from what we have just seen – individuals who are aware of disasters and who are finally attaining adulthood – how do we logically imagine the following step: organizations of adult people? Strong, caring and supportive organizations, through which we can 'feel safer, feel more joy, construct a future, build a new culture'.[51]

Our societies are torn between generalized fear and an anxious need for community. We know that the big changes do not come just from whistle-blowers; they involve collective realizations, communities who share a vision. What though is a community? Your nation? Your family? Your village or neighbourhood? Your football club? If the world collapses, with which group would you like to spend the rest of your life?

Adult communities

Community, which in today's parlance usually means proximity or a mere network, is a much deeper kind of connection than that: it is a sharing of one's being, an expansion of one's self. To be in community is to be in personal, interdependent relationship, and it comes with a price: our illusion of independence, our freedom from obligations. You can't have it both ways. If you want community, you must be willing to be obligated, dependent, tied, attached. You will give and receive gifts that you cannot just buy somewhere. You will not be able to easily find another source. You *need* each other.[52]

We probably all appreciate that it is very difficult to maintain a community, an ecovillage or an eco-neighbourhood without that problematic human factor coming one day to shatter them. Emotional and relational intelligence – being able to express one's emotions, to resolve conflict, feel empathy, share in a common story and the like – is just as important as the practical skills of eco-construction or agri-culture, if not more. Conflicts and tensions will arise, that is a certainty, and it is better to become competent sooner rather than later.

When we talk about community, looking forward to pos-sible extreme upheavals, we mean a group of people who have chosen to live together, to cooperate, with a common goal and by finding a shared meaning in life. Such a commu-nity is a group of people (between 30 and 150[53]) who weave very powerful connections and attachments to a territory, between each other, with other-than-humans, with humans outside the community, and also with the sacred.

The networks of initiation and mutual aid that we men-tioned earlier work precisely on the establishment of authentic connections and trust between people. In this sense, they can be seen as a good breeding ground for creat-ing authentic and effective communities. What they do is the opposite to what a cult does. Cults work to separate people from those around them so as to make them weaker, the same in fact as what our society does through television or the cult of competition. The practices of the ManKind Project or the Work that Reconnects workshops build our self-confidence, strengthen us, make us more resilient, because they teach us how to make effective connections with those to whom we are attached, and also beyond.[54]

For Chris Martenson, who is famous for his extremely informative Crash Course: 'Whatever the future holds, I'd rather face it surrounded by people I respect, admire, and love in my local community, people whom I trust and know I can count on. That's my measure of true wealth.'[55]

For some survivalists, the time has come to create 'Sustainable Autonomous Zones' (in French, BAD or *bases autonomes durables*[56]), places to ensure the autonomy of their occupants, with the necessary things for life (water, food, medicine, energy, shelter, security, socialization). Among the transitioners, there is a tendency to the ecovillage, less self-contained and less focused on the goal of autonomy. Among the direct-action activists (*zadistes* in French), it is not Sustainable Autonomous Zones, but Defended Zones (*zones à defendre*, ZAD), collectives which are held in a place by a shared struggle and by strong connections with local inhabitants (human and non-human).

When you form communities, whatever the basis, you realize that unity is strength. Taking this one step further, we arrive at the desire to create 'rough-weather networks', through building bridges between Defended Zones, Sustainable Autonomous Zones and other ecovillages, in order to increase our resilience capacity and protect our communities from destruction. We need to work on hybridization, building connections in all directions, among the ruins of a dying world.

The mycelium network keeps growing

The three of us have been living with the idea of collapse now for almost ten years. And if we are beginning – despite everything – to get better at living with it, it is because, after beginning completely on our own, we have become several. Collapsonauts make connections easily around topics that become essential: basic needs, emotions (including fear, imaginary futures and so on), not to say the feeling of being in the same boat!

A small network has begun to emerge from the various 'subcultures' we came from (permaculture, biomimicry,

Schumacher College,[57] popular education, Work that Reconnects, transition initiatives, etc.). When the expression 'rough-weather networks' emerged in 2013 during a memorable Work that Reconnects workshop with Joanna Macy, we immediately recognized ourselves in it. We felt connected in every sense, with people sometimes geographically distant, but united by a shared initiatory experience (brothers and sisters), also by the awareness of being in a situation of extreme urgency and fragility. This network grew, like mycelium, that invisible network of whitish filaments, hidden in the topsoil, which establishes underground and symbiotic connections between different organisms, and especially allows the transmission of excess energy from one to another. So why not consider connecting together the Defended Zones, Sustainable Autonomous Zones and other ecovillages, supported by a galaxy of collapsonauts and other Earth-Dwellers in the process of coming back to the earth?

In Belgium, this mysterious mycelium generated an external form, an organization or network that is itself aptly named 'Mycelium',[58] and aims to connect more quickly the various initiatives related to resilience and collapse, and to give them tools to reinforce and 'warm up' the connections between them (organizations and people), and make those connections thicker and more flowing.

Mycelium grows by itself, and very quickly – via social networks, initiatory networks, networks growing out of Work that Reconnects workshops, through popular education courses, and through other associations in France, Switzerland, even as far as Colombia.[59] Operated laterally, in a decentralized, quiet and unpredictable way, it also has the potential to connect beyond the borders, into the non-French-speaking world. This is good, because while the community is becoming extensive and dispersed, it is also becoming more solid, and we feel that we can count on it if we suffer a serious blow. This embryonic network fore-shadows what could be networks of solidarity 'during the collapse', and also starting-points for 'after'.

Becoming a 'user' of the collapse does not imply a hermit's life. The loneliness of he who preaches in the wilderness comes out of the fact that he preaches. It is wiser to let everyone evolve at their own pace and connect to others by affinity. The important thing is to understand that we are not alone. Far from it. Connections are made very quickly, and these networks are all the more effective as they are composed of people who have both voyaged internally and engaged in the outer world.

Listening and sharing groups

Many of us have already had trouble finding an ear to listen when talking about possible collapse. When we first discover all this, especially if we are on our own, the initial reflex is to want to share it quickly with the people we are close to, so as to feel less alone, or because we love them and believe that this information is crucial for their safety. But as we discover, when others are not ready to hear, which is often the case, people's reactions can often be unpleasant. So can the feelings of loneliness and misunderstanding to which they can lead.

The first thing to do is perhaps to take the time to integrate all this for yourself. Those who are not lucky enough to have people close to them who are sensitive to these issues can easily communicate through social networks. Reading an article, a commentary or a book, or seeing a documentary on a subject that you had thought of as taboo, and talking about it freely, gives the heart comfort. 'Putting a name onto this diffuse and persistent feeling that everything is going to collapse', Alexia Soyeux explains, 'gave me immense relief.

Being able to make a connection between the facts, the articles, the data, and my feelings, comforted me. Everything may collapse. That's it, it's been said. It doesn't mean that I'm crazy, or at least I'm not alone in my craziness.'[60]

That moment of insight when we realize that we are no longer alone also lets us become more relaxed about convincing everyone around us. It's important for our well-being to be listened to, to be able to speak the truth as we see it, sincerely and in depth. Speaking, unloading, relaxing . . . This probably means that 'one of the most important skills we can develop for collapse is the capacity to listen'.[61] In fact, there are plenty of people around you waiting to speak their own truth.

As with refugees, the traumatized, the injured, sick and so on, the mere presence of an attentive and caring ear allows us to let go, to unload our sorrows and fears, the unbelievable stories we have lived, and our unbelievable stories of what is to come. In the process of grieving, too, one of the most important and beneficial factors is the 'subjective perception of a quality support network'.[62]

When you are speaking, do not try to convince. When you are listening, do not judge, do not answer, do not try to console or reassure, or be constructive. Hugs and opportunities to recover will come later. Just let it flow and accept it, listen to the stories of others, about loss, grief and mourning, about fears and expectations, not omitting moments of joy and laughter.

Knowing this, it makes sense to build local listening and exchange groups around global disasters and collapse. Creating spaces appropriate for people at the different stages of 'digestion' of the collapse (see the Chefurka scale, in the Introduction); spaces to share experiences and *feelings*, without judgements or justifications. Because what makes you suffer is the feeling of being isolated and misunderstood, of never being listened to. If this frustration persists in extreme forms, it can drive people to violence, sabotage or self-destruction.

But to be able to open up, and to speak our truth with authenticity, we need to create 'secure' circles or spaces, with a strong protective membrane, so that we feel confident. They need good operating rules (speaking times, confidentiality, a non-judgemental attitude, good will, etc.) and they need a reliable person to make sure the rules are followed. Very effective relationships of reciprocity and trust can arise by natural empathy from such trusting, authentic exchanges.

Welcoming and being welcomed

Listening groups are very effective with refugees, who arrive loaded with traumatic baggage. Even though accepting foreigners can be difficult (depending on the people concerned), it is perhaps the best way to reduce future tensions. Because the worst situation in which we could find ourselves, in case of serious disruption of the social order, is to be alone, in other words having strangers all around you, or being seen as a stranger by everyone else. Imagine yourself lost in the middle of Uganda, without resources, and learning about the outbreak of riots related to a coup d'état. We know how 'the foreigner' can easily be used as a scapegoat for the expression of popular anger. The easiest and most effective way to avoid this kind of situation is to include as many 'foreign' people as possible inside our 'membranes', whether we are at home surrounded by foreigners, or alone in a foreign country, and so to expand our circles of identities.

If you are comfortably installed in your home with no intention of moving, this proposal may seem crazy. But we shouldn't see refugees only in terms of people from Mali or Syria fleeing their country. In a destabilized region, most migrations are internal. If social order breaks down in France or elsewhere in Europe, we can well imagine thousands or millions of displaced Europeans, with suitcases and children, walking along the roads to get to wherever they think is the safest place to live in uncertain times, or to get back to their family members, or even to leave for another country where there has not yet been a major industrial accident.

The future risks being largely nomadic. If we imagine half of France on the roads, we will also realize that the other half will have no choice but to accept them. While the possibility of armed gangs cannot be ruled out, most travellers, whether moving voluntarily or forcibly displaced, will be ordinary families, for the most part peaceful, driven by the impetus to live elsewhere. Solitary wanderers, nomadic travellers, refugees who have lost everything, refugees arriving from a remote region in a distressed state, will be numerous. They will need food and empathy, a bowl of soup or just an attentive and caring ear, the opportunity to tell their incredible stories, and then to continue their journey, or try their luck where they have arrived.

These chaotic displacements will also be occasions of intense connections for the mega-mycelium! But we will only be able to make these connections, as in the fable of the three little pigs, if the feeling of fraternity and the opening of our 'membranes' have been cultivated in advance, that is to say *now*.

To prepare for it, why not already start travelling without material objects, without money, vulnerable, as Guillaume Mouton and Nans Thomassey have done for years?[63] They depend for a period of time just on the goodwill of the people they meet on their way. It may sound elitist or ridiculous for those who are still living in a situation of abundance.

It's a good way, however, to experience our resilience and our ability to cope, and to learn skills and even new habits, of reciprocity, of empathy, of modesty, of humility, of sobriety and of hospitality. Because we are all potential migrants.

Conclusion:
Apocalypse or 'happy collapse'?

The central feature of our epoch is a sudden return to Earth, to *living on the earth*. The shock is gigantic. The most vulnerable will be overwhelmed. The invincible self-confidence of the political and financial elites of this thermo-industrial world will be broken. This is a time when everything has to be rethought. 'From now on', Bruno Latour says, 'we benefit, so to speak, from help offered by unleashed agents that oblige us to revisit the definition of what it means to be a human, a territory, a politics, a civilization.'[1]

The crash of the Modern dream reveals a field of ruins: beliefs smashed into pieces, a horizon of dust, of human victims (the immature and the vulnerable), burned forests, terrified animals. What can emerge from such a landscape? Other worlds, probably. With organisms whose minds work laterally, who 'think' like mushrooms, who patiently recreate the conditions for other forms of life to return. In contrast to industrial logic, smooth, top-down, sharp and noisy, they are flexible, quiet, adaptable, resilient, lateral, interconnected, creative. Human or other-than-human, soft, joyful, sad or austere, they wait for the end to arrive, defend territories and invent furiously.

The collapse of our present world sets into motion a new narrative, starting with catastrophic figures, feelings and intuitions. This narration makes it possible to bring the end of our thermo-industrial period into the story (whether that end is chosen or imposed), and so to give a new meaning to this tumultuous century. As Alexia Soyeux,[2] a key collapse reporter, realizes very clearly, there are no ready-made formulas. Everything needs to be invented: 'Here we don't parrot the refrain, "it was better before". Still less, "it's going to be better after"'.[3] And, as Dominique Bourg ironically notes, we are not going to go to find a spare planet in some pathetic burst of energy, from this devastated base camp.

Plunging into this story can be overwhelming at first, even paralysing. Susanne Moser, who is a specialist in climate change adaptation, recalls: 'A friend of mine, a coral researcher, once told the story how when the truth about a future without corals finally sank in, she had to run to the bathroom and vomit, it was so devastating. It took her years to accept it.'[4] And that is far from the only bad news that we are and will be facing.

How do we move on from this state of paralysis? First, we learn to live with our fears: the fear of violence (including fascism), of the irrational, the unknown, the loss of our values and of our points of reference, the depoliticization, and even the fear of being afraid. The answer to fear isn't hope or optimism, it's courage. We cannot be sure of getting through these storms unscathed, but we have no choice, we have to get moving. That aside, we will undoubtedly have to learn plenty about loss, grief and bereavement. We don't need to look for or cultivate so-called 'negative' emotions such as fear, anger, sadness or despair, even less to indulge in them, but if they arrive we just need to accept them and share them in order to find a little peace, joy and pleasure in being together. Hiding them under the rug, on the contrary, by focusing only on the 'positive' aspects of what the transition may bring with it, seems to us to be a good recipe for an explosion at a moment when we least expect it. As the British philosopher Peter Kingsley wisely notes, 'it's impossible to reach the light at the cost of rejecting darkness'.[5] The philosopher and veteran of the Iraq war Roy Scranton says:

'Many thinkers [. . .] have argued that studying philosophy is learning how to die. If that's true, then we have entered humanity's most philosophical age – for this is precisely the problem of the Anthropocene. The rub is that now we have to learn how to die not as individuals, but as a civilization.'[6]

Collapse is a magnifying mirror for our shadows and our fear of death. So, Paul Chefurka says, 'perhaps all we can do is to grow up, and become bigger than the pain'.[7] To accept death (the end of our world) is to give ourselves the opportunity to live well what time remains for us to live. Paradoxically, it opens up to us opportunities to create something else. So we have to learn how to die well . . . but we still have our whole life in front of us.

The narrative of the collapse, however, has one major risk. It can flatten the future; in other words, it can reduce our ability to act, all the while spoiling our present life. We need to learn to see it, paradoxically in terms of being able to make other worlds emerge and to invent other futures for ourselves. What matters is not to focus on the end or the supposed end. In any case, we may well not live through a moment where everything changes at once, more a slow degradation in fits and starts. What matters is to imagine how we will live *until then*, and keep this idea in mind. In other words, it's about finding out how the narrative of collapse can transform our present in a joyful and creative way.

As exciting as it may be, inventing a future is not a simple matter. And no matter what we imagine, the changes will be beyond our imagination: dizzying, overwhelming, traumatic or even marvellous. To anticipate and imagine an upheaval of our lives, then, implies radically changing our outlook on the world. For this, we suggest three directions to follow. First, break down the walls that split up the practice of science into different disciplines, so we can create knowledge more anchored in the Earth system, more lateral and more democratic. Then, continue the pathways traced by daring anthropologists and other peoples in situations of resistance: open ourselves to other perspectives on the world (ontologies) so as to imagine alliances, improbable but necessary, with other cultures and with other Earth-Dwellers. Last, set off on an extraordinary expedition, in which we recreate stories based on other mythologies to discover and explore new horizons.

We can already start developing our ability to respond to stress, our empathy, compassion, generosity, resilience, endurance and so on, by organizing listening groups around the subject of collapse, hosting refugees or, for example, volunteering in a hospice to learn how to accompany a world in pain. The skills of group life will also be vital, as will learning how to live in the wild.

Perhaps, with all this, it will be possible to regenerate life from the ruins, through creating alliances in all directions: with ourselves (our emotions and intuition), among humans (between Moderns, also between cultures), with other living beings (with diplomacy and acceptance of the wild) and with what is beyond us (the relation to the sacred).

Here, we have clearly left the usual tracks of scientific discourse about the collapse. We are not about to make an enemy of reason or rationality; they are vital. To begin to change our direction, though, or begin our descent for a landing on earth, we need to appreciate that we *also* need a much richer spiritual, ethical, artistic and emotional life.

What we call collapsosophy is intended as a support and complement to collapsology. Its point is to help us not to lose our reason. What this book suggests is that we *simultaneously* give as much importance to what is happening outside, at the material and political level, and to the inner, spiritual path. Collapsology is engaging and useful for these two paths, but it is also lame and blind if not accompanied by compassion and wisdom. To put it otherwise, playing with Rabelais' famous sentence, 'science without soul . . . is only awareness of the ruins'.[8]

The inner path and the outer effect

The great challenge of our time, then, is to bring about a great rapprochement with all that is alive, and to find our place on this Earth. To begin this, we need to find a common language with as many as possible of the beings living on Earth, by listening to them, by exchanging, and why not also by beginning to sketch a great treaty of political alliances and inter-species diplomacy.

To have some power available after the end of fossil energy, it will be necessary to turn to other beings than humans, but this time without considering them as inexhaustible reservoirs of material resources. To make alliances with them (if they accept!) implies to *exchange* energy and material resources, and so to think beforehand of what we could give to them.

But the rapprochement with the living world cannot be reduced to making business agreements. We must also reconnect ourselves with our wild nature and our mortal status, which requires a degree of humility, and an acceptance of something that goes beyond our power to control. For the artist and educator Martín Prechtel, 'true initiations [will] be impossible until the modern world surrenders to the grief of its origins and seeks a true comprehension of the sacred. A tangible relationship with the divine must be found: a relationship to ritual that actively feeds the invisible forces behind all this visible life.'[9]

None of this will immunize us against a catastrophic future, but it will allow us to live it in a less catastrophic way. It will make us more mature, and if our hearts grow, they will become available for this great work of love and giving. This is what Francis Weller calls 'soul activism'.

We have no intention of painting an over-rosy picture; in fact it is more a question of finding the strength to open our eyes to the dark sides of the world. The New Age movement of the 1970s simply refused to accept the dark side. By being too 'positive', by cultivating denial, it probably also contributed to the deterioration of the situation.

Some people will call us irrational or mystical, and we understand why that might be so. But we would oppose that judgement with these words of Bruno Latour, in which he points out that the so-called rationality of our civilization is really anything but:

> How could we deem 'realistic' a project of modernization that has 'forgotten' for two centuries to anticipate the reactions of the terraqueous globe to human actions? How could we accept as 'objective' economic theories that are incapable of integrating into their calculations the scarcity of resources whose exhaustion it had been their mission to predict? How could we speak of 'effectiveness' with respect to technological systems that have not managed to integrate into their

design a way to last more than a few decades? How could we call 'rationalist' an ideal of civilization guilty of a forecasting error so massive that it prevents parents from leaving an inhabited world to their children?[10]

The return of spirituality is driven by deep and powerful needs. The future will probably produce countless variations of it. Some of them will be frauds, other will be very beautiful. Rather than holding our noses in disdain, it might be useful to learn how to sort them out, in other words to plunge our hands into the sludge, and become competent. Frankly, at the point we have reached, what do we have to lose? Our reputation? An offer of a job?

In our society, if you want to be 'at the service of the living' and you declare it publicly, you are likely to be seen as abnormal, naive or utopian. We know that many people secretly want to be of service, from the bottom of their heart, but they are afraid of how they will be judged by those around them. What we, along with many others, propose in this book will not make it easier for them, for sure, but perhaps it will give them some courage to get back into authentic life. It is high time to drop our inhibitions.

Survival as the first step

We need everyone. There is a certain irenicism in stating this, a downplaying of differences and disagreements, but we take it for granted. We will need everyone, simply to take care of the different aspects of life, and to have the best chance of recovering after the shocks. We need people who aren't too excitable, but we also need the hyper-sensitive. We need the resilient and the vulnerable. To look after knowledge, we need scientists and teachers; to look after our imagination and stimulate our emotions, we need artists; to look after material aspects, we need low-tech engineers, crazy inventors, peasant agroecologists and survivalists; to defend what we achieve, we need activists, *zadists*, 'militants'; to look after our bodies and our psyches, we need meditators and people involved in spiritual paths; to take care of our relationship to the living, we need anthropologists, ecopsychologists and organizers of immersion courses in the wild; to look after human organizations, we need pioneers in human permaculture and facilitators in collective intelligence; to look after ourselves, we need our loved ones, even if they do not believe in the possibility of a collapse.

We also need to get rid of all the labels, because they stick easily, and they hang on stubbornly. Survivalists, transitioners, artists, bohemians, creative types, inventors, artisans, peasants, ecopsychologists, all the careers of the 'world-of-before' (computer scientist, advertising, industrial designer, and so on). They enclose us in a certain comfort, a way of thinking, feeling or acting. Over time, many people settle comfortably into their favourite areas, and lose the ability to understand the world of others. Fortunately, these categories are not closed off from each other, and there are always 'multifunctional' people who navigate through the walls between different worlds.

We can schematize our life in terms of passing two thresholds. The first takes us from childhood to adolescence. It represents the effort to get out of *dependence* – living off others – and find *independence* – living from our own resources. In the case of collapse, this typically corresponds to the survivalist phase, where we build our own means of subsistence, our autonomy, outside the framework of the State and industrial society.

'Independence is more functional than dependence, but it has its limits', notes Carolyn Baker. 'Nobody can stock enough food to last for the rest of his or her life. Eventually, independence must be transcended.'[11] Then comes the second passage, when one realizes that independence is only an illusion and that everything is *interdependence*, living with and in mutual dependence with others. Symbolically, this is the passage to adult life: the discovery of finiteness and vulnerability, connections (which liberate) with everyone else, and *self-restraint*. 'For some, especially for those who feel safer being independent, interdependence is challenging, perhaps even emotionally threatening. All the more reason for cultivating it sooner rather than later.'[12] In the case of collapse, this stage, which is the heart of our book, could finally be called *creating life together*.

Given the urgency, it's very tempting to take action as quickly as possible, and to draw up broad policies for collapse without managing to go through the internal journey first. It can be done, but doing this risks falling back into the same traps that caused our problems in the first place. An internal journey, as proposed in this book, is not a rejection of politics. On the contrary, it should be an essential prerequisite for rethinking our politics completely and radically, and for having the resources to do it.

But how do we include other cultures in our political project? How do we rethink the law so as to include other-than-humans? How do we learn to share the riches of the Earth, knowing that among those that we used to exploit are . . . our new political partners?

Making breaches and holding on to them

There will be conflicts in the years to come around places where people have decided to become *Earth-Dwellers* again, to find themselves a territory and defend it. This act of rebel-

lion in Modern 'airspace' implies for the Earth-Dwellers
the commencement of resistance against all that is destroying and breaking their connections with the earth. On both
sides, there is the question of access to the Earth. 'It is a situation of colonization, of the occupation of the soil of others,
which is a pretty good definition of war.'[13] Worse, the war
has a global dimension: for example, when the industrialized
countries send CO_2 to other countries, does that not constitute a *casus belli*?

In this state of war, the Modern camp is invisible, and it
still has the means to harm considerably. How do we make
sense of the conflicts and the stakes along the front that
unfolds between the Earth-Dwellers and the militants of
the extreme Modern, between those who defend territories
intended for recreating common goods and regenerating
life, and those who keep on destroying the common bases of
our livelihood?

Between conflicts and alliances, between resistance and
resilience, thousands of collectives are emerging and working to restore polluted rivers and soils, to produce healthy
food, find somewhere to live, take care of others, teach
and organize a different way of life. Others fight to reduce
inequalities and injustices, or campaign against the capitalist hydra and international finance. Others, real laboratories
these, set up spaces of creativity (zones to go crazy, zones
to disinhibit ourselves) where people can innovate, explore,
invent other ways to survive and live, recover the knowledge
of the old and the social memories of the dark periods (from
people who have lived through wars, migrations and the like)
to mix them into their time, or to take advantage of the last
moments of stability to experience the beginnings of the politics of collapse.

There are three dimensions to what Joanna Macy calls
The Great Turning. The first consists of actions and strug-

gles to slow down or stop the damage to the Earth, to ecosystems, to communities and to vulnerable people. This, whether spectacular or quiet, is activism as we usually think of it. The second brings together analysis and understanding of the current situation (collapsology) and the creation of concrete alternatives (ecovillages, transition towns, alternative economies, agroecology and so on). Finally, the third dimension is that of a deep change of consciousness, an inner change. None is more important than another. We need all three at once.

So that's where we have got to. The end of this world announces a great breaking down of divisions and the growth of unlikely alliances. Those who do not understand this, who are offended by it, or who do not wish it, are depriving themselves of whole areas of life, many of which may be critical for their survival. The situation is complex because there are desirable aspects of collapses and others that we would rather did not occur. We will need to decide what we want to support and what we want to see collapse, while being aware that everything is intimately connected . . . Alliances and relations of solidarity will therefore be strategic choices. We are not all from the same worlds, but we are all living in the same boat.

The situation is also complex in that we will simultaneously be undergoing feelings of both pain and joy. The pain of observing the collapse of life, of the places where we live, of our futures and our attachments; the joy of seeing (at last!) the collapse of the thermo-industrial world and of many other toxic things, of being able to invent new worlds, of returning to a simple existence, of recovering memory (against *amnesia*) and feeling (against *anaesthesia*), of regaining autonomy and power, of cultivating beauty and authenticity, and of weaving real bonds with the rediscovered wild. It is entirely possible to live both an apocalypse *and* a 'happy collapse'.

Afterword

I've just finished this book, like you. And it leaves me with many emotions, thoughts and impressions.

Paradoxically, reading it makes me feel a little more at peace. The prospect of an ecological collapse, even if it's already partially under way, even if it is a gradual process rather than a sudden apocalypse, has been a source of continuous anxiety since, in 2012, I read the study[1] that finally decided me to make the film *Demain* (*Tomorrow*). This prospect is a source of creativity, of action, as well, but it keeps me in a state of a deep restlessness. Now, reading this book, it seems to me that a kind of acceptance is growing within me. It is already too late to return to normal as far as the climate is concerned. Many of us have thought this for some years now, but as I am writing, groups of scientists are beginning to emerge from their professional restraint to suggest or even confirm it themselves. Among them are the international team who published a new report on 6 August 2018 in the *Proceedings of the National Academy of Sciences*[2] highlighting feedback loops that would take over even if we managed to limit warming to +2°C (we are already over one degree). They would cause phenomena – among them the release of methane trapped under Arctic and Siberian permafrost – which would easily bring us up to four to five degrees of global warming before the end of the century. With the frightening consequences about which we all know.

Why the hell, are you wondering, would such a prospect make me less anxious? Because, as this book explains, to face reality, to stop going back and forth between some vague hope that we can still, by God only knows what miracle, stabilize the situation, and the general feeling that this hope rests on a damp sand dune, is a relief. When the situation is clear, we can give a clear response.

What kind of response will this be? Complex, as our Three Musketeers of Collapsology have described it here, especially when it comes to implementation.

Certainly we are about to enter, by choice or by compulsion, and not without a lot of noise, into a new age of humanity, and doubtless also of the Earth system. This new age will force us to develop a new consciousness of ourselves, of the world around us and of the relationship between the two. Today, we are behaving like some adolescent species exploring its limits and, like any adolescent, quite capable of putting its life in danger in order to work out the lines it can't cross. At fifteen, I got myself into an alcoholic coma after a hundred shots back to back of vodka, gin, whiskey, Baileys and Curaçao. They had to drag me physically away from the bottle (with a few punches) before I finally stopped and my body and my mind sank into darkness. That's more or less what we are doing with oil, gas and money: we're drinking ourselves to death to see how far we can go. Pushing our morbid drive to the extreme, in search of the borderland between exultation, frenetic enjoyment and death. And some days, it seems that we will actually need to be forced to drag ourselves away from this horribly powerful addiction to fossil fuels and comfort. Because even if we now know where the limit is, this theoretical knowledge isn't enough to stop us. We need to transform it into awareness. A new kind of awareness.

For me, we will succeed when we have collectively replied to a question: What useful function can the human species serve, among all the other species? What is its role in the chain of life? Scientists studying ecosystems highlight the interdependence of mineral, plant, animal and microbial organisms. All have a function which participates in creating and maintaining a kind of dynamic equilibrium. We alone, as a species, have found out how to break this beautiful mechanism, for our short-term benefit. If we draw up a balance sheet of what our species has been able to bring to the animal and plant kingdoms, the balance is very certainly on the side of destruction. So much so that we are now jeopardizing our own survival. Yet we are an integral part of life. That is a fact. So we should have a part to play. I can't believe that we only exist to destroy and disappear. We are a very specific species: mammals endowed with consciousness, with language and, thanks to these abilities, able to bring about the cooperation of millions of individuals to achieve remarkable things. How do we put these qualities at the service of the restoration of ecosystems, and of a new alliance of the living, human beings included?

Finding an answer to this question is for me the central issue of the coming years.

It implies, in my opinion, abandoning the petty squabbles which we humans are so fond of. Who is the purest ecologist? Who is the traitor? Who is right and who is wrong? Because, while we are playing these games, the situation continues to deteriorate all too quickly. Even if we agree that we are not going to find a solution, let's not forget that anything that we can do to limit the impact of a systemic ecological collapse will save lives, in our species and in others. If we let the temperature rise to an average +7°C, not +3°C or +4°C, which would already be a terrifying situation, then far more people will suffer and die, and far more ecosystems will disappear.

We need both to stop the destruction and the warming, to build up the resilience of our territories (to absorb the shock) and to engage in regeneration (planting forests, rewilding, regenerating the Great Barrier Reef, etc.). Involving millions of people on this path requires, in my opinion, a profound cultural change, a different story of the future, of who we are, of the civilizations which we want to build, a story which breaks with predatory capitalism and neoliberalism, with the obsessive search for profit and for material accumulation. But it will also require a huge mobilization that will itself create power relations. These changes will not occur, even under the battering brought about by collapse, without a broad, well-organized movement, ready to embody these new civilizations in political, economic and social structures. As Indian activist Vandana Shiva told me a few years ago:

When a disaster happens people do not change, they panic. It is on this soil that dictatorships develop and coups d'état take place. The idea that the most exploited people in the depths of a society will rise up miraculously is not realistic. It is an illusion to imagine that a catastrophe could awaken consciousness in a day. It's a process that requires education, that's why our work is so important to everyone. However, solidarity does work. Opposition to all forms of exploitation connects all these beings and can bring about real transformations. At least this is what we see everywhere where the change has taken place.[3]

We have no time to lose to ask whether it is the collapsologists or the 'positive ecologists' (as I've been called) who are right. We have an immense project before us, one which, by the way, seems to me an extremely exciting one, not a sea of privations as the pessimists like to portray ecology.

Because, in essence, do we really have anything to do with the flat screens, smartphones, networked cars, and smart speakers, the continuous flow of series, movies and sports which are broadcast twenty-four hours a day on the hundreds of channels distributed by our boxes, the stacks of clothes that gather dust in our closets? What do we really want? If I had to answer this question, and if I exclude the basic necessities such as to eat, drink, be cared for and sheltered, what the answer would look like would be: to be able to walk, in town or in the nature, facing the wind, warmed by the sun, to have genuine good friends with whom I can share what matters most to me, who will be there in case of hard knocks and for whom I will be there too, to love deeply a dear partner, children, to be loved deeply for who I am, to do what I'm passionate about, what I'm good at, every day, to be useful, to read, to write, to create, to listen to or to make music, to discover what I do not yet know, to eat good, healthy products, to have the choice, to have time, to understand what I'm doing on this planet. In this small inventory in the style of Jacques Prévert,[4] very few items depend on advanced technology, very few require extravagant use of fossil energy, or of energy at all. They all require, though, a human organization that does not make exploitation, competition and enslavement of others into cardinal values, but places cooperation, sharing, intelligence and interdependence with the rest of the living, at the centre of its institutions. Material possession is one strategy for meeting deeper needs such as security, self-fulfilment and connections with others. But it's not the only one; far from it.

We are standing face to face with a precipice. I think it's time to drop the bottle and move on to something else . . .

Cyril Dion
Writer, director

Notes

Foreword

1 The reference is to Serge Reggiani's 1967 song, 'Les loups sont entrés dans Paris' ('The wolves have entered Paris') – Tr.
2 Pablo Servigne and Raphaël Stevens, *How Everything Can Collapse: A Manual for Our Times* (Cambridge: Polity Press, 2020).

Preface

1 A neologism we proposed to refer to the emerging field of research in the scientific community that studies global catastrophic risks (GCRs), the category of risks that could cause mass deaths and disasters on a global scale. See Gorm E. Shackelford et al., 'Accumulating evidence using crowdsourcing and machine learning: a living bibliography about existential risk and global catastrophic risk', *Futures* 116, 2020: 102508.
2 Jean-Laurent Cassely and Jérôme Fourquet, *La France: Patrie de la collapsologie?* (Paris: Fondation Jean Jaures and IFOP, 2020). https://bit.ly/37jzvOv. For a press dispatch in English, see https://bit.ly/2XKNWaU
3 M. Ivanova, 'Global risks: a survey of scientists' perceptions', in *Our Future on Earth* (Future Earth, 2020), pp. 14–17.
4 Pablo Servigne and Raphaël Stevens, *Comment tout peut s'effondrer* (Paris: Seuil, 2015).
5 Asher Moses, '"Collapse of civilisation is the most likely outcome": top climate scientists', *Voice of Action* (5 June 2020). https://bit.ly/2MI2H8j
6 The Doomsday Clock was created during the Cold War, and is maintained by the editors of the Bulletin of the Atomic Scientists

at the University of Chicago. Since 23 January 2020, the clock has been displaying midnight minus 100 seconds (23:58:20), for the first time since 1953, due to the inability of world leaders to deal with the imminent threats of nuclear war and climate change, and the proliferation of 'fake news' as a weapon to destabilize democracies.

7 Le Petit Robert, *Les mots nouveaux du Petit Robert* (15 May 2020). https://bit.ly/3dS3Zt4

8 European Environment Agency, 'Climate change and its impact in Europe' (EEA, 2020). https://bit.ly/3f7xuHJ

Introduction: Learning to live with it

1 Kevin Anderson and Alice Bows, 'Beyond "dangerous" climate change: emission scenarios for a new world', *Philosophical Transactions of the Royal Society A: Mathematical, Physical and Engineering Sciences* 369, 2011: 20–44.

2 Ben Chapman, 'BP and Shell planning for catastrophic 5°C global warming despite publicly backing Paris climate agreement', *The Independent*, 27 October 2017.

3 Henry Kendall (coordinator), 'World Scientists' Warning to Humanity', Union of Concerned Scientists, 1992.

4 Michel Salomon (coordinator), 'Scientific ecology: The Heidelberg appeal to Heads of States and Governments', *Interdisciplinary Science Reviews* 17(4), 1992: 299–300. See also Stéphane Foucart, 'L'appel d'Heidelberg, une initiative fumeuse', *Le Monde*, 16 June 2012.

5 William J. Ripple et al., 'World scientists' warning to humanity: a second notice', *BioScience* 67(12), 2017: 1026–8.

6 For an analysis of the phenomenon of 'gated communities' in relation to the collapse, see Renaud Duterme, *De quoi l'effondrement est-il le nom? La fragmentation du monde* (Paris: Les Éditions Utopia, 2016).

7 'Millionaire migration in 2015', *New World Wealth*, March 2016.

8 Alec Hogg, 'As inequality soars, the nervous super rich are already planning their escapes', *The Guardian*, 24 January 2015.

9 Evan Osnos, 'Doomsday prep for the super-rich', *The New Yorker*, 23 January 2017; Yarra Elmasry, 'The super-rich are buying luxury apocalypse-safe bunkers for protection against

natural disasters and nuclear attack', *The Independent*, 10 July 2017; Emmanuèle Peyret and Coralie Schaub, 'Fin du monde: les survivalistes à bunker ouvert', *Libération*, 23 March 2018.

10 Bruno Latour, *Down to Earth: Politics in the New Climatic Regime* (Cambridge: Polity, 2018). Translation by Catherine Porter from *Où atterrir? Comment s'orienter en politique* (Paris: La Découverte, 2017).

11 For example, John Wiseman, *The SAS Survival Handbook: The Ultimate Guide to Surviving Anywhere*, 3rd edn (New York: HarperCollins, 2014); Bob Arnot and Mark Cohen, *Your Survival: The Complete Resource for Disaster Planning and Recovery* (Hobart, NY: Hatherleigh Press, 2007); Jim Cobb, *Prepper's Long-Term Survival Guide* (Berkeley, CA: Ulysses Press, 2014).

12 Bertrand Vidal, *Les Représentations collectives de l'événement-catastrophe. Étude sociologique sur les peurs contemporaines*, Thèse de doctorat en sociologie, université Montpellier 3, 2012, p. 499.

13 Abraham H. Maslow, 'A theory of human motivation', *Psychological Review* 50, 1943: 370–96. This somewhat simplistic theory is used in most business schools.

14 Ruth Stégassy, 'Devenir autonome. Entretien avec Kim Pasche', broadcast by Terre à Terre, France Culture, 5 September 2015, https://bit.ly/2LU59dG. Developed in Frederika Van Ingen, *Sagesses d'ailleurs pour vivre aujourd'hui* (Paris: Les Arènes, 2016), p. 37.

15 Stégassy, 'Devenir autonome. Entretien avec Kim Pasche'.

16 There are other theories which take account of the complex relations between different fundamental needs. See, for example, that of the Chilean economist Manfred Max-Neef, *Development and Human Needs* (New York: The Apex Press, 1992).

17 Carolyn Baker, *Collapsing Consciously* (Berkeley, CA: North Atlantic Books, 2013), p. 13.

18 Pablo Servigne and Raphaël Stevens, *How Everything Can Collapse: A Manual for Our Times* (Cambridge: Polity, 2020). Translation by Andrew Brown from *Comment tout peut s'effondrer. Petit manuel de collapsologie à l'usage des générations présentes* (Paris: Le Seuil, 2015).

19 See Clive Hamilton, *Requiem for a Species: Why We Resist the Truth About Climate Change* (Crows Nest, NSW: Allen and Unwin, 2010); Carolyn Baker, *Sacred Demise* (Bloomington, IN: iUniverse, 2009); Joanna Macy and Chris Johnstone, *Active Hope: How*

To Face the Mess We're In Without Going Crazy (Novato, CA: New World Library, 2012).

20 Baker, *Collapsing Consciously*, p. 15.
21 See his blog at http://www.paulchefurka.ca/
22 This simplified schematic structure is useful for situating ourselves, but we should be aware that the reality can be much more complex and dynamic.
23 Paul Chefurka, 'Climbing the Ladder of Awareness', 19 October 2012, http://www.paulchefurka.ca/LadderOfAwareness.html, accessed 15 August 2019.
24 Ibid.
25 Ibid.
26 Ibid.
27 Adapted from Baruch Spinoza, *Ethics*, Part III, Preface.
28 Dominique Bourg, *Une nouvelle Terre* (Paris: Desclée De Brouwer, 2018).
29 John Michael Greer, 'Bringing It Down to Earth', https://carolynbaker.net/2011/11/25/bringing-it-down-to-earth-by-john-michael-greer/, accessed 5 March 2020. Originally posted in *Energy Bulletin*.
30 Ibid. See also John Michael Greer, *Ecotechnic Future: Envisioning a Post-Peak World* (Gabriola Island, BC: New Society Publishers, 2009).
31 Documentary written and directed by Iolande Cadrin-Rossignol, *La Terre vue du cœur*, distribution Ligne 7, May 2018.
32 Baker, *Collapsing Consciously*, p. 98.
33 Latour, *Down to Earth*, p. 5. I've slightly changed Catherine Porter's translation to avoid losing the 'earth' imagery which is important for Servigne et al. (*terrestre, territoire, atterrir*). – Tr.

Chapter 1: Experiencing the impact

1 See, for example, Hamilton, *Requiem for a Species*.
2 Daniel S. Levine and Samuel J. Leven, *Motivation, Emotion, and Goal Direction in Neural Networks* (London: Psychology Press, 2014).
3 Keith E. Stanovich and Richard F. West, 'On the relative independence of thinking biases and cognitive ability', *Journal of Personality and Social Psychology* 94(4), 2008: 672–95.

4 Hang Lu and Jonathon P. Schuldt, 'Exploring the role of incidental emotions in support for climate change policy', *Climatic Change* 131(4), 2015: 719–26.

5 Bamboo recovers easily. It bends, but does not break, unlike the oak that breaks when the wind is too strong.

6 Joan Brunkard, Gonza Namulanda and Raoult Ratard, 'Hurricane Katrina deaths, Louisiana, 2005', *Disaster Medicine and Public Health Preparedness* 2(4), 2008: 215–23.

7 Kevin Quealy, 'The cost of hurricane Harvey. Only one recent storm comes close', *The New York Times*, 1 September 2017.

8 Lennart Reifels et al., 'Lessons learned about psychosocial responses to disaster and mass trauma: an international perspective', *European Journal of Psychotraumatology* 4, 2013: article 22897.

9 A. Hasegawa, T. Ohira, M. Maeda, S. Yasumura and K. Tanigawa, 'Emergency responses and health consequences after the Fukushima accident: evacuation and relocation', *Clinical Oncology* 28(4), 2016: 237–44; 'Real cost of Fukushima disaster will reach ¥70 trillion, or triple government's estimate: think tank', *The Japan Times*, 1 April 2017.

10 Emily Goldmann and Sandro Galea, 'Mental health consequences of disasters', *Annual Review of Public Health* 35(1), 2014: 169–83.

11 Ronald C. Kessler et al., 'Posttraumatic stress disorder in the National Comorbidity Survey', *Archives of General Psychiatry* 52(12), 1995: 1048–60.

12 Alexander C. McFarlane and Richard Williams, 'Mental health services required after disasters: learning from the lasting effects of disasters', *Depression Research and Treatment*, 2012: article 970194.

13 George S. Everly, Jr and Jeffrey M. Lating, *The Johns Hopkins Guide to Psychological First Aid* (Baltimore, MD: Johns Hopkins University Press, 2017).

14 Yuval Neria, A. Nandi and S. Galea, 'Post-traumatic stress disorder following disasters: a systematic review', *Psychological Medicine* 38(4), 2008: 467–80. For a detailed description of the symptoms, see also American Psychiatric Association, *Diagnostic and Statistical Manual of Mental Disorders (DSM-5)* (Washington, DC: American Psychiatric Association Publishing, 2013).

15 Michael T. Compton and Ruth S. Shim, 'The social determinants of mental health', *Focus* 13(4), 2015: 419–25.

16 Fran H. Norris et al., '60,000 disaster victims speak. Part I. An empirical review of the empirical literature, 1981–2001', *Psychiatry: Interpersonal and Biological Processes* 65(3), 2002: 207–39.

17 Hiroyuki Hikichi et al., 'Increased risk of dementia in the aftermath of the 2011 Great East Japan earthquake and tsunami', *PNAS* 113(45), 2016: E6911–E6918.

18 Lorraine de Meaux, 'La fin de l'URSS ou la seconde mort de l'Empire russe', in Patrice Gueniffey and Thierry Lentz (eds.), *La Fin des Empires* (Paris: Perrin, 2016), p. 440.

19 Namely hyperinflation, mass dismissals, blackouts, confusion, the emergence of mafias, Russian oligarchs, dictators and autocratic governments (Belarus, Uzbekistan and Kazakhstan), civil wars (Georgia and Tajikistan), endemic corruption (Kyrgyzstan and Turkmenistan), or just extreme poverty (Moldova and Armenia).

20 The scientific literature is full of population health studies for this period. For a review, see Steven Stillman, 'Health and nutrition in Eastern Europe and the former Soviet Union during the decade of transition: a review of the literature', *Economics & Human Biology* 4(1), 2006: 104–46.

21 Tamma A. Carleton, 'Crop-damaging temperatures increase suicide rates in India', *PNAS* 114(33), 2017: 8746–51.

22 Marshall Burke et al., 'Higher temperatures could increase suicide rates across the United States and Mexico', *Nature Climate Change* 8, 2018: 723–9.

23 'Focus on climate change and mental health', *Nature Climate Change* 8(4), 2018: 259. See also Pablo Servigne and Raphaël Stevens, 'Le côté lumineux du désespoir', *Kairos*, 33, March–April 2018.

24 Ashlee Cunsolo and Neville R. Ellis, 'Ecological grief as a mental health response to climate change-related loss', *Nature Climate Change* 8(4), 2018: 275–81.

25 Stephanie Morrice, 'Heartache and Hurricane Katrina: recognising the influence of emotion in post-disaster return decisions', *Area* 45(1), 2013: 33–9.

26 Cunsolo and Ellis, 'Ecological grief'.

27 Glenn Albrecht et al., 'Solastalgia: the distress caused by environmental change', *Australasian Psychiatry* 15(supplement), 2007: S95–8.

28 Ashlee Cunsolo and Karen E. Landman (eds.), *Mourning Nature: Hope at the Heart of Ecological Loss and Grief* (Kingston, ON: McGill-Queen's University Press, 2017), p. 277.

29 Cunsolo and Ellis, 'Ecological grief'.

30 Ibid.

31 Ashlee Cunsolo, 'Climate change as the work of mourning', in Cunsolo and Landman, *Mourning Nature*, pp. 169–89; also in *Ethics and the Environment* 17(2), 2012: 137–64.

32 Dale Dominey-Howes, 'Seeing "the dark passenger". Reflections on the emotional trauma of conducting post-disaster research', *Emotion, Space and Society* 17, 2015: 55–62.

33 Émilie Hermant and Valérie Pihet, *Le Chemin des possibles. La maladie de Huntington entre les mains de ses usagers* (Dijon: Dingdingdong éditions/Les presses du réel, 2017), p. 40.

34 This is related to the 'eco-anxiety' that can appear, for example, when disasters make the fate of future generations uncertain, resulting in feelings of abandonment, fatalism and resignation. See Glenn Albrecht, 'Chronic environmental change: Emerging "psychoterratic" syndromes', in Inka Weissbecker (ed.), *Climate Change and Human Well-Being* (New York: Springer, 2011), pp. 43–56.

35 Donella Meadows, 'Feeling our feelings might not be a trivial exercise', *The Donella Meadows Archive: Global Citizen Columns*, 30 January 1997. http://donellameadows.org/archives/feeling-our-feelings-might-not-be-a-trivial-exercise/, accessed 1 April 2020.

36 Donald W. Winnicott, 'Fear of Breakdown'. *International Review of Psycho-Analysis* 1, 1974: 103–7.

37 Saffron O'Neill and Sophie Nicholson-Cole, '"Fear won't do it": promoting positive engagement with climate change through visual and iconic representations', *Science Communication* 30(3), 2009: 355–79.

38 Nicholas Smith and Anthony Leiserowitz, 'The role of emotion in global warming policy support and opposition', *Risk Analysis* 34(5), 2014: 937–48.

39 Joanna Macy and Molly Brown, *Coming Back to Life: The Updated Guide to the Work That Reconnects* (Gabriola Island, BC: New Society, 2014).

40 Susanne C. Moser and Lisa Dilling, 'Communicating climate change: closing the science-action gap', in John S. Dryzek, Richard

B. Norgaard and David Schlosberg (eds.), *The Oxford Handbook of Climate Change and Society* (Oxford: Oxford University Press, 2011), pp. 161–74; See also Rusi Jaspal and Brigitte Nerlich, 'When climate science became climate politics: British media representations of climate change in 1988', *Public Understanding of Science* 23(2), 2014: 122–41.

41 Susanne C. Moser, 'Navigating the political and emotional terrain of adaptation: community engagement when climate change comes home', in Susanne C. Moser and Maxwell T. Boykoff (eds.), *Successful Adaptation to Climate Change. Linking Science and Policy in a Rapidly Changing World* (Abingdon: Routledge, 2013), pp. 289–305.

42 Lesley Head and Theresa Harada, 'Keeping the heart a long way from the brain: the emotional labour of climate scientists', *Emotion, Space and Society* 24, 2017: 34–41.

43 Hamilton, *Requiem for a Species*, pp. viii–ix.

44 'Focus on climate change and mental health', *Nature Climate Change* 8(4), 2018: 259. These fields, such as climatology, geology, ecology and oceanography, are now often referred to as 'survival sciences'.

45 Keynyn Brysse, Naomi Oreskes, Jessica O'Reilly and Michael Oppenheimer, 'Climate change prediction: erring on the side of least drama?', *Global Environmental Change* 23(1), 2012: 327–37.

46 See also Carol Farbotko and Helen V. McGregor, 'Copenhagen, climate science and the emotional geographies of climate change', *Australian Geographer* 41(2), 2010: 159–66; George Marshall, *After the floods: Communicating climate change around extreme weather* (Climate Outreach Information Network report, 2014).

47 Sabine Roeser, 'Risk communication, public engagement, and climate change: a role for emotions', *Risk Analysis* 23(6), 2012: 1033–40.

48 Naomi Oreskes, 'The scientist as sentinel', *Limn* 3, 2012, at https://limn.it/articles/the-scientist-as-sentinel/, accessed 15 June 2020.

49 The police and the military are concerned as well. See, for example, Mary N. Hall, 'Law enforcement officers and death notification: a plea for relevant education', *Journal of Police Science and Administration* 10(2), 1982: 189–93; Paul Cowkill, 'Death in the

armed forces: casualty notification and bereavement support in the UK military', *Bereavement Care* 28(2), 2009: 25–30.

50 Hamilton, *Requiem for a Species*, pp. x–xi.

51 Cunsolo and Ellis, 'Ecological grief'.

52 Eva Gifford and Robert Gifford, 'The largely unacknowledged impact of climate change on mental health', *Bulletin of the Atomic Scientists* 72(5), 2016: 292–7.

53 *Manifeste de Dingdingdong*, Dingdingdong éditions, 2013, p. 57. English translation by Damien Bright at https://dingdingdong. org/wp-content/uploads/DingdingdongManifesto.pdf, accessed 8 March 2020, p. 3.

54 *Manifeste*, p. 75. English by Bright, p. 11.

55 *Manifeste*, p. 84. English by Bright, p. 14.

56 Hermant and Pihet, *Le Chemin des possibles*, p. 13.

57 Ibid., p. 122.

58 Ibid., p. 263.

59 *Manifeste de Dingdingdong*, p. 74. English by Bright, p. 10.

60 *Manifeste*, p. 90.

61 *Manifeste*, p. 85. English by Bright, p. 15.

62 Ibid.

63 Ibid.

64 Hermant and Pihet, *Le Chemin des possibles*, p. 74.

65 Ibid., p. 88.

66 Maiko Fujimori and Yosuke Uchitomi, 'Preferences of cancer patients regarding communication of bad news: a systematic literature review', *Japanese Journal of Clinical Oncology* 39(4), 2009: 201–16.

67 Robert Buckman, 'Breaking bad news: why is it still so difficult?', *British Medical Journal* 288(6430), 1984: 1597–9.

68 Ibid.

69 Walter F. Baile et al., 'SPIKES – a six-step protocol for delivering bad news: application to the patient with cancer', *The Oncologist* 5(4), 2000: 302–11.

70 John T. Ptacek and Tara L. Eberhardt, 'Breaking bad news: a review of the literature', *The Journal of the American Medical Association* 276(6), 1996: 496–502.

71 Fujimori and Uchitomi, 'Preferences of cancer patients'.

72 Baile et al., 'SPIKES'.

73 Naoko T. Miyaji, 'The power of compassion: truth-telling among

American doctors in the care of dying patients', *Social Science & Medicine* 36(3), 1993: 249–64.

74 Edgar Landa-Ramírez et al., 'Comunicación de malas noticias en urgencias médicas: Recomendaciones y retos futuros', *Revista Médica del Instituto Mexicano del Seguro Social* 55(6), 2017: 736–47.

75 Tim Rayner and Asher Minns, 'The challenge of communicating unwelcome climate messages', *Tyndall Centre Working Paper* 162, 2015 (Tyndall Centre for Climate Change, University of East Anglia, 2015.)

76 Ibid.

Chapter 2: Regaining our spirits

1 George A. Bonanno, 'Resilience in the face of potential trauma', *Current Directions in Psychological Science* 14(3), 2005: 135–8.

2 For disaster psychologists, resilience to disaster is characterized by the 'absence of dysfunction or psychopathology after a highly undesirable event'. It does not mean the total absence of traumatic symptoms, but their spontaneous and relatively rapid decrease. Bonanno, 'Resilience'; Steven M. Southwick, George A. Bonanno, Ann S. Masten, Catherine Panter-Brick and Rachel Yehuda, 'Resilience definitions, theory, and challenges: interdisciplinary perspectives', *European Journal of Psychotraumatology* 5(1), 2014: article 25338.

3 Traumatized people, that is, who are attempting to recover after the shock, and who are not resilient by the psychologists' definition.

4 George A. Bonanno, Chris R. Brewin, Krzysztof Kaniasty and Annette M. La Greca, 'Weighing the costs of disaster: consequences, risks, and resilience in individuals, families, and communities', *Psychological Science in the Public Interest* 11(1), 2010: 1–49.

5 J. Irene Harris, Susan Thornton and Brian Engdahl, 'The psychospiritual impact of disaster: an overview', in Grant H. Brenner, Daniel H. Bush and Joshua Moses (eds.), *Creating Spiritual and Psychological Resilience. Integrating Care in Disaster Relief Work* (Abingdon: Routledge, 2010), pp. 83–93.

6 Christine Eriksen and Tamara Ditrich, 'The relevance of mindfulness practice for trauma-exposed disaster researchers', *Emotion, Space and Society* 17, 2015: 63–9.

7   See Pablo Servigne and Gauthier Chapelle, *L'Entraide. L'autre loi de la jungle* (Paris: Éditions Les Liens qui Libèrent, 2017).

8   See, for example, James R. Elliott, Timothy J. Haney and Petrice Sams-Abiodun, 'Limits to social capital: comparing network activation in two New Orleans neighborhoods devastated by Hurricane Katrina', *The Sociological Quarterly* 51, 2010: 624–48.

9   Daniel P. Aldrich, 'Social, not physical, infrastructure: the critical role of civil society after the 1923 Tokyo earthquake', *Disasters* 36(3), 2012: 398–419.

10 Krzysztof Z. Kaniasty and Fran H. Norris, 'Distinctions that matter: received social support, perceived social support, and social embeddedness after disasters', in Yuval Neria, Sandro Galea and Fran H. Norris (eds.), *Mental Health and Disasters* (Cambridge: Cambridge University Press, 2009), pp. 175–200.

11 Angelo J. Imperiale and Frank Vanclay, 'Experiencing local community resilience in action: learning from post-disaster communities', *Journal of Rural Studies* 47, 2016: 204–19.

12 Melissa Bernstein and Betty Pfefferbaum, 'Posttraumatic growth as a response to natural disasters in children and adolescents', *Current Psychiatry Reports* 20(5), 2018: 37.

13 Jacques Lecomte, *La Bonté humaine. Altruisme, empathie, générosité* (Paris: Éditions Odile Jacob, 2012).

14 Daniel P. Aldrich, *Building Resilience: Social Capital in Post-Disaster Recovery* (Chicago, IL: University of Chicago Press, 2012).

15 Susan Clayton, Christie Manning and Caroline Hodge, *Beyond Storms & Droughts: The Psychological Impacts of Climate Change* (American Psychological Association and ecoAmerica, 2014), p. 37.

16 Susan K. Whitbourne, 'When disaster strikes others: how your brain responds', *Psychology Today*, 15 March 2011. https://www.psychologytoday.com/us/blog/fulfillment-any-age/201103/when-disaster-strikes-others-how-your-brain-responds, accessed 1 April 2020.

17 R. Nathan Spreng and Raymond A. Mar, 'I remember you: a role for memory in social cognition and the functional neuroanatomy of their interaction', *Brain Research* 1428, 2012: 43–50.

18 Joanna Macy, 'Working through environmental despair', in Theodore Roszak, Mary E. Gomes and Allen D. Kanner (eds.),

Ecopsychology: Restoring the Earth, Healing the Mind (San Francisco, CA: Sierra Club Books, 1995; now handled by Berkeley, CA: Counterpoint), p. 242.

19 Francis Weller, *The Wild Edge of Sorrow: Rituals of Renewal and the Sacred Work of Grief* (Berkeley, CA: North Atlantic Books, 2015), p. xii.

20 Ibid., p. xx.

21 Ibid., p. xix.

22 Ibid., p. 9.

23 Baker, *Collapsing Consciously*, p. 58.

24 Weller, *Wild Edge of Sorrow*, p. xii.

25 Ibid., p. xvi.

26 According to Weller, many people in the self-help groups he facilitates even apologize for crying or feeling sad. Shame is a kind of disease of the soul; it disconnects us from life and from our soul. To get rid of this shame which follows us and shapes us, Weller suggests moving through three stages: the first is not to see yourself as useless, but as wounded; then to shift your attitude from despising yourself to compassion; and finally to break the silence and share with people you trust.

27 Weller, *Wild Edge of Sorrow*, p. 31.

28 Ibid., p. xv.

29 Quoted in Macy and Brown, *Coming Back to Life*.

30 Jean Liedloff, *The Continuum Concept: In Search of Happiness Lost* (London: Penguin Arkana, 1975).

31 Weller, *Wild Edge of Sorrow*, p. xvi.

32 C. Fauré, *Vivre le deuil au jour le jour* (Paris: Albin Michel, 2012).

33 Ibid., p. 70.

34 Ibid., p. 129.

35 Ibid., p. 131.

36 Ibid., p. 134.

37 Cunsolo and Landman, *Mourning Nature*, p. 275.

38 See also Vinciane Despret's book, *Au bonheur des morts* (Paris: La Découverte, 2017). She describes people who continue an inner dialogue with the deceased.

39 Fauré, *Vivre le deuil*, p. 317.

40 This is what some of the rituals of the Work that Reconnects workshops, which we discuss in chapter 8, suggest. Macy and Brown, *Coming Back to Life*.

41 https://www.next-laserie.fr/ – Several episodes are available on YouTube with English subtitles. – Tr.

42 Vincent Lucchese, 'Entretien avec Clément Monfort: "Parler de solutions au problème climatique, c'est mentir aux gens."' Usbek & Rica, 14 October 2017. https://bit.ly/2ynS8Bj.

43 Roy Scranton, 'Learning how to die in the Anthropocene', *The New York Times*, 10 November 2013.

Chapter 3: Moving on

1 Incidentally, 88 per cent thought that businesses try to sell them things they do not need. Joe Tucci, Janise Mitchell and Chris Goddard, *Children's Fears, Hopes and Heroes: Modern Childhood in Australia* (Ringwood, VIC: Australian Childhood Foundation, 2007).

2 Charles S. Carver, Michael F. Scheier and Suzanne C. Segerstrom, 'Optimism', *Clinical Psychology Review* 30, 2010: 879–89.

3 Jean-Pierre Dupuy, *Pour un catastrophisme éclairé. Quand l'impossible est certain*. (Paris: Éditions du Seuil, 2004); 'The precautionary principle and enlightened doomsaying', *Revue de Métaphysique et de Morale* 76(4), 2012: 577–92; English translation available from https://www.cairn.info/revue-de-metaphysique-et-de-morale-2012-4-page-577.htm – Tr.

4 Gabriele Oettingen, Doris Mayer and Sam Portnow, 'Pleasure now, pain later: positive fantasies about the future predict symptoms of depression', *Psychological Science* 27(3), 2016: 345–53.

5 Ulrich Beck, 'The anthropological shock: Chernobyl and the contours of the risk society'. *Berkeley Journal of Sociology* 32, 1987: 153–65; *The Metamorphosis of the World. How Climate Change is Transforming Our Concept of the World* (Cambridge: Polity, 2016).

6 See Gabriele Oettingen, *Rethinking Positive Thinking. Inside the New Science of Motivation* (New York: Current, 2015).

7 Gabrielle Oettingen et al., 'Mental contrasting and goal commitment: the mediating role of energization', *Personality and Social Psychology Bulletin* 35(5), 2009: 608–22.

8 The opposite is also true: fantasizing about an undesirable future while opposing it with thoughts about the actions that might prevent or mitigate it helps to face fears with courage and reduces anxiety. Gunnar Brodersen and Gabrielle Oettingen, 'Mental

contrasting of a negative future with a positive reality regulates state anxiety', *Frontiers in Psychology* 8, 2017: article 1596.

9 Steven Pinker, *The Better Angels of Our Nature: Why Violence Has Declined* (New York: Viking Books, 2011).

10 Jacques Lecomte, *Le Monde va beaucoup mieux que vous ne le croyez* (Paris: Les Arènes, 2017).

11 Johan Norberg, *Progress: Ten Reasons to Look Forward to the Future* (London: Oneworld, 2017).

12 A metaphor used by Bertrand Russell and taken up by Nassim N. Taleb in *The Black Swan: The Impact of the Highly Improbable* (New York: Random House, 2007).

13 Derrick Jensen, *Endgame: Volume 1: The Problem of Civilization* (New York: Seven Stories Press, 2006), p. 329.

14 Ibid., pp. 325–6.

15 Macy and Johnstone, *Active Hope.*

16 Joanna Macy, talk in Grass Valley, California, 24 August 2012. http://peakmoment.tv/journal/joanna-macy-active-hope-recon nects-us-to-life/, accessed 2 June 2020.

17 Jensen, *Endgame*, p. 329.

18 Letter to Lucilius, quoted by A. Comte-Sponville, J. Delumeau and A. Farge, *La Plus Belle Histoire du Bonheur* (Paris: Éditions du Seuil, 2004).

19 Michel M. Egger, *La Terre comme soi-même. Repères pour une écospiritualité* (Geneva: Labor et Fides, 2012), pp. 27–9.

20 Maria Ojala, 'Hope and climate change: the importance of hope for environmental engagement among young people', *Environmental Education Research* 18(5), 2012: 625–42.

21 Z. Janet Yang and LeeAnn Kahlor, 'What, me worry? The role of affect in information seeking and avoidance', *Science Communication* 35(2), 2013: 189–212.

22 Jensen, *Endgame*, p. 331.

23 A quote from Thomas Merton, also known as 'Father Louis' (1915–1968), a spiritual writer, poet and social activist who was interested in interreligious and inter-monastic dialogue. Merton, *The Seven-Storey Mountain* (Boston, MA: Houghton Mifflin Harcourt, 1998), p. 116.

24 Jensen, *Endgame*, pp. 332, 334.

25 Václav Havel, *Disturbing the Peace: A Conversation with Karel Hvížd'ala* (New York: Vintage Books, 1991), pp. 181–2.

26 Margaret J. Wheatley, *Turning to One Another. Simple Conversations to Restore Hope to the Future*, expanded 2nd edn (San Francisco, CA: Berrett-Koehler Publishers, 2002), p. 23.

27 Wilfrid Lupano and Paul Cauuet, *Les Vieux Fourneaux, tome 1, Ceux qui restent* (Paris: Dargaud, 2014).

28 Maggie Astor, 'No children because of climate change? Some people are considering it', *The New York Times*, 18 July 2018. https://nyti.ms/2vsjiVn; Roy Scranton, 'Opinion. Raising my child in a doomed world', *The New York Times*, 19 July 2018; https://nyti.ms/2LnOE5w

29 For example, our society's habit of bringing everything back to numbers and carbon balances; the excessive scale of our groups and political systems (and of the power exerted by them), which leads to equally excessive consequences; the pyramidal and patriarchal hierarchical structure of political systems; our lack of presence within our bodies; our not listening to women; our lack of consideration for intergenerational equity, etc. The subject of the birth rate is difficult because it challenges the pillars of modernity, the individual and personal freedom.

30 Elisabeth Kübler-Ross, *On Children and Death: How Children and Their Parents Can and Do Cope with Death* (New York: Collier Books, 1983).

31 Ursula K. LeGuin, 'The child and the shadow', *The Quarterly Journal of the Library of Congress*, 32(2), 1975: 147–8. First published in Le Guin's novel, *The Tombs of Atuan* (New York: Atheneum, 1971).

Chapter 4: Integrating other ways of knowing

1 A term used by the philosopher Timothy Morton. Climate change or radioactive plutonium are typical examples of this, because even though they can be experienced in real life, they are very difficult for humans to access from a cognitive and theoretical point of view (at any rate not in the way in which classical science could hope to). See Timothy Morton, *Hyperobjects. Philosophy and Ecology after the End of the World* (Minneapolis, MN: University of Minnesota Press, 2013).

2 Ernst F. Schumacher, *A Guide for the Perplexed* (New York: Harper Perennial, 1977).

3 A term introduced by C. West Churchman, 'Guest Editorial: Wicked problems', *Management Science* 14(4), 1967: B141–2. See Valerie A. Brown, John A. Harris and Jacqueline Y. Russell (eds.), *Tackling Wicked Problems: Through the Transdisciplinary Imagination* (London: Earthscan, 2010).

4 Joachim Schellnhuber, 'Terra quasi-incognita: beyond the 2°C line', International Climate Conference in Oxford, 28–30 September 2009.

5 John R. Turnpenny, 'Lessons from post-normal science for climate science-sceptic debates', *Wiley Interdisciplinary Reviews: Climate Change* 3(5), 2012: 397–407.

6 See Pablo Jensen, *Pourquoi la société ne se laisse pas mettre en équations?* (Paris: Éditions du Seuil, 'Science ouverte', 2018).

7 At the turn of the last century, the two largest peer-reviewed journals, *Science* and *Nature*, both devoted special issues to this new discipline. See 'Beyond reductionism', *Science* 284(5411), 1999; 'Complex systems', *Nature* 410(6825), 2001.

8 Arturo Escobar, *Sentir-penser avec la Terre. Une écologie au-delà de l'Occident* (Paris: Éditions du Seuil, 'Anthropocène', 2018), p. 122. Translated from *Sentipensar con la tierra: Nuevas lecturas sobre desarrollo, territorio y diferencia* (Medellín, Colombia: UNAULA – Universidad Autónoma Latinoamericana, 2014). There is no English version of the book as yet, but see Escobar's article, 'Thinking-feeling with the Earth: territorial struggles and the ontological dimension of the epistemologies of the South', *Revista de Antropologia Iberoamericana* 11 (2016): 11–32.

9 See the map of the complexity sciences by Brian Castellani of Kent State University, 2018; https://www.art-sciencefactory.com/complexity-map_feb09.html, accessed 17 April 2020.

10 See for example Chiang H. Ren, *How Systems Form and How Systems Break: A Beginner's Guide for Studying the World* (Cham, Switzerland: Springer, 2017).

11 Brian Goodwin, 'From control to participation via a science of qualities', *ReVision* 21(4), 1999.

12 Goodwin taught this 'holistic science' for many years at Schumacher College, an international centre based in the UK which organizes educational courses on environmental and social issues (http://schumachercollege.org).

13 Adapted from the definition given by the University of Plymouth

(UK) in relation to its Masters of Science course in Holistic Science, taught jointly with Schumacher College. See https://bit.ly/2MvjJEV, accessed 17 April 2020.

14 Phenomenology is a philosophical current directed towards the study of phenomena, lived experience and the contents of consciousness.

15 University of Plymouth, MSc in Holistic Science (as above).

16 See, for example, Pieter H. Punter, 'Free choice profiling', in Sarah E. Kemp, Joanne Hort and Tracey Hollowood (eds.), *Descriptive Analysis in Sensory Evaluation* (Hoboken, NJ: Wiley-Blackwell, 2018), pp. 493–511.

17 See, for example, Stephan P. Harding, Sebastian E. Burch and Françoise Wemelsfelder, 'The assessment of landscape expressivity: a free choice profiling approach', *PLoS ONE* 12(1), 2017: article e0169507.

18 See, for example, Françoise Wemelsfelder, 'The scientific validity of subjective concepts in models of animal welfare', *Applied Animal Behaviour Science* 53(1–2), 1997: 75–88.

19 Goodwin, 'From control to participation'.

20 Baker, *Collapsing Consciously*, p. 8.

21 'Les Trente Glorieuses' – the period from 1945 to 1975, following the end of the Second World War in France. – Tr.

22 Michael Egan, 'Survival science: crisis disciplines and the shock of the environment in the 1970s', *Centaurus* 59 (1–2), 2018: 26–39.

23 Epistemology is the study of forms of knowledge, of our connection to knowledge, structure and the scientific method.

24 Michael E. Soulé, 'What is conservation biology?', *Bioscience* 35(11), 1985: 733.

25 Daniel Kahneman, *Thinking Fast and Slow* (New York: Farrar, Straus and Giroux, 2011).

26 C. Chet Miller and R. Duane Ireland, 'Intuition in strategic decision making: friend or foe in the fast-paced 21st century?', *The Academy of Management Executive* 19(1), 2005: 9–30.

27 Brian Walker and David Salt, *Resilience Thinking. Sustaining Ecosystems and People in a Changing World* (Washington, DC: Island Press, 2006).

28 Jean-François Dortier, 'L'abîme ou la métamorphose? Rencontre avec Edgar Morin', *Sciences Humaines*, February 2009; https://bit.ly/2N1hlWv

29 Isabelle Stengers, *Another Science is Possible: Manifesto for Slow Science* (Cambridge: Polity, 2018), p. 6. Translated by Stephen Muecke from *Une autre science est possible!* (Paris: La Decouverte, 2013).

30 Tom Dedeurwaerdere, *Les Sciences du développement durable pour régir la transition vers la durabilité forte* (Université Catholique de Louvain/Fonds National de la Recherche Scientifique, 2013); also available in English as *Sustainability Science for Strong Sustainability* (London: UCL/FNRS, 2013).

31 Silvio O. Funtowicz and Jerome R. Ravetz, 'Science for the post-normal age', *Futures* 25(7), 1993: 739–55.

32 See, for example, M. Saif, 'World Medical Association Declaration of Helsinki: Ethical Principles for Medical Research Involving Human Subjects', *Journal of the American Medical Association* 284(23), 2000: 3043–5.

33 Stengers, *Another Science is Possible*, p. 4.

34 Latour, *Down to Earth*, p. 25.

35 Arun Agrawal, 'Dismantling the divide between indigenous and scientific knowledge', *Development and Change* 26(3), 1995: 413–39.

36 Fulvio Mazzocchi, 'Western science and traditional knowledge: despite their variations, different forms of knowledge can learn from each other', *EMBO reports* 7(5), 2006: 463–6.

37 The term 'traditional ecological knowledge' refers to 'a cumulative body of knowledge and beliefs, handed down through generations by cultural transmission, about the relationship of living beings (including humans) with one another and with their environment'. Fikret Berkes, 'Traditional ecological knowledge in perspective', in Julian T. Inglis (ed.), *Traditional Ecological Knowledge. Concepts and Cases* (Ottawa: International Development Research Centre, 1993).

38 Henry P. Huntington, 'Using traditional ecological knowledge in science: methods and applications', *Ecological Applications* 10(5), 2000: 1270–4.

39 Daniel Nepstad et al., 'Inhibition of Amazon deforestation and fire by parks and indigenous lands', *Conservation Biology* 20(1), 2006: 65–73.

40 A network of NGOs working on land rights and resources of indigenous peoples and local communities. https://rightsand resources.org/en/#.WjmJeSPyuX0, accessed 2 June 2020.

41 For example, Henry P. Huntington, Robert S. Suydam and Daniel H. Rosenberg, 'Traditional knowledge and satellite tracking as complementary approaches to ecological understanding', *Environmental Conservation* 31(3), 2004: 177–80.

42 Adopted by the United Nations Intergovernmental Science and Policy Platform on Biodiversity and Ecosystem Services (IPBES).

43 Maria Tengö et al., 'Connecting diverse knowledge systems for enhanced ecosystem governance: the multiple evidence base approach', *AMBIO* 43(5), 2014: 579–91.

44 Huntington, 'Traditional knowledge and satellite tracking'.

45 Presentation of the Co-Create research programme by Innoviris (Brussels Institute for Research and Innovation) on http://www.cocreate.brussels

46 Presentation of Co-Create research programme.

47 Cuthbert C. Makondo and David S.G. Thomas, 'Climate change adaptation: linking indigenous knowledge with western science for effective adaptation', *Environmental Science & Policy* 88, 2018: 83–91.

48 John Tharakan, 'Indigenous knowledge systems for appropriate technology development', in Purushothaman Venkatesan (ed.), *Indigenous People* (Rijeka, Croatia: InTechOpen, 2017).

49 Madhav Gadgil, Fikret Berkes and Carl Folke, 'Indigenous knowledge for biodiversity conservation', *AMBIO* 22, 1993: 151–6.

50 Mason H. Durie, 'Understanding health and illness: research at the interface between science and indigenous knowledge', *International Journal of Epidemiology* 33(5), 2004: 1138–43.

51 Gloria Snively and John Corsiglia, 'Discovering indigenous science: implications for science education', *Science Education* 85(1), 2001: 6–34.

52 Alejando Espinoza-Tenorio, Matthias Wolff, Ileana Espejel and Gabriela Montaño-Moctezuma, 'Using traditional ecological knowledge to improve holistic fisheries management: transdisciplinary modeling of a lagoon ecosystem of southern Mexico', *Ecology and Society* 18(2), 2013: article 6.

53 John Parrotta, Youn Yeo-Chang and Leni D. Camacho, 'Traditional knowledge for sustainable forest management and provision of ecosystem services', *International Journal of Biodiversity Science, Ecosystem Services & Management* 12(1–2), 2016: 1–4.

54 Billie R. Dewalt, 'Using indigenous knowledge to improve agri-

culture and natural resource management', *Human Organization* 53(2), 1994: 123–31.

55 Uichol Kim, Young-Shin Park and Donghyun Park, 'The challenge of cross-cultural psychology: the role of the indigenous psychologies', *Journal of Cross-Cultural Psychology* 31(1), 2000: 63–75.
56 David W. Orr, *Ecological Literacy: Education and the Transition to a Postmodern World* (Albany, NY: State University of New York Press, 1992), p. 32.
57 Jerome R. Ravetz, *Scientific Knowledge and its Social Problems* (Oxford: Oxford University Press, 1971).
58 Funtowicz and Ravetz, 'Science for the post-normal age'.
59 Silvio O. Funtowicz and Jerome R. Ravetz, 'Uncertainty, complexity and post-normal science', *Environmental Toxicology and Chemistry* 13(12), 1994: 1882.
60 Giacomo D'Alisa and Giorgos Kallis, 'Post-normal science', in Giacomo D'Alisa, Federico Demaria and Giorgos Kallis, *Degrowth: A Vocabulary for a New Era* (Abingdon, Oxon.: Routledge, 2014).
61 Ibid.
62 Latour, *Down to Earth*, p. 74.
63 Ibid., p. 78.
64 Scientism (or technoscience) is the ideology, perhaps it would be better to say religion, which claims that all the problems of humanity can be solved by applying the scientific method, and believes that this method should have priority over other modes of knowing and representing the world.

Chapter 5: Opening to other visions of the world

1 Paul Kingsnorth and Dougald Hine, *Uncivilisation. The Dark Mountain Manifesto* (East Reydon, Suffolk: Dark Mountain Project, 2014), p. 9.
2 David Abram, *The Spell of the Sensuous: Perception and Language in a More-than-Human World* (New York: Vintage Books, 1997).
3 Bourg, *Une nouvelle Terre*, p. 29.
4 Ibid., p. 27.
5 Nicolas Casaux, 'Le narcissisme pathologique de la civilisation', *Le Partage*, 2018, https://www.partage-le.com/2018/07/21/le-narcissisme-pathologique-de-la-civilisation-par-nicolas-casaux/, accessed 3 April 2020.

6 Latour, *Down to Earth*, p. 64.
7 See Christophe Bonneuil and Jean-Batoste Fressoz, *L'Événement Anthropocène: La Terre, l'histoire et nous* (Paris Éditions du Seuil, 'Points Histoire', 2016), pp. 41–6. English translation by David Fernbach, *The Shock of the Anthropocene: The Earth, History and Us* (London: Verso, 2017).
8 Philippe Descola, *Beyond Nature and Culture* (Chicago, IL: University of Chicago Press, 2013), pp. 197–8. Translated by Janet Lloyd from *Par-delà nature et culture* (Paris: Gallimard, 2005).
9 Pope Francis, *Lettre encyclique Laudato si'. La sauvegarde de la maison commune*, Vatican, 18 June 2015.
10 Ibid., § 116. English version from Vatican website.
11 Ibid., § 117.
12 Bruno Latour, *We Have Never Been Modern* (London: Harvester-Wheatsheaf, 1993). Translation by Catherine Porter from *Nous n'avons jamais été modernes. Essai d'anthropologie systématique* (Paris: La Découverte, 1991); *An Inquiry into Modes of Existence: An Anthropology of the Modern* (Cambridge, MA: Harvard University Press, 2013). Translation by Catherine Porter from *Enquête sur les modes d'existence. Une anthropologie des modernes* (Paris: La Découverte, 2012); Latour, *Down to Earth*.
13 Latour, *Down to Earth*, pp. 63–4.
14 In the Middle Ages Westerners were closer to analogical thinking (alchemy, emblems, interpretation of the virtues of plants from their form, etc.) than to naturalism. In its history, the West has not always been modern. There is therefore one (or more) pre-modern ontology or ontologies which we can dig up and take on in order to extract elements that could help us to imagine new ones.
15 Even though this separation is seriously undermined by ethology and the study of cognitive evolution. See Frans de Waal, *Sommes-nous trop bêtes pour comprendre l'intelligence des animaux?* (Paris: Éditions Les Liens qui Libèrent, 2016). English version, *Are We Smart Enough To Know How Smart Animals Are?* (New York: W.W. Norton, 2016).
16 Escobar, *Sentir-penser avec la Terre*, p. 10.
17 Ibid., p. 122.
18 Arne Næss, 'The shallow and the deep, long-range ecology movement: a summary', *Inquiry* 16(1–4), 1973: 95–100.

19 Valeria Wagner, 'Récits à bascule: Les cas de La villa de César Aira et Embassytown de China Miéville', *EU-topias* 12, 2016: 119–31.

20 For the 'pluriverse', see also Arturo Escobar, *Designs for the Pluriverse: Radical Interdependence, Autonomy, and the Making of Worlds* (Durham, NC: Duke University Press, 2018); Ashish Kothari, Ariel Salleh, Arturo Escobar, Federico Demaria and Alberto Acosta, *Pluriverse: A Post-Development* Dictionary (Tulika Books: New Delhi, 2019), also https://www.radicalecologicaldemocracy.org/pluriverse/ – Tr.

21 Latour, *Down to Earth*.

22 Interview with Hugues Dorzée: 'Bruno Latour: "Les climatosceptiques nous ont déclaré la guerre"', *Imagine demain le monde*, May–June 2018, pp. 85–8.

23 Philippe Descola, *La Composition des mondes. Entretiens avec Pierre Charbonnier* (Paris: Flammarion, 2017), pp. 347–8, quoted in Léna Balaud and Antoine Chopot, 'Nous ne sommes pas seuls: Les alliances sylvestres et la division politique', Intervention à la semaine 'Greffer de l'ouvert: matériaux pour des écoles de la terre', Lachaux, 28 August–1 September 2017. http://ladivision-politique.toile-libre.org/nous-ne-sommes-pas-seuls-rencontres-greffer-de-louvert/, accessed 3 April 2020.

24 Escobar, *Sentir-penser avec la Terre*, p. 26.

25 Valérie Cabanes, *Un nouveau droit pour la Terre. Pour en finir avec l'écocide* (Paris: Éditions du Seuil, 'Anthropocène', 2016).

26 At the international level, it is reflected in the Universal Declaration of Rights of Mother Earth, adopted in Cochabamba in Bolivia in 2010. See https://www.rightsofmotherearth.com, accessed 5 April 2020.

27 Valérie Cabanes, 'Les rivières et les océans sont des personnes', *Orbs, l'autre Planète*, no spécial #Eau, 2018.

28 Latour, *Inquiry into Modes of Existence*, p. 143.

29 Ibid., p. 17.

30 Escobar, *Sentir-penser avec la Terre*, p. 131.

31 Dorzee, 'Bruno Latour: "Les climatosceptiques nous ont déclaré la guerre"'.

32 Quoted in Escobar, *Sentir-penser avec la Terre*, p. 137.

33 Christophe Bonneuil, in Jade Lingaard (ed.), *Éloge des mauvaises herbes. Ce que nous devons à la ZAD* (Paris: Les Liens qui Libèrent, 2018), p. 106.

34 'Feeling-thinking [*sentir-penser*] with the territory implies think-ing simultaneously with the heart and the mind, or, as the col-leagues of Chiapas, inspired by the Zapatista experience, put it so well, "reasoning with the heart". Feeling-thinking is the way in which territorialized communities have learned to live.' Escobar, *Sentir-penser avec la Terre*, p. 29.

35 Latour, *Down to Earth*, p. 90.

36 See Alessandro Pignocchi, *Anent. Nouvelles des Indiens Jivaros* (Paris: Éditions Steinkis, 2016).

37 A region in northern France. – Tr.

38 Alessandro Pignocchi, *Petit traité d'écologie sauvage*, Vols 1 and 2 (Paris: Éditions Steinkis, 2017, 2018).

39 The reference is to a text by Déborah Danowski and Eduardo Viveiros de Castro, 'L'arrêt de monde', translated from Portuguese into French and published in June 2014 in Émilie Hache (ed.) *De l'univers clos au monde infini* (Bellevaux, Rhone-Alpe: Editions Dehors 2014), pp. 221–339. An updated and expanded version was published in English as Déborah Danowski and Eduardo Viveiros de Castro, *The Ends of the World* (Cambridge: Polity, 2017) – Tr.

40 Anna Lowenhaupt Tsing, *The Mushroom at the End of the World: On the Possibility of Life in Capitalist Ruins* (Princeton, NJ: Princeton University Press, 2015). – Tr.

41 Olivier Julien, *Tchernobyl, Fukushima: vivre avec*, ARTE France, Bellota Films, April 2016.

42 Hermant and Pihet, *Le Chemin des possibles*, p. 283.

43 Christophe Bonneuil in Lingaard, *Éloge des mauvaises herbes*, p. 111.

44 ZAD (*Zone à defendre*) refers to a direct-action occupation of a specific area to physically prevent a development project. – Tr.

45 Geneviève Pruvost, in Lingaard, *Éloge des mauvaises herbes*, p. 83.

46 Escobar, *Sentir-penser avec la Terre*, p. 107.

47 Ibid., p. 107.

48 Latour, *Down to Earth*, p. 53. During the Second World War, the Vichy regime in France encouraged a 'back to the land' movement, including reforestation, the draining of marshes, etc. – Tr.

49 A location near Nantes where there was a long-term ZAD, a resistance movement against plans to build a new airport. The

collection *Éloge des mauvaises herbes (In Praise of Weeds)*, cited several times in this book, grew out of the experience of this ZAD. – Tr.

50 John Seed, Joanna Macy, Pat Fleming and Arne Næss, *Thinking Like a Mountain. Toward a Council of all Beings* (Philadelphia, PA: New Society Publishers, 1988), p. 36. John Seed's words, in his essay, 'Spirit of the Earth', are 'If we enter the rainforest and allow our energies to merge with the energies we find there . . . a most profound change in consciousness takes place. We realize that our psyche is itself a part of the rainforests. I am protecting the rainforest becomes I am part of the rainforest protecting myself. I am that part of the rainforest recently emerged into thinking.' – Tr.

51 The French word I have translated here and elsewhere as 'Earth-Dwellers' or 'dwellers on the earth' is *terrestres*, but the English 'terrestrials' does not fully capture how this term is used by Latour and particularly in later sections of the present book. – Tr.

52 Latour, *Down to Earth*, p. 86; translation modified.

53 Bonneuil in Lingaard, *Éloge des mauvaises herbes*, p. 112.

54 Starhawk in Lingaard, *Éloge des mauvaises herbes*, pp. 125–7.

55 Latour, *Down to Earth*, p. 56.

56 Lingaard, *Éloge des mauvaises herbes*, p. 26.

57 Vandana Shiva in Lingaard, *Éloge des mauvaises herbes*, p. 62.

58 Balaud and Chopot, 'Nous ne sommes pas seuls'.

59 Danowski and Viveiros de Castro, 'L'arrêt de monde'.

60 Paul Hawken, *Blessed Unrest: How the Largest Social Movement in History is Restoring Grace, Justice, and Beauty to the World* (London: Penguin Books, 2008), p. 4.

61 Balaud and Chopot, 'Nous ne sommes pas seuls'.

62 Jodi Dean, quoted in Balaud and Chopot, 'Nous ne sommes pas seuls'.

63 Balaud and Chopot, 'Nous ne sommes pas seuls'.

64 See, for example, Emma Donada, 'Argentine: ces banlieues qui ont fait plier Monsanto', *Reporterre*, February 2018; https://bit.ly/2AWCyj5

65 Baptiste Morizot, *Les Diplomates. Cohabiter avec les loups sur une nouvelle carte du vivant* (Marseille: Wildproject, 2016).

66 Balaud and Chopot, 'Nous ne sommes pas seuls'.

Chapter 6: Telling other stories

1 David Graeber, preface to Lingaard, *Éloge des mauvaises herbes*, p. 13.
2 Nicholas Carr, 'Technology: techno-fix troubles', *Nature* 495, 2013: 45.
3 Kingsnorth and Hine, *Uncivilisation*, p. 4.
4 Thomas Berry, 'The new story: Comments on the origin, identification and transmission of values', *CrossCurrents* 37, 1987: 187–99.
5 Lev Grossman, 'Zombies Are the New Vampires', *Time*, 9 April 2009.
6 Nancy Huston, *The Tale-Tellers: A Short Study of Humankind* (Toronto: McArthur & Co. 2008). Translated by the author from *L'Espèce fabulatrice* (Arles: Actes Sud, 2008).
7 Cyril Dion, *Petit Manuel de résistance contemporaine. Récits et stratégies pour transformer le monde* (Arles: Actes Sud, 2018).
8 Ibid., p. 57.
9 Ibid., p. 96.
10 Yuval Noah Harari, *Sapiens: A Brief History of Humankind* (London: Harvill Secker, 2014), n.p.
11 Mircea Eliade, *Myth and Reality* (New York, NY: Harper and Row, 1963), p. 2.
12 Joseph Campbell, *The Power of Myth* (New York, NY: Anchor Books, 1991), p. 15.
13 Harari, *Sapiens*, n.p.
14 George Marshall, *Don't Even Think About It: Why Our Brains are Wired to Ignore Climate Change* (London: Bloomsbury, 2014), p. 105.
15 Huston, *The Tale-Tellers*.
16 See Frankl, *Man's Search for Meaning*.
17 Ibid., p. 85.
18 Quoted in Émilie Hache (ed.), *Reclaim. Recueil de textes écoféministes* (Paris: Éditions Cambourakis, 2016), p. 18.
19 See Peter Kropotkin, *Mutual Aid: A Factor in Evolution*, rev. edn (London: William Heinemann, 1904), pp. 215–62.
20 The so-called 'glorious years' of the French economy. See earlier note. – Tr.
21 Luc Semal, 'Politiques locales de décroissance', in Agnes Sinaï

(ed.), *Penser la décroissance. Politiques de l'Anthropocène* (Paris: Presses de Sciences Po, 2013), pp. 139–58.

22 Ursula Le Guin, *The Language of the Night* (New York: Ultramarine Publishing, 1979), p. 78.

23 Isabelle Stengers, 'Sf antiviral ou comment spéculer sur ce qui n'est pas là', in *Cahiers d'enquêtes politiques* (Vaulx-en-Velin: Les Éditions du Mondes à faire, 2016), pp. 107–24.

24 Isabelle Stengers, 'Ma science-fiction', conférence dans le cadre de la résidence d'écrivain d'Alice Rivières à l'Espace Khiasma, November 2015; http://www.khiasma.net/rdv/ma-science-fiction/, accessed 4 April 2020.

25 Philippe Vion-Dury, 'Alain Damasio: "Rendre désirable autre chose que le transhumanisme"', socialter.fr, 7 June 2018; http://www.socialter.fr/fr/module/99999672/682/alain_dama sio__qrendre_dsirable_autre_chose_que_le_transhumanismeq, accessed 2 June 2020.

26 Le Guin, *The Language of the Night*, p. 58.

27 Stengers, 'Ma science-fiction'.

28 See Kathleen M. Weigart and Robin J. Crews (eds.), *Teaching for Justice. Concepts and Models for Service-Learning in Peace Studies* (Washington, DC: American Association for Higher Education, 1999).

29 Margaret Atwood's 'MaddAddam' trilogy consists of three novels, *Oryx and Crake* (London: Bloomsbury, 2003), *The Year of the Flood* (London: Virago, 2010) and *MaddAddam* (London: Bloomsbury, 2013) – Tr.

30 Richard A. Northover, 'Ecological apocalypse in Margaret Atwood's *MaddAddam* trilogy', *Studia Neophilologica* 88(Suppl. 1), 2016: 81–95.

31 Andrew S. Greer, 'Final showdown: *MaddAddam* by Margaret Atwood', *The New York Times*, 6 March 2013.

32 Dion, *Petit Manuel*, p. 111.

33 Jean Hegland, *Into the Forest* (New York: Bantam Books, 1997).

34 Chris Martenson, *The Crash Course: The Unsustainable Future of Our Economy, Energy, and Environment* (New York: Wiley, 2011).

35 Bill McKibben, 'A world at war', *The New Republic*, 15 August 2016.

36 The research and development programme that led to the first atomic bomb.

37 Dennis Bartels, 'Wartime mobilization to counter severe global climate change', *Human Ecology* 10, 2001: 229–32.

38 See Servigne and Chapelle, *L'Entraide*, ch. 5.

39 Laurence L. Delina and Mark Diesendorf, 'Is wartime mobilisation a suitable policy model for rapid national climate mitigation?', *Energy Policy* 58, 2013: 371–80.

40 Johannes Kester and Benjamin K. Sovacool, 'Torn between war and peace: critiquing the use of war to mobilize peaceful climate action', *Energy Policy* 104, 2017: 50–5.

41 The National Council of Resistance (Conseil national de la Résistance or CNR) co-ordinated the various French resistance groups working against the Axis forces during the Second World War. – Tr.

42 An idea which we owe to our friends Marc Pier and Luc Sonveau.

43 An initiative that began in the Basque region of France in 2013 and now operates throughout Europe. See https://alternatiba.eu/en/ – Tr.

44 The Décroissance or 'degrowth' movement developed in the 1980s around the ideas of the Romanian-American mathematician and economist Nicholas Georgescu-Roegen and the French historian and philosopher Jacques Grinevald. It has been particularly influential in France. – Tr.

45 https://transitionnetwork.org/ – Tr.

46 A documentary directed by Cyril Dion and Mélanie Laurent. It was released in 2015: https://www.demain-lefilm.com/en/film – Tr.

47 See Christopher Landry's documentary film, *Joanna Macy and the Great Turning*, 2014.

48 Paul Kingsnorth, 'Why I stopped believing in environmentalism and started the Dark Mountain Project', *The Guardian*, 29 April 2010.

49 Ibid.

50 Ibid.

51 Kingsnorth and Hine, *Uncivilisation*.

52 Kingsnorth, 'Why I stopped believing'.

53 Ibid.

54 Ibid.

55 Kingsnorth and Hine, *Uncivilisation*.

56 Ibid., p. 2.

57 Ibid., p. 7.
58 Ibid., p. 8.

Interlude: Entry to collapsosophy

1 See Michel M. Egger, *Soigner l'esprit, guérir la Terre. Introduction à l'écopsychologie* (Geneva: Labor et Fides, 2015); Michel M. Egger, *Écopsychologie. Retrouver notre lien avec la Terre* (Saint-Julien-en-Genevois: Éditions Jouvence, 2017).
2 Much of the methodology is described in Macy and Brown, *Coming Back to Life.*
3 See http://roseaux-dansants.org
4 See http://terreveille.be Two of us are facilitators within this organization.
5 Egger, *Soigner l'esprit*, p 247.
6 Hache, *Reclaim*, p. 14.
7 Ibid., p. 40.
8 Ibid., p. 33.

Chapter 7: Weaving connections

1 The distancing of the structures of religion from public life has led to a desacralization of the world, or more precisely, according to Jean-Pierre Dupuy, a denial of the sacred character of our rational thought. See Jean-Pierre Dupuy, *The Mark of the Sacred* (Redwood City, CA: Stanford University Press, 2013). Translated by M.B. Debevoise from *La Marque du sacré* (Paris: Flammarion, 2010).
2 Abdennour Bidar, *Les Tisserands. Réparer ensemble le tissu déchiré du monde* (Paris: Les Liens qui libèrent, 2018).
3 About forty different types of metal are required to make a smart-phone. See Guillaume Pitron, *The Rare Metals War: The Hidden Face of the Energy and Digital Transition*, translated by Bianca Jacobsohn (London: Scribe, 2020); *La Guerre des métaux rares. La face cachée de la transition énergétique et numérique* (Paris: Les liens qui libèrent, 2018).
4 Servigne and Chapelle, *L'Entraide.*
5 Daniel Smith et al., 'Cooperation and the evolution of hunter-gatherer storytelling', *Nature Communications* 8(1), 2017: 1–9.

6 David S. Wilson and Edward O. Wilson, 'Rethinking the theoretical foundation of sociobiology', *The Quarterly Review of Biology* 82(4), 2007: 327–48. Original English from p. 335. This theme is developed in Wilson, *The Social Conquest of Earth*.

7 See Servigne and Chapelle, *L'Entraide*, chs 3 and 4.

8 Jonathan Haidt, *The Righteous Mind. Why Good People are Divided by Politics and Religion* (New York: Vintage, 2012), p. 221.

9 Projections for 2050 vary between 200 million and 1 billion displaced people due to environmental factors (floods, droughts, etc.). These do not take into account other factors that may occur such as wars or epidemics. See Susanne Melde, 'Data on environmental migration: how much do we know?', *Global Migration Data Analysis Centre Data Briefing Series Issue 2* (Geneva: International Organization for Migration, 2016); Robert McLeman and Franccois Gemenne (eds.), *Routledge Handbook of Environmental Displacement and Migration* (London: Routledge, 2018); Suchul Kang and Elfatih A.B. Eltahir, 'North China plain threatened by deadly heatwaves due to climate change and irrigation', *Nature Communications* 9, 2018: article 2894.

10 It is generally accepted that we have to wait for agriculture, sedentarization and the first cities to emerge first, that is, hierarchical social structures date from less than 8,000 years ago.

11 Personal communication. See also Marc Halévy, *Réseaux, l'autre manière de vivre* (Escalquens: Éditions Oxus, 2015).

12 Quoted by Isabelle Attard, 'Plutôt que Parcoursup ... si on essayait l'école anarchiste?', *Reporterre*, 26 June 2018; https://bit. ly/2KLVvEH

13 Frederic Laloux, *Reinventing Organizations: A Guide to Creating Organizations Inspired by the Next Stage of Human Consciousness* (London: Nelson Parker, 2014).

14 Macy and Brown, *Coming Back to Life*, p. 56.

15 Baker, *Collapsing Consciously*, p. 66.

16 See Janine Benyus, *Biomimétisme. Quand la nature inspire des innovations durables* (Paris: Rue de l'Échiquier, 2011). Also, for a critical look at the use that society has made of this concept, see G. Chapelle and M. Decoust, *Le Vivant comme modèle. La voie du biomimétisme* (Paris: Albin Michel, 2015).

17 Aldo Leopold, *A Sand County Almanac* (Oxford: Oxford University Press, [1949] 1968), p. 189.

18 For our civilization, see Alan Weisman's stylish exercise in *The World Without Us* (New York: Thomas Dunne Books, St Martin's Press, 2007).

19 Liisa Tyrväinen, Stephan Pauleit, Klaus Seeland and Sjerp de Vries, 'Benefits and uses of urban forests and trees', in Cecil Konijnendijk, Kjell Nilsson, Thomas Randrup and Jasper Schipperijn (eds), *Urban Forests and Trees* (Cham, Switzerland: Springer, 2005), pp. 81–114.

20 Agnes E. Van Den Berg and Mariëtte H.G. Custers, 'Gardening promotes neuroendocrine and affective restoration from stress', *Journal of Health Psychology* 16(1), 2011: 3–11.

21 Roger S. Ulrich, 'View through a window may influence recovery from surgery', *Science* 224(4647), 1984: 420–1.

22 See, for example, Frances E. Kuo and William C. Sullivan, 'Environment and crime in the inner city: does vegetation reduce crime?', *Environment and Behavior* 33(3), 2001: 343–67.

23 Monica Gagliano and Mavra Grimonprez, 'Breaking the silence – language and the making of meaning in plants', *Ecopsychology* 7(3), 2015: 145–52.

24 Steve Fierens, *L'Impact des théories de l'effondrement sur le mouvement des ZAD. Étude de cas chez les zadistes de Roybon et de Notre-Dame-des-Landes.* Mémoire présenté en vue de l'obtention du grade de master en sciences de la population et du développement, Université Libre de Bruxelles, 2018, p. 64.

25 Watch the videos of the L214 association on industrial breeding (http://l214.com/video), or Gabriella Cowperthwaite's movie *Blackfish* (2013), denouncing the captivity of whales and dolphins.

26 See, for example, Julie K. Schutten, 'Perspectives on human–animal communication: internatural communication', *Environmental Communication* 9(1), 2015: 137–9; Raymond T. Bradley, 'The psychophysiology of intuition: a quantum-holographic theory of nonlocal communication', *World Futures* 63(2), 2007: 61–97; Harald Walach and Nikolaus von Stillfried, 'Generalised quantum theory. Basic idea and general intuition: a background story and overview', *Axiomathes* 21(2), 2011: 185–209.

27 Maja Kooitstra and Benjamin Stassen, *Communiquer avec les arbres. Expériences spirituelles entre l'Homme et la Nature* (Paris: Le Courrier du Livre, 2000).

28 Stefano Mancuso and Alessandro Viola, *Brilliant Green: The Surprising History and Science of Plant Intelligence* (Washington, DC: Island Press, 2015). Translated into English by Joan Benham from *Verde brillante: Sensibilità e intelligenza del mondo vegetale* (Florence and Milan: Giunti, 2013).

29 Brian J. Pickles et al., 'Transfer of 13C between paired Douglas-fir seedlings reveals plant kinship effects and uptake of exudates by ectomycorrhizas', *New Phytologist* 214(1), 2017: 400–11.

30 František Baluška, 'Recent surprising similarities between plant cells and neurons', *Plant Signaling & Behavior* 5(2), 2010: 87–9.

31 Alessandro Pelizzon and Monica Gagliano, 'The sentience of plants: animal rights and rights of nature intersecting?', *Australian Animal Protection Law Journal* 11, 2015, 5–14.

32 Stephen H. Buhner, *Plant Intelligence and the Imaginal Realm: Beyond the Doors of Perception into the Dreaming of Earth* (Rochester, VT: Inner Traditions/Bear & Company, 2014), p. 122.

33 Suzanne W. Simard, 'Mycorrhizal networks facilitate tree communication, learning, and memory', in *Memory and Learning in Plants* (New York: Springer, 2018), pp. 191–213.

34 Ibid.

35 Terr'Eveille, 'Earthawake', is an organization that runs Work that Reconnects workshops based on the work of Joanna Macy in Belgium, France and the French-speaking areas of Switzerland; Gauthier Chapelle was one of the founders. See http://www.ter-reveille.be/ – Tr.

36 In contact with Bill Plotkin and Geneen Haugen at a seminar, 'Coming home to an animate world: a way of ceremony and conversation', Schumacher College, 7–11 September 2015.

37 Ram Dass (Richard Alpert), *Be Here Now* (San Cristobal, NM: Lama Foundation, 1971).

38 Despite their bad reputation in our pasteurized culture, only one bacterium in a hundred thousand is pathogenic for us, the others being indifferent (and most often beneficial, directly or indirectly). Margaret McFall-Ngai, 'Adaptive immunity: care for the community', *Nature* 445(7124), 2007: 153.

39 Nicholas J. Butterfield, 'Modes of pre-Ediacaran multicellularity', *Precambrian Research* 173(1), 2009: 201–11.

40 Appearance of the first liverworts (a 'primitive' group of mosses still represented on our pavements), from a group of freshwater

algae. Claudia V. Rubinstein et al., 'Early Middle Ordovician evidence for land plants in Argentina (eastern Gondwana)', *The New Phytologist* 188(2), 2010: 365–9.

41 Christine Strullu-Derrien, Paul Kenrick and Marc-André Selosse, 'Origins of the mycorrhizal symbioses', in Francis Martin (ed.) *Molecular Mycorrhizal Symbiosis* (Hoboken, NJ: Wiley-Blackwell, 2016), pp. 1–20.

42 Sean P. Modesto et al., 'The oldest parareptile and the early diversification of reptiles', *Proceedings of the Royal Society B: Biological Sciences* 282(1801), 2015: article 20141912.

43 Shundong Bi et al., 'Three new Jurassic euharamiyidan species reinforce early divergence of mammals', *Nature* 514(7524), 2014: 579–84.

44 Simon Tavaré et al., 'Using the fossil record to estimate the age of the last common ancestor of extant primates', *Nature* 416(6882), 2002: 726–9.

45 Recent discoveries have increased the age of *Homo sapiens* from 200,000 to 315,000 years; see Jean-Jacques Hublin et al., 'New fossils from Jebel Irhoud, Morocco and the pan-African origin of *Homo sapiens*', *Nature* 546(7657), 2017: 289–92.

46 Quoted by Irina Ionita, 'L'empathie et les générations futures: une leçon iroquoise', *Finance & Bien Commun* 37–38(2), 2010: 122.

47 Ibid., p. 157.

48 See Frank White, *The Overview Effect. Space Exploration and Human Evolution* (Reston, VA: American Institute of Aeronautics and Astronautics, 1987); Jean-Pierre Goux, *Admirer la Terre en entier*, TEDxVaugirardRoad, 2016 (Version with English subtitles, 'Seeing the Earth like never before', at https://www.youtube.com/watch?v=Boe8F09OvWI); Sebastian V. Grevsmuhl, *La Terre vue d'en haut. L'invention de l'environnement global* (Paris, Éditions du Seuil, 'Anthropocène', 2014), p. 205.

49 The short film *Overview* can be viewed at https://vimeo.com/55073825 – for the subsequent feature-length film, *Planetary*, see https://vimeo.com/60234866 – Tr.

50 Alain Damasio's novels include *La Zone du Dehors* ('The Outer Zone', 1999), *La Horde du Contrevent* ('The Windwalkers', 2004), and *Les furtifs* ('The Stealthy Ones', 2019). So far, none have been translated into English. – Tr.

51 Vion-Dury, 'Alain Damasio'.
52 Egger, *Écospiritualité*, p. 78.
53 Dupuy, *La Marque du sacré*, p. 29.
54 Corine Pelluchon, *Éthique de la consideration* (Paris: Éditions du Seuil, 2018).
55 Baker, *Collapsing Consciously*, p. 6.
56 Macy and Johnstone, *Active Hope*, p. 43–5.
57 Baker, *Collapsing Consciously*, p. 6.
58 Macy and Brown, *Coming Back to Life*, n.p.
59 Bourg, *Une nouvelle Terre*, p. 104.
60 Ibid., p. 69.
61 Ibid., p. 16.
62 Ibid., p. 104.

Chapter 8: Growing up and settling down

1 Bill Plotkin, *Nature and the Human Soul: Cultivating Wholeness and Community in a Fragmented World* (Novato, CA: New World Library, 2010), p. 9.
2 See Pitron, *The Rare Metals War*.
3 Christian Arnsperger, *Éthique de l'existence post-capitaliste. Pour un militantisme existentiel* (Paris: Éditions du Cerf, 2009).
4 Fauré, *Vivre le deuil*, p. 194
5 Ernest Becker, *The Denial of Death* (New York: Free Press, 1973).
6 Baker, *Collapsing Consciously*, p. 8.
7 Vion-Dury, 'Alain Damasio'.
8 B. Kauth, 'MKP in evolutionary context: who we have become', *ManKind Project*, 14 February 2012; https://bit.ly/2w3ZDKZ
9 Plotkin, *Nature and the Human Soul*.
10 Ibid., p. 304.
11 Also known as the 'New Warrior Training Adventure'; see https://mankindproject.org/
12 Pema Chödrön, *When Things Fall Apart: Heart Advice for Difficult Times* (Boston, MA: Shambhala, 2010), p. 3.
13 Carl Gustav Jung, *Psychology and Religion*, quoted in Le Guin, 'The Child and the Shadow', p. 143.
14 Kauth, 'MKP in evolutionary context'.
15 Hache, *Reclaim*, p. 18.

16 Françoise d'Eaubonne, *Le Féminisme ou la mort* (Paris: Pierre Horay, 1974), p. 220–1.

17 Jeanne Burgart Goutal, 'Amazones et sorcières: deux récits d'origine dans la pensée écoféministe', communication aux Journées d'étude de l'Association Charles Gide, 'Fictions originelles, états hypothétiques et conjectures historiques dans la pensée économique', 2016.

18 Anne L. Barstow, *Witchcraze. New History of the European Witch Hunts* (London: Pandora, 1994), cited in Silvia Federici, *Caliban and the Witch* (Brooklyn, NY: Autonomedia, 2004), p. 208.

19 Francis Bacon [1620], quoted in Pierre Hadot, *Le Voile d'Isis. Essai sur l'histoire de l'idée de nature* (Paris, Gallimard, 2004), p. 107.

20 Francis Bacon [1620], quoted in Carolyn Merchant, *The Death of Nature. Women, Ecology, and the Scientific Revolution* (New York: HarperOne, [1980] 1990), p. 169.

21 Lorène Lavocat, 'Violences sexuelles, violence à la Terre, une même culture', *Reporterre*, 28 October 2017; https://bit.ly/2OHtTmD

22 Francis Bacon [1623] quoted in Merchant, *The Death of Nature*, p. 168.

23 Federici, *Caliban and the Witch*, p. 164.

24 Starhawk, *Dreaming the Dark: Magic, Sex and Politics* (London: Unwin Paperbacks (Mandala), 1990), p. xxvii.

25 Patrick Blennerhassett, 'Many of my childhood friends are dead. Is masculinity to blame?', *The Guardian*, 20 June 2018.

26 Dan Bilsker, Andrea S. Fogarty and Matthew A. Wakefield, 'Critical issues in men's mental health', *Canadian Journal of Psychiatry* 63(9), 2018: 590–6.

27 Hache, *Reclaim*, p. 39.

28 http://womanstandsshining.strikingly.com; https://youtu.be/vCLWJr9sXNo

29 Annie Adams, 'Pat McCabe: The healing of an archetypal wounding of humanity', Schumacher College Blog, 6 April 2016; https://www.schumachercollege.org.uk/blog/the-healing-of-an-archetypal-wounding-of-humanity

30 Jacques Ferber, *L'Amant tantrique. L'homme sur la voie de la sexualité sacrée* (Gap, France: Le Souffle d'Or, 2007).

31 Kauth, 'MKP in evolutionary context'.

32 Yinon M. Bar-On, Rob Phillips and Ron Milo, 'The biomass distribution on Earth', *Proceedings of the National Academy of Sciences* 115(25), 2018: article 201711842.

33 James E.M. Watson et al., 'Catastrophic declines in wilderness areas undermine global environment targets', *Current Biology* 26(21), 2016: 2929–34.

34 Kendall R. Jones et al., 'The location and protection status of earth's diminishing marine wilderness', *Current Biology* 28(16), 2018: 1–7.

35 James R. Allan, Oscar Venter and James E.M. Watson, 'Temporally inter-comparable maps of terrestrial wilderness and the Last of the Wild', *Nature Scientific Data* 4, 2017: article 170187.

36 'Indoor air pollution: new EU research reveals higher risks than previously thought', *European Commission*, Press release IP/03/1278, 22 September 2003; https://bit.ly/2Mg9oAC

37 'The not-so great outdoors?', Ribble Cycles Blog, 15 February 2017; https://www.ribblecycles.co.uk/blog/not-great-outdoors/, accessed 5 April 2020.

38 That is, less than an hour each day. Damian Carrington, 'Three-quarters of UK children spend less time outdoors than prison inmates', *The Guardian*, 25 March 2016.

39 See Masashi Soga and Kevin J. Gaston, 'Extinction of experience: the loss of human-nature interactions', *Frontiers in Ecology and the Environment* 14(2), 2016: 94–101.

40 Richard Louv, *Last Child in the Wood: Saving our Children from Nature-Deficit Disorder* (New York: Algonquin Books, 2005).

41 For a survey of these studies, see Florence Williams, *The Nature Fix. Why Nature Makes Us Happier, Healthier, and More Creative* (New York: W.W. Norton & Company, 2017).

42 Michael Soulé and Reed Noss, 'Rewilding and biodiversity: complementary goals for continental conservation', *Wild Earth* 8(3), 1998: 18–28.

43 Jamie Lorimer et al., 'Rewilding: science, practice, and politics', *Annual Review of Environment and Resources* 40(1), 2015: 39–62.

44 Paul Shepard, *Coming Home to the Pleistocene* (Washington, DC: Island Press, 1998).

45 Edward O. Wilson, *Half-Earth. Our Planet's Fight for Life* (New York: Liveright Publishing, 2016).

46 Mark Nord, A.E. Luloff and Jeffrey C. Bridger, 'The association of forest recreation with environmentalism', *Environment and Behavior* 30(2), 1998: 235–46; Caren Cooper, Lincoln Larson, Ashley Dayer, Richard Stedman and Dan Decker, 'Are wildlife recreationists conservationists? Linking hunting, birdwatching, and pro-environmental behavior', *The Journal of Wildlife Management* 79(3), 2015: 446–57.

47 Silvia Collado, José A. Corraliza, Henk Staats and Miguel Ruiz, 'Effect of frequency and mode of contact with nature on children's self-reported ecological behaviors', *Journal of Environmental Psychology* 41, 2015: 65–73.

48 Carina R. Fernee, Leiv E. Gabrielsen, Anders J.W. Andersen and Terje Mesel, 'Unpacking the black box of wilderness therapy: a realist synthesis', *Qualitative Health Research* 27(1), 2017: 114–29.

49 Baker, *Collapsing Consciously*, p. 17.

50 Plotkin, *Nature and the Human Soul*, p. 3.

51 Bill Kauth and Zoe Alowan, *We Need Each Other: Building Gift Community* (Ashland, OR: Silver Light Publications, 2011), p. 13.

52 Charles Eisenstein, *Sacred Economics: Money, Gift, and Society in the Age of Transition* (Berkeley, CA: North Atlantic Books, Evolver Editions, 2011), pp. 424–5.

53 Robin I.M. Dunbar, 'Coevolution of neocortical size, group size and language in humans', *Behavioral and Brain Sciences* 16(4), 1993: 681–94, cited in Kauth and Alowan, *We Need Each Other*, p. 15. See also Marco Casari and Claudio Tagliapietra, 'Group size in social-ecological systems', *Proceedings of the National Academy of Sciences* 115(11), 2018: 2728–33.

54 For sceptical readers, the Mankind Project has been officially classified by French and Swiss organizations as not being a cult. Nicole Durisch Gauthier and Brigitte Knobel, *Rapport annuel 2004*, Centre intercantonal d'information sur les croyances (CIC), 2005.

55 Martenson, *Crash Course*, n.p.

56 Piero San Giorgio, *Survivre à l'effondrement économique* (Lyon: Le retour aux sources, 2011). English translation, *Survive the Economic Collapse: A Practical Guide* (Augusta, GA: Radix/ Washington Summit Publishers, 2013).

57 https://schumachercollege.org.uk/

58 http://mycelium.cc, accessed 17 April 2020.
59 http://terreveille.be/colombia, accessed 17 April 2020.
60 Alexia Soyeux, 'L'Effondrement et la Joie', *Medium*, 21 December 2017; https://medium.com/@alexiasoyeux/https-medium-com-alexiasoyeux-leffondrement-et-la-joie-70215e8271ff, accessed 5 April 2020.
61 Baker, *Collapsing Consciously*, p. 68.
62 Fauré, *Vivre le deuil*, p. 268.
63 Guillaume Mouton, Nans Thomassey and Charlène Gravel, *Nus et culottes*. TV series, France 5 (France TV), 2012 onwards.

Conclusion: Apocalypse or 'happy collapse'?

1 Latour, *Down to Earth*, pp. 88–9.
2 Since 2018, Alexia Soyeux has run a podcast, *Presages*, on the theme of the climate crisis, the Anthropocene, and the risk of collapse – https://www.presages.fr/ – Tr.
3 Soyeux, 'L'Effondrement et la Joie'.
4 Susanne C. Moser, 'Getting real about it: meeting the psychological and social demands of a world in distress', in Deborah R. Gallagher (ed.), *Environmental Leadership: A Reference Handbook* (Thousand Oaks, CA: Sage Publications, 2012), p. 904.
5 Peter Kingsley, 'In the dark places of wisdom', *Parabola*, Winter 1999; https://goldensufi.org/publications/books/in-the-dark-places-of-wisdom/, accessed 2 June 2020.
6 Scranton, 'Learning how to die in the Anthropocene'.
7 Interview with Paul Chefurka for the Adrastia Association, 22 April 2015; https://bit.ly/2w61COE
8 In *Pantagruel*, Rabelais wrote, 'Science sans conscience n'est que ruine de l'âme' ('Science without awareness is only the ruin of the soul'). – Tr.
9 Quoted in Kauth and Alowan, *We Need Each Other*. Martín Prechtel, 'A tadpole's tale', from *Long Life, Honey in the Heart: A Story of Initiation and Eloquence from the Shores of a Mayan Lake* (Wellingborough, UK: Thorsons, 2002), pp. 355–62. http://www.kanzeon.nl/prechtel_tadpole.pdf, accessed 5 April 2020.
10 Latour, *Down to Earth*, p. 66.
11 Baker, *Collapsing Consciously*, p. 66.
12 Ibid., p. 67.

13 Dorzee, 'Bruno Latour: "Les climatosceptiques nous ont déclaré la guerre"'.

Afterword

1 Anthony D. Barnosky et al., 'Approaching a state shift in Earth's biosphere', *Nature* 486(7401), 2012: 52–8.

2 Will Steffen et al., 'Trajectories of the Earth system in the Anthropocene', *Proceedings of the National Academy of Sciences* 115(33), 2018: 8252–9.

3 Vandana Shiva, interview with Cyril Dion in *Kaizen*, 13 November 2012; https://kaizen-magazine.com/article/vandana-shiva/

4 Popular French poet, 1900–1977 – Tr.